FIELD GUIDE TO OREGON RIVERS

TEXT AND PHOTOS BY TIM PALMER

DRAWINGS BY WILLIAM E. AVERY

Oregon State University Press   Corvallis

The paper in this book meets the guidelines for permanence and durability of the Committee on Production Guidelines for Book Longevity of the Council on Library Resources and the minimum requirements of the American National Standard for Permanence of Paper for Printed Library Materials Z39.48-1984.

The John and Shirley Byrne Fund for Books on Nature and the Environment provides generous support that helps make publication of this and other Oregon State University Press books possible. The Press is grateful for this support.

Library of Congress Cataloging-in-Publication Data

Palmer, Tim, 1948-
    Field guide to Oregon rivers / text and photos by Tim Palmer; drawings by William E. Avery.
        pages cm.
    Includes bibliographical references and index.
    ISBN 978-0-87071-627-0 (alk. paper) — ISBN 978-0-87071-737-6 (e-book)
    1. Rivers—Oregon—Guidebooks. 2. Rivers—Oregon—Pictorial works.
    3. Natural history—Oregon. I. Avery, William E. II. Title.
    GB1225.O7P35 2014
    551.48'309795–dc23
                                          2014012117

Cover photo: McKenzie River upstream of Trail Bridge
Half-title page: Willamette River, Middle Fork below Dexter
Title page: John Day River below Service Creek
Contents page: South Umpqua River

Oregon State University Press
121 The Valley Library
Corvallis OR 97331-4501
541-737-3166 • fax 541-737-3170
www.osupress.oregonstate.edu

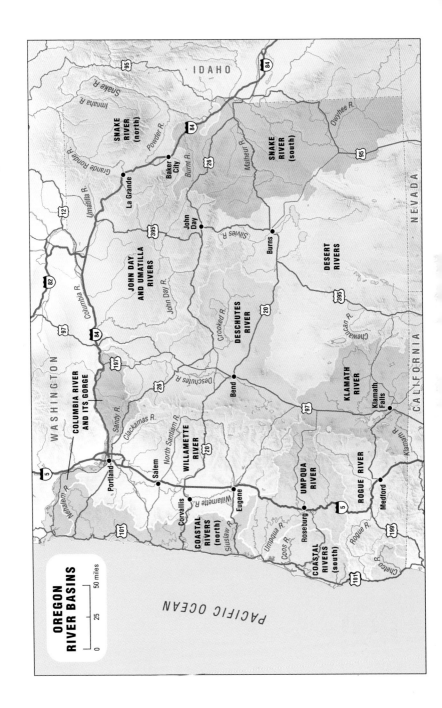

OREGON
RIVER BASINS

0 25 50 miles

PACIFIC OCEAN

WASHINGTON

IDAHO

NEVADA

CALIFORNIA

COLUMBIA RIVER
AND ITS GORGE

SNAKE RIVER
(north)

SNAKE RIVER
(south)

JOHN DAY
AND UMATILLA
RIVERS

DESCHUTES
RIVER

DESERT
RIVERS

WILLAMETTE
RIVER

COASTAL
RIVERS
(north)

COASTAL
RIVERS
(south)

UMPQUA
RIVER

ROGUE RIVER

KLAMATH
RIVER

Snake R.

Imnaha R.

Grande Ronde R.

Powder R.

Umatilla R.

Columbia R.

John Day R.

Malheur R.

Silvies R.

Owyhee R.

Crooked R.

Chewaucan R.

Deschutes R.

Sandy R.

Clackamas R.

North Santiam R.

Willamette R.

Nehalem R.

Siuslaw R.

Umpqua R.

Coos R.

Rogue R.

Chetco R.

Klamath R.

Klamath R.

Baker
City

La Grande

John
Day

Burns

Bend

Portland

Salem

Corvallis

Eugene

Roseburg

Medford

Klamath
Falls

95

84

84

26

395

82

97

112

197

26

20

20

97

5

101

5

101

199

395

ALSO BY TIM PALMER

Field Guide to California Rivers
California Glaciers
Oregon: Preserving the Spirit and Beauty of Our Land
Rivers of California
Luminous Mountains: The Sierra Nevada of California
Trees and Forests of America
Rivers of America
California Wild
Pacific High: Adventures in the Coast Ranges from Baja to Alaska
Lifelines: The Case for River Conservation
Endangered Rivers and the Conservation Movement
The Heart of America: Our Landscape, Our Future
America by Rivers
The Columbia
Yosemite: The Promise of Wildness
The Wild and Scenic Rivers of America
California's Threatened Environment
The Snake River: Window to the West
The Sierra Nevada: A Mountain Journey
Youghiogheny: Appalachian River
Stanislaus: The Struggle for a River
Rivers of Pennsylvania

PLEASE NOTE!

Much of this book describes the nature of Oregon's rivers, but it also includes tips about hiking, fishing, and boating. These river sports can be hazardous, to one degree or another. Regardless of anything that any guidebook says, river users need to know about their own limitations as well as conditions at the time of their outing. This book assumes that each person is responsible for his or her own safety, and each accepts all risks. The author and publisher assume no responsibility or liability with respect to personal injury, property damage, loss of time or money, or other loss or damage caused directly or indirectly by activities in or near the rivers covered here. With recognition of a wide range of readers and respective abilities, information here cannot be construed to be a recommendation for any particular individual to visit the rivers covered, and this book makes no representations that any activity mentioned here is safe particularly for you or your party. In other words, information here is no substitute for experience, training, skill, prudence, common sense, adequate equipment, safe levels of flow, and competent personal assessment of dangers.

The book has been written as accurately as possible, but mistakes can occur and conditions change. Information is included from other books written by other experienced authors. Owing to the large number of river reaches in Oregon and to the difficulty of paddling some of these, not all the information from these other sources has been verified by this author. People paddling or rowing in difficult whitewater should consult other guides and other sources for further details. But always beware: judgments of hazards—even in the international system of whitewater difficulty—vary with the individual. Fluctuations in water level and weather can alter risks greatly from assessments covered here or elsewhere, and hazards such as fallen logs or landslides can happen at any time and change conditions dramatically.

Be prepared. Being safe requires not only the ability to cope with dangers as they arise, but even more the ability to identify potential dangers before they occur. This requires experience, good judgment, and training. Get the necessary instruction for your activity; paddling clubs, kayak schools, and others offer training courses, and of course, much can be learned from competent friends. If you go boating, see the American Whitewater Safety Code and follow it, and read important explanations at the beginning of Part II. All that said, let's knowledgably and prudently head out for these rivers and have fun!

CONTENTS

INTRODUCTION

Rivers provide our water, nourish the land, and sustain entire systems of life. They make it possible—if not irresistible—to paddle in silvery currents, to cast a fishing line, and to walk along green shores that reveal the brilliant beauty and timeless wonder of the natural world. Flowing from the Coast, Cascade, and eastern Oregon mountain ranges, 114,500 miles of streams create pathways and lifelines across Oregon. Of these streams, 77 run 50 miles or more; 190 or so are "rivers," and hundreds of smaller ones are "creeks"—all are considered rivers in this book.

A STATE OF RIVERS

Oregon excels as a state of outstanding waterways. The Rogue—a classic wild river of America—draws people from all around the country for river running and fishing. Its tributary, the Illinois, remains one of the most pristine waterways on the West Coast, and the nearby Chetco tops this list as well. Smaller, but exquisite, the Elk has some of the finest salmon and steelhead habitat for a stream of its size. The Nehalem, Wilson, Nestucca, Siletz, Alsea, Siuslaw, and Smith are exceptional rivers of the central and north coast. At the border with Washington, the Columbia ranks as the fourth-largest river in the United States. The Willamette is crucial to Oregon, flowing through the largest cities and farming valley. Cascade rivers including the Sandy, Clackamas, Santiam, McKenzie, Umpqua, and Metolius plunge down from their mountain sources as premier streams of the Northwest. The Deschutes and John Day run as dryland arteries. The Klamath begins its California-bound descent with headwaters in Oregon. At the eastern border of the state, the Owyhee carves remarkable desert wilds, and the Snake River thunders through Hells Canyon. A stellar group of Snake tributaries gather in the Wallowa Mountains. Hundreds of other waterways are no less valuable to the people and life around them.

Oregon's rivers are legendary as salmon, steelhead, and trout fisheries. Whitewater here ranks with the best, and our gentler waters are among the most beautiful. More multiday river trips can be taken here than in any other western state; no less than 10 expeditions are truly epic. And I've concluded that Oregon also has the best riverfront hiking in America.

Two-thirds of Oregonians depend on rivers or streams for drinking water while the rest tap groundwater that's intimately tied to the surface flow, and so everyone needs healthy streams. Rivers underpin the statewide economy in ways beyond the obviously essential water they provide; 600,000 people buy fishing licenses, and the Department of Fish and Wildlife estimates that $2.5 billion are spent on fish and wildlife recreation annually.

Beyond the exuberance of whitewater or the simple pleasures of a quiet day going with the flow, rivers create an opportunity to see and experience the real and authentic nature of Oregon. Paddling, rowing, and drifting on our longer rivers offers an unparalleled way to travel for days and even weeks through the heart of a landscape that's usually seen only through the windshield of a car. Enjoying rivers can be done close to home, without the long drives that many other tourist destinations require.

A BOOK OF RIVERS

This field guide provides information, travel tips, and perhaps a bit of inspiration so that we might know our network of rivers better and enrich our lives by visiting these alluring places and also by taking better care of them. As an all-around rivers enthusiast, I've explored and enjoyed streams throughout the state off and on for 45 years, and more thoroughly since I moved to Oregon full-time in 2002. Wanting to see it all, I've paddled my canoe or rowed my whitewater raft on scores of waterways and made a point of doing most of the multiday trips possible—some for a week or two. I've walked along the shorelines of any waterway where I could find a trail and in a lot of places where I couldn't. I've found other guidebooks to boating, fishing, and hiking useful, but none offered a full view of the rivers, and none featured the rivers, themselves, as the prime focus. For several decades, I've also been writing about rivers and photographing them nationwide, so I realized that our Oregon streams are among the best. In this process, I've consulted books, articles, and experts by the dozen, and with all that material in hand I decided that a consolidation of information would be useful to me and hopefully to others. This first comprehensive guide to Oregon rivers is the result.

Inflatable kayak on the Chetco River above Steel Bridge

Fly-fishing on the Rogue River

The book might be useful as a field reference to be kept in your pack, dry bag, or glove box for a day, weekend, or vacation. It might become a source of data and tips for recreation, work, or just playful curiosity. Where can you go canoeing if you want to relax and enjoy nature, and where can you go for the ultimate paddling challenge? Where are the best hikes along Oregon rivers? Where can you still see salmon leaping up waterfalls? How can I best experience the Willamette, Wallowa, or Winchuck?

I don't want to dampen the sense of adventure that each of us can feel when we head out into the natural world. I think that exploring on my own and without expectations is the best way to go. Adventure is good! But much can be gained by learning about a river and its surroundings, and having some help along the way can save a lot of gasoline and time while avoiding unwelcome danger. In short, I'd be honored to help you figure out where to go. Yet I make no pretenses about running your trip. Unlike some guides, I don't offer advice about how to run the rapids, I don't tell you what's around the next bend in the trail, and I don't tell you what kind of lures or bait to put on your line. That's for you to determine, to see, and to do. But with recreation in mind (think *re-creation*), I identify which rivers, and which sections of them, are appealing given different interests, skills, and commitments of time, and I tell you how to get there. I hope that all of this complements—and does not detract from—the remarkable feeling of going out and discovering something new and rewarding for yourself.

Writing a guidebook presents a dilemma: some favorite places that I used to have all to myself might become more visited. Yet each of us deserves our share of nature, and without knowing and thereby appreciating it, our commitment to protecting what's natural and wild will be less. So I'd like to help everyone to know and experience our rivers better.

While I note significant waterworks, this is not a book about delivery systems. For that, see *The Oregon Water Handbook*. Nor does this *Field Guide* consider recreation on reservoirs. When rivers are dammed, they are rivers no more; the man-made flatwater completely alters a river's appearance, hydrology, and biology. While I briefly cover the history of river protection, I leave general history to other authors, who have written thoroughly in that field. This book is principally a guide to nature, not to culture, and so you'll find that my photos reveal the less altered rather than human-made scenes.

Some people might think that rivers are the province of the skilled angler or the trained whitewater paddler. Yet Oregon's astonishing collection of waterways offers appeal not just to the seasoned aficionado, but to everybody, whether we paddle through easy or difficult rapids, fish with flies or lures or bait, or simply walk along, sit beside, or appreciate the water that flows. With an extra pitch of excitement in my voice, I cover rivers that demand advanced paddling, but I give even more attention to streams not requiring expert skills. I recommend casual strolls that almost anybody can take, and also extended hikes for the assiduously fit. River exploration can be a sport, a pastime, and a passion for everyone.

The guide is presented in two unequal parts. The first begins with Natural History, about the world of geology, climate, hydrology, plants, animals, and ecology. In Chapter 2, fifty sketches by biology professor and artist Bill Avery identify typical flora and fauna in and along the streams while my text covers distinguishing highlights. Realizing the importance of better stewardship, Chapter 3 provides an overview of the challenges our rivers face. I note reform efforts underway, proposed, or needed, and I suggest where you can see the problems and solutions on the ground.

Canoeing on the South Fork Coos River

Part II forms the heart of the book—10 chapters organized by watersheds. For each stream I present a summary of the waterway and its character, notes about its nature and fish, and comments about ongoing threats along with protection efforts. Then I point to opportunities for seeing the stream, hiking along its shores, fishing, and exploring by canoe, kayak, raft, or drift boat.

In the space available I try to include enough information so that the reader can select which stream and which section to visit, and enough guidance to get adventurous people to the water for their own discoveries. Anglers may want detailed tips available in guides such as *Fishing Oregon*, and for those paddling difficult whitewater I recommend *Soggy Sneakers: A Guide to Oregon Rivers* and *Paddling Oregon*.

A state highway map is essential—my directions begin with a place you can locate there. I also find the Oregon *DeLorme Atlas* requisite for my travels. National Forest and BLM (Bureau of Land Management) maps show more—especially trails—and U.S. Geological Survey topographic maps offer detail. All are available at outdoor stores or on the Internet.

Oregon's collection of streams is unlike any other on earth, and it offers enticing opportunities for all. I hope that these chapters help you to know and understand our rivers better, and to enjoy them by dipping your paddle, your feet, and your fishing line into the flow. I'm inspired by an old friend, Bob Potter, one of the founders and the first manager of the state's Scenic Waterways program. In an article about the Deschutes he wrote, "This river is mine. When you have joined it for a quiet float, moved with it, and felt the country passing, it will, I hope, be yours as well."

The rivers, of course, belong to everyone, and they're governed by the great natural systems that surround them. Geologic processes and climate shape the hydrologic makeup of each stream and ultimately determine what plants and animals will thrive. The first two chapters of Part I feature those natural processes and the lifeforms they support.

Facing page: North Fork Sprague River at Lee Thomas Meadow

Imagine the rivers of Oregon loosely resembling spokes of a wheel radiating out from interior regions. The coastal rivers flow west to the ocean. The Willamette, Sandy, Hood, Deschutes, John Day, and Umatilla push north to the Columbia. Snake River tributaries flow east to that northbound artery, and southcentral waters trend to land-locked basins in the desert or southward to the California-bound Klamath. The Oregon Water Resources Department recognizes 18 basins; I simplify to 10 watersheds or groupings of them, organized by chapters in Part II.

Scribing the border with Washington, the Columbia is the largest river—five times the volume of the Snake, which is runner-up. The lion's share of water in both comes from upstream states. The Willamette is by far the largest river entirely within Oregon. The following table lists the 21 largest rivers, ranked by volume (average or "mean" cubic feet per second—cfs) and also the longest in mileage, plus the watershed area in square miles and the stream's rank in each category (see Part II for data methods).

Oregon's Largest Rivers, and Their Rank in Flow, Length, and Watershed Area

River	Avg flow (mean cfs)	Length (miles)	Watershed (sq mi)
Columbia	265,000 (1)	1,257 (1); 307 in OR	260,000 (1)
Snake	56,255 (2)	1,056 (2); 235 in OR	109,000 (2)
Willamette	33,054 (3)	187; 272 with MF (6)	11,400 (4)
Klamath	17,397 (4); 1,767 in OR	257; 364 with Williamson (3); 46 in OR; 153 with Williamson in OR	14,831 (3); 5,702 in OR
Umpqua	7,729 (5)	108; 226 with SF & Castle Rock Fork (8)	4,668 (10)
Santiam	7,726 (6)	12; 105 with North Santiam	1,804
Rogue	6,730 (7)	216 (9)	5,159 (8)
McKenzie	5,916 (8)	88	1,216
Deschutes	5,827 (9)	255 (7)	9,934 (6)
Coquille	4,526 (10)	36; 100 with SF	1,053
Willamette, MF	4,078 (11)	85	1,365
Umpqua, North	3,705 (12)	106	1,356
Grande Ronde	3,053 (13)	209 (10); 173 in OR	3,308 (12)
South Santiam	2,951 (14)	66	1,040
Clackamas	2,925 (15)	84	942
Umpqua, South	2,755 (16)	102; 118 with Castle Rock Fork	1,801
Nehalem	2,660 (17)	128	852
Siuslaw	2,285 (18)	109	773
Sandy	2,278 (19)	57	501
Chetco	2,244 (20)	57	353
John Day	2,060 (21)	180; 293 with NF (5)	7,880 (7)
Owyhee	1,213	347 (4); 198 in OR	10,569 (5)
Crooked	1,553	127; 203 with SF (11)	4,338 (11)
Malheur	201	190 (12)	4,703 (9)

CHAPTER 1

NATURAL HISTORY OF OREGON RIVERS

Rivers provide for plants and animals and, even more importantly, they support whole ecosystems and natural cycles that underpin the very basis of life.

The fundamental nature of any river—the way it looks and works—depends on five factors. First, geologic events created the mountain ranges, topography, and bedrock through which a river flows—the big backdrop. Second, climate prescribes the amount and timing of the crucial rain and snow. Third, the forces of geology and climate together determine hydrology—characteristics of flow, including cycles of flood and drought. This flow has sculpted valleys and canyons into the profiles we recognize today, and it continues to shape riverbeds, shorelines, and floodplains. Fourth, the combined effects of geology, climate, and hydrology govern what plants can live in and along a river. Finally, all these factors influence what insects, fish, and other wildlife will thrive, and ultimately how we can use and appreciate the streams. The diversity of Oregon rivers owes to the multitude of ways that all these interactions vary across the state.

GEOLOGY

The geologic processes that forge the rivers of today begin with plate tectonics and seismic activity, which directly cause mountains to form and indirectly cause volcanism—the dominant force that has shaped the face of Oregon and created the terrestrial template on which the rivers flow. Subsequent geologic forces of erosion—mostly by water—sculpt valleys and canyons and direct the paths of rivers. This section will consider the geologic history that fashioned our riverscape, followed by aspects of rivers' flow that continue to be governed by geologic forces.

The earth is composed of crustal plates that float on top of a semisolid and deeper molten layer. Plates of lighter rocks buoy up as continents, while those made of heavier rocks lie undersea. The plates move, and seismic ruptures form at intersections where the plates collide or scrape against each other, thrusting up crust that forms mountains.

The Pacific Plate, beneath the ocean, creeps north relative to the lighter North American Plate. The intersection defines the San Andreas Fault to the south. The famous shear-line, however, veers out to sea in northern California, and this detour in its northern trajectory leaves the relatively small Farallon Plate as a separate undersea crust wedged against North America offshore from Oregon. Unlike the Pacific Plate, which slides northwest, the east-moving Farallon collides head-on with the North American Plate, and being denser, it plunges underneath the lighter North American mass. This subduction has been occurring for millennia, and most of the Farallon has disappeared, but fragments remain and continue their march to subduction offshore from the Oregon coast.

The advance of the Farallon and related microplates have fundamentally shaped western Oregon and thereby the rivers that run across it. As the oceanic plate is driven underground it pushes up a block of ancient seafloor to become the Coast Range, which by some accounts is still rising 1 inch/year (erosion constantly lowers the mountains, but slower). As the relative westward movement of the continent continues to override the Farallon, remnants of that smaller plate migrate east underground and continue to drop at a steady angle beneath the surface of the continent. When this subducted mass reaches 60 vertical miles beneath the surface, the temperature of the earth's interior causes overlying rock to melt into magma, which then pushes up through cracks and periodically erupts a hundred miles inland from the ocean at the chain of Cascade volcanic peaks—from Mount Hood in Oregon's north to McLoughlin in the south. On all these mountain masses the rivers take form and flow as underlying topography dictates.

Predating the Farallon's collision and buildup of the current Coast Range, similar ranges formed at ancestral oceanfronts that now lie to the east where they were uplifted to become the Klamath, Ochoco, and Blue Mountains. Lava flows later covered much of eastern and northern Oregon, creating the Columbia Plateau in the northcentral state and spreading basalt layers southward in the Basin and Range Province. Where lava flows were thin, they cooled quickly, forming the signature hexagonal basalt columns seen along many rivers.

While the modern Coast Range continues to rise as a result of the Farallon subduction, and while molten rock still activates the Cascade volcanoes to the east, the Willamette Valley seismically drops in elevation and may be widening in the trough that the river follows between the Coast and Cascade Mountains.

One of the most obvious signs of mountains' influence on rivers is the radial pattern that streams take from major peaks down to lower terrain. The Hood, Sandy, Salmon, and White Rivers flowing from Mount Hood graphically illustrate this starfish pattern of rivers flowing away from a summit, as do Wallowa Range streams in the northeast.

Since the Cascade Mountains are new and high, they cause the steepest gradients and most dramatic drops of rivers: the Sandy, for example, plunges from the flanks of Mount Hood. The White, Metolius, and Deschutes fall from the east side of the Cascades, where headwaters drop sharply owing to volcanism and to the east face of the Cascades being drier and therefore less eroded than the wetter west side. The precipitous plunge is seen in the White as it foams to the lower Deschutes.

In contrast, the Coast Range has softer rocks that have enabled its rivers to carve gentler gradients extending far inland. The Siuslaw, for example, fingers eastward almost to the Willamette Valley. Low-gradient

Columnar basalt along the Deschutes River below Island Rapids

streams north of Cape Blanco offer better habitat for coho salmon, which gravitate toward rivers with "flats" and associated gravel beds suitable for spawning. As they near the ocean, many rivers have eroded into even softer and more pliable marine sediments and abraded them to sea level, producing long estuaries; tidal reaches of the Columbia, Nehalem, Siletz, Alsea, Siuslaw, Umpqua, and Coquille reach far inland.

Where they finally disgorge into the ocean, Oregon's rivers both shape and are shaped by geologic conditions of the coastline, and by its surf. The seacoast's sand comes principally from rivers—the final disposition of soil eroded from the banks. Oceanographer Paul Komar reported that most sand on the Oregon coast came from just two rivers: the Columbia and Klamath, whose volume and sediment-transporting abilities far exceed other streams. Sand disgorged from the two mega-rivers during the Ice Ages was somewhat evenly spread along the Oregon coast because a lower sea level at that time exposed a narrow coastal plain that allowed ocean-current transport of sand freely north and south. With higher sea level today lapping up against rocky outcrops, coastal sand is largely constrained in isolated cells between headlands.

The coastal rivers, in turn, are affected by the sand that they have delivered. Their final trajectory is directed north or south by localized sand that has been rearranged as waves and wind shape beaches and dunes. The lower Siuslaw, for example, is diverted 3 miles north by a sand barrier in its way. The New is an 8-mile river paralleling the coast and formed entirely by a berm of windblown sand only one dune (or bar) wide.

South of the Coquille River, soft mudstones and sandstones of the Coast Range transition upstream to harder volcanic and metamorphic rocks of the Siskiyou Mountains, yielding steeper river gradients. The South Fork Coquille bridges the two geological provinces; upper reaches sport harder rocks and steep rapids of the Siskiyous; lower mileage more uniformly embeds into erodible shales and mudstones of the Coast Range and wends languidly to sea.

Other than the Columbia—in a class by itself—the only two rivers that cut entirely through Oregon's coastal mountains are the Umpqua and Rogue. Their routes plunged from the Western Cascades to sea before the uplift of the Coast Range. As its emergence began, they maintained their westward direction by crosscutting down at a rate roughly matching the Coast Range's uplift, producing the magnificent canyons and valleys we know today.

Rivers' underlying bedrock is one of the principal reasons that rapids appear. The largest drops indicate resistance points where the toughest bedrock is exposed. One of Oregon's most notorious rapids—boulder-ridden Blossom Bar on the Rogue—indicates the river's encounter with erosion-resistant sandstones and conglomerates of the Riddle Formation. In the lower Umpqua basin, the Smith River drops over sandstone ledges that cross the river like stair-steps. Taking the resistance of hard-rock strata a step further, waterfalls of Columbia tributaries in the great gorge east of Portland showcase the durability of volcanic basalt; cliffs persist in spite of water flowing directly over them.

Forming rapids across much of the state, the fine-grained, black or brown basalt was deposited in viscous flows of lava, like layers of cake batter. These cooled, hardened, and fractured into columns sometimes resembling giant packs of pencils. Turbulent rapids at sharp basalt outcrops in the upper Deschutes River indicate the edges, seams, and cracks in lava flows that periodically oozed across much of eastern Oregon. The river has not yet worn the rock down into the steadier gradients typical of rivers in older terrain. Lava flows also account for steep cliffs of the Owyhee canyonlands and the golden walls above the John Day—among the most spectacular basalt and rhyolite formations anywhere.

Exceptionally hard and erosion-resistant, granite forms as molten rock in underground plutons but cools slowly and develops a coarse crystalline structure that's nearly white or mixed with salt-and-pepper pink and black. Distinctive granite cobble bars appear in scattered locations through the Siskiyou Mountains of southwest Oregon, but the purest granite exposures are the gleaming streambeds of the Wallowa Range in the northeast.

Rapids are caused by other geologic forces as well. Landslides sometimes terminate in streams and congest the current, occasionally damming rivers until the overflow creates turbulent drops. Flood-induced bedload movements of cobbles and boulders take on rapid-forming patterns in a pool-and-drop sequence. Other rapids are formed when steep tributaries reach their confluences with larger rivers and force a backup of water; the currents slow, and drop the heaviest rocks, which then create rapids at the tributary mouths.

While the geologic force of ancient volcanoes and lava flows dominate much of Oregon's riverscape, glaciers have also played a role. Continental glaciers of the Ice Ages stopped north of Oregon but affected the Columbia via the Missoula Floods, whose waters backed up as a giant eddy in the Willamette Valley (see Chapter 8). Localized mountain glaciers grew without connection to the continental icefields but existed at the same time, 18,000 years ago. The impressive Cascade ice mass covered Mount Hood and ramped southward at elevations above 5,800 feet along the crest for 170 miles, continuous from Olallie Butte (north of Mount Jefferson) through Mount McLoughlin. Icy runoff affected all the rivers flowing from this palisade and delivered glacier-tumbled cobbles and gravel still populating the riverbeds and forming both rapids and fish-spawning habitat today. Smaller glaciers persist on Mounts Hood and Jefferson, the Three Sisters, and a few other peaks where the ice produces milky or pale green flows saturated with rock dust that's pulverized by the glaciers' movement—best seen in the White River.

Other glaciers formed on the eastern Oregon peaks of the Steens, Wallowa, Elkhorn, Strawberry, and Greenhorn Mountains, and they fed rivers below with dramatically greater flows than exist today. Rivers and lakes of southcentral Oregon survive as remnants of those once-vast glacial outwashes and inland seas. Evidence of the icy past is obvious in tributaries of the Donner und Blitzen River; capacious U-shaped canyons were carved by ice in a landscape incongruously surrounded by today's desert.

Another river-connection to the geologic past can be seen where streams adhere to fault lines, exploiting and following weak erodible rock. The northward direction of the Willamette at Portland follows faults, as do sections of rivers in the Western Cascades, which lie west of our High Cascades and now appear as older foothills. The narrow gorge of the Rogue's Mule Creek Canyon follows a fault line between the Dothan Formation of sandstone and siltstone on the south side and the Rogue Formation of hard volcanic lava that was metamorphosed undersea.

Geology also governs groundwater—an abundant, dominant hydrologic feature in Oregon's volcanic landscape. Cracks and voids permeate hardened lava and absorb, retain, and carry water underground. The ultimate volcanic conveyances are lava tubes. These resulted because the initial cooling of lava began at the surface, which hardened, leaving molten lava to continue flowing underground in subsurface conduits or "tubes" through the jelling mass of lava around it. In some places these tubes transported liquid lava until the source dried up, suddenly leaving the tube empty. Rain and snowmelt accumulated in the voids, and the tubes are now underground water pipelines, ultimately disgorging at springs. At Natural Bridge, the Rogue enters one of the more remarkable tubes where

Lava tubes along the upper Rogue River near Union Creek

the entire river disappears and then—a short walk downstream—foams back up. The McKenzie and Williamson likewise disappear into lava fissures and later reappear below.

Throughout much of the state, underlying lava rock absorbs rain and snowmelt into porous underground cavities, especially apparent in the High Cascades and along their eastern flank. Unlike surface runoff that flashes off quickly, the movement of groundwater within lava slows in intricate seeps and settles into dark grottos that even out flows. These ultimately emerge via springs with steady yields. Protected from surface erosion and pollution, the groundwater is pure. And without exposure to sunlight, it's extremely cold. Thus, streams of the Cascades' volcanic landscape have some of the steadiest hydrographs known, and their waters are clean, cold, excellent for trout. The Metolius rises in a large spring and exemplifies the groundwater legacy of volcanic landscapes. Rivers of the upper Klamath basin also benefit from volcanic groundwater sources.

Part II of this guide offers river-specific notes about geology.

Plate tectonics, volcanism, and erosion create the landscape across which all rivers flow, but without rain and snow delivered by Oregon's climate, the rivers would not exist.

CLIMATE

Patterns of precipitation shape the rivers from beginning to end, and the temperature of the air affects the water and all its life.

Owing to global atmospheric patterns, cool, descending air in summer forms the sunny Pacific High Pressure system at mid-latitudes spanning the length of California and Oregon. When the high-pressure zone retreats southward in autumn, its absence allows encroachment of rain-laden low-pressure systems. This gives Oregon wet winters, with precipitation beginning in autumn, peaking November–January, and continuing through spring. The rivers respond accordingly, rising with winter rains and springtime snowmelt, falling in summer and fall. The lowest flows statewide come August–September, abruptly ending with the first big autumn storms.

As these eastbound storms are pushed up over Oregon's mountains, they cool; the temperature typically drops 3 degrees for each 1,000-foot rise. Because cold air holds less water vapor, it sheds moisture as it rises, so higher elevations get more precipitation. While rainfall offshore might total 30 inches a year, the upraised coast gets 60–80 inches, and Coast Range mountaintops can receive 200. In winter, clouds that deliver rain to lower elevations drop snow at higher levels.

Mountains also create rain shadows. Once the moisture-laden, prevailing western winds top the summits, the air descends the east side, and as it does, it warms and regains capacity to hold water vapor, so precipitation sharply decreases on this downwind side. The change is evident when crossing the Cascade crest; the forest suddenly turns from hemlocks to ponderosa pines, which require less moisture, and then to junipers at lower, drier levels. East-side streams have far less flow per acre of watershed than do their nearby counterparts on the west slope of the Cascades.

Owing to the rain shadows of the Cascades and other mountains, much of eastern Oregon is exceptionally dry, its streams small or intermittent. In the eastern shadow of monumental Steens Mountain, Alvord Desert receives a scant 5 inches a year—barely more than America's driest place in Death Valley. Most of Oregon's desert gets about 12 inches of rain, which largely evaporates, leaving little runoff.

On Oregon's coastal streams dominated by rainfall rather than snowmelt and groundwater, rivers rise and subside in cadence with the storms.

Heavy winter snow cover at Tumalo Creek, Deschutes watershed

Peak runoff often occurs only hours after the most intense rainfall. Flows in coastal basins as well as the Umpqua, Rogue, and Willamette typically top out during storms in December and January. Coast Range rivers flash up and down the fastest because they lack snowpacks to store water, their watersheds are short and shunt rainfall quickly, and their soils have been damaged by erosion and compaction that accompanied heavy clearcutting across about 98 percent of the coastal mountains. To see these streams at their turbulent, heart-pounding heights, you usually have to go out while the storms are still raging. These rivers spike high repeatedly through winter, then gradually decline from spring through autumn.

Streams fed by snowmelt, on the other hand, have steadier flows that extend well into summer. Snow piles up on the Cascades and summits of eastern Oregon and accounts for 80 percent or more of runoff there. Cascade elevations above 4,000 see twice the precipitation of nearby valley areas, and the accumulated snow produces high flows April–July, with peak runoff often in late May. The Columbia, whose greatest volume comes a long distance from slower-melting heights of the Rocky Mountains, doesn't crest until June.

Immense storms, and thus floods, occur inevitably and at irregular intervals from late autumn through spring, governed in large part by El Niño and La Niña events—climatic and oceanic phenomena linked to continental winds and long-term cycles of warming and cooling in the eastern Pacific. El Niño causes warm ocean conditions off the Oregon shore and southward. These produce heavy winter storms in California and occasional deluges in Oregon, but more likely drier conditions from the California border north. In contrast, La Niña causes cool ocean conditions and northern storms brought by the polar jet stream. These are sometimes combined with the subtropical jet stream, which makes landfall in Oregon with intense rains called the "Pineapple Express," and big floods result. Oregon's highest known flows came in 1861, and also with the Christmas Day flood of 1964 when some coastal rivers crested 30 feet above normal. That and floods of 1996, 1997, and 2012 are attributable to La Niña. Regardless of heavy precipitation in winter and spring, low stream flows occur in late summer and fall, and many waterways that surge powerfully in winter go nearly dry, especially in the Coast Range and eastern drylands.

Reflecting the interplay between geology, climate, and hydrology, the north sides of mountains and the north-facing slopes of canyons receive shade from the sun and are cooler, and so stream temperatures on those aspects are cooler as well. Volcanic peaks are especially significant where north-side meltwater continues through summer. Mount Hood's glaciers and permanent snowfields provide water to the Hood River even in autumn when other snow-fed streams are dry. These high-elevation and north-side streams are vital to cold-water species such as salmon and trout, and will become increasingly important as the climate warms further.

The life of the rivers has slowly adapted to climate-caused fluctuations in flow that go back millennia. However, the climate is now changing rapidly (see Chapter 3), and the effects on rivers will be profound.

Cape Creek alder forest with flood flows

HYDROLOGY

Geology and climate together determine characteristics of river flow, including volume, direction, gradient, chemistry, color, and temperature of the water. The science of river flow is hydrology.

As climate dictates, rivers follow cycles of high and low runoff. Many of the flood flows in Oregon arrive December–January, and these high waters do the most to shape the riverbeds. The massive Christmas Day flood of 1964 and its rearrangement of rock along Oregon rivers still affects many streams.

Floods cause economic loss and suffering where people have built in harm's way, but periodic high water is essential to the health of streams. Floods scour out pools where fast water picks up silt, sand, gravel, and cobbles and flushes them downstream. Alternately, floods deposit their heaviest and densest cargo—large cobbles—at riffle and rapid sites where the incoming rocks further congest the runoff and create whitewater. The resulting pools keep water cold in summer and provide shelter for fish and other life. Meanwhile the riffles aerate the water and increase its oxygen supply while shallow rocks provide anchoring structures for invertebrates at the base of the food chain. The combined pool-and-riffle sequence—maintained by floods—is essential to a healthy river.

Seasonal flow variation is crucial not only to the stream channel but to the shorelines and riparian corridor. High water dislodges silt, sand, and gravel from channels and banks on the outsides of bends, carries them downstream, and later deposits this bedload on the insides of bends where the current slows. The entire process constantly renews the shape and condition of the shores. The biological health of floodplains and riparian forests depend on this periodic flooding and cyclical erosion and deposition in what's called a "disturbance ecosystem."

Keystone species such as cottonwoods require occasional flooding for reproduction. Fish also benefit from floods. Aside from their dependence on the flood-sculpted maintenance of the riverbed, fish need seasonal high water that makes the rich food source of wetlands and floodplains accessible. Plus, flooded areas are temporary but important refuges from predators, including alien species of fish. Fourteen fish species—11 of them native—use inundated Willamette floodplains for breeding or rearing.

Floods and other natural processes result in channel complexity—the mix of pools, riffles, overflow areas, riverfront wetlands, and sloughs. Seen often with large rivers such as the Willamette, back channels that carry water in high flows are crucial for wildlife. Willamette research has shown that gravel-bottomed back channels contain not only warm water that one would expect in languid pools, but also exceptionally cold water; two-thirds of the sloughs were surprisingly colder than the main stem. This owes to deep gravel deposits, established by past flooding, which hold cold water that percolates up—crucial to fish that need cool relief in summer. Diking and filling the back channels has in many places eliminated this important bio-hydrologic phenomenon.

Where floods have been prevented by dams or the channel made uniform by levees, pools tend to fill in with sediment, and riffles subside by erosion, evening out the gradient and leading to a constant glide of current with less biological productivity.

High water also plays a critical role in nourishing riparian forests and wetlands beyond the riverbank. But with development and farming, wide swaths of habitat along many streams have been reduced to narrow remnants, or eliminated. Once miles in width, the Willamette's floodplain and riparian corridor are now thin and meager in comparison.

Logjam on the Nestucca River below Fan Creek

Illustrating another connection between hydrology, plants, and wildlife, trees that fall into streams during floods play a vital role in the ecosystem. Large logs partially block the flow and redirect the current, and one stranded log entraps another, eventually making a logjam. These form pools where water backs up, and rapids where water is forced around the blockage. Wood in the streams provides anchorage and habitat to invertebrates that fish and other animals depend upon and offers underwater cover from predators. The wood's breakdown nourishes microbes, insects, and invertebrates important in rivers, estuaries, and the sea. In the past, massive logjams backed up water enough to spill over the banks, cover low flats alongside, and deposit the bedload, which included gravels needed by spawning salmon. Fish, mammals, and riparian plants thrived in the resulting forested wetlands, and the log-induced overflows also recharged groundwater tables, enabling them to discharge back into streams as summer levels waned, evening out the flow for the benefit of many species.

One of these species is coho salmon—now imperiled. Unlike most Chinook salmon, coho remain in freshwater a year before going out to sea, and to do that they need logs in streams for refuge during winter floods. They also need deep pools and shaded water that the logs provide in summer. Some fallen trees that are flushed the whole way down rivers become grounded in shallow estuaries, providing young salmon the cover they need from predators such as cormorants. Efforts to eliminate those birds might be better directed to adding fallen trees to estuarine shallows.

The ecological benefits of fallen trees in streams went unrealized until recent decades; from 1890–1917 the Army Corps of Engineers removed 470 trees per river mile from some estuaries and large rivers. Later, virtually all major logjams were removed, often with dynamite. This misguided effort caused streams to downcut their banks and channelize their corridors, separating rivers from their floodplains, eliminating riparian habitat, and depleting groundwater reserves. With reduced flows after the end of the rainy season, water temperatures climbed beyond the tolerance of native fishes, and alien species took hold. Large conifers create the best logjams, but today's post-logging-era shortage of big conifers means it will take many years until significant logjams again become common—and never if the trees aren't allowed to grow large. Biologists agree that large woody debris must be reinstated into waterways to restore streams and the life that depends on them. The benefit of logjams is one among many compelling reasons to protect and reinstate riparian old-growth forests.

Many of the logs, and much of the gravel deposited in the flats that occur behind logjams, come from cataclysmic events that are at once geologic, climatic, and hydrologic in nature—big landslides that deliver the logs and gravel to the streams. On rivers of the Coast Range, these naturally occurred on roughly 300-year cycles (in contrast to more frequent slides that result from man-made watershed disturbance). The heavy bedload temporarily eliminates good local fish habitat, but in about 80 years the disturbance transforms into highly beneficial areas for fish, according to biologist Gordon Reeves and others in *Forest and Stream Management in the Oregon Coast Range*. The cycle is long-term on a rotating scale; while one section of stream suffers disturbance, many others reach their prime. Apparent disorder at the local scale aggregates to an elegant order at a larger scale, but only if nature is allowed to act on a truly grand stage of landscape and time.

Hydrology and the rhythms of runoff affect everything from logjams to the flooding in communities built along the riverfronts, to the spawning of fish, to the plants that grow along the streams.

PLANTLIFE

In natural river systems, trees and shrubs shade the streams, keep them cool, and protect banks from erosion. Roots exposed by the current give fish cover, and fallen trees provide food, spawning habitat, and shelter. Riverfront vegetation delivers essential nutrients to the water in the form of leaves, organic detritus, and insects that drop from overhanging branches.

The health of riparian (river-related) plantlife is a key indicator of the health of streams themselves. The *Oregon State of the Environment Report* estimated that riparian areas total 23,000 square miles—15 percent of the state. With similar ecosystem benefits, wetlands including swamps, marshes, and tidal estuaries cover 2,190 square miles (down from 3,750 before drainage and filling).

Owing to the availability of water, depth of productive soil, shelter from wind, and deterrence of fire, floodplains along rivers often support the largest trees. This is true of Sitka spruce, which normally grow within a few hundred yards of the coast but extend up the floodplains of some coastal river valleys such as the Siletz. Grand firs likewise grow largest on floodplains. However, old-growth conifers that once dominated riparian zones in Oregon have been cut, and old conifers now account for only 20 percent of riparian forests in the Cascades and 3 percent in the heavily logged coastal mountains.

Black cottonwoods reign as Oregon's largest riparian trees and serve as a keystone species. They cast the most shade and produce the greatest quantities of nutrient-bearing leaves. They deliver food for beavers, deer, and elk. Their crowns form nesting habitat for songbirds, and dead snags provide homes for ospreys, eagles, and herons. Trunk cavities become nests for woodpeckers, wood ducks, mergansers, and raccoons. Cottonwoods might be considered the ultimate riparian tree not just because they serve other riverfront life so well, but also because they require floods to reproduce: their seeds ripen just after high waters of springtime and generally need a freshly scoured floodplain or new deposit of sand or silt to germinate. An entire "class" of young trees will arise in the wake of a specific flood. Cottonwood corridors thrive especially along the Columbia, Willamette and lower reaches of its tributaries, and some coastal streams. Where dams control floods, cottonwood forests lack the fresh silt or scoured sand and often die out.

Cottonwood forest along the Willamette River downstream of Corvallis

Also specializing on Oregon floodplains, alder trees are uniquely suited to the riverfront. Because high water washes away fallen leaves and organic detritus, the remaining sand and gravel is low in nitrogen. Adapted for this problem, alders host nitrogen-fixing microbes in their roots, extracting this element from the atmosphere, where it's plentiful, and converting it to a form consumable by the tree (atmospheric gasses permeate the soil and are available to roots). Through the alders' leaf litter and roots, nitrogen is laced into the soil where it nourishes other plants. Alders and willows are also the preferred food of beavers, deer, and elk.

Stream corridors with their riparian (river-related) forests have been heavily cut, but thanks to the Northwest Forest Plan, which limits logging along federally owned streams west of the Cascade crest, and to nominal setback requirements of the State Forest Practices Act, even heavily logged basins such as the Smith and Coos have riparian groves remaining partially intact. With improved forest management, riparian forests are recovering. If the Forest Practices Act were upgraded, the improvement could be much greater.

Some Cascade Mountain riparian corridors still support great conifers in deep soils; French Pete Creek in the McKenzie basin and short reaches of other Cascade rivers are excellent places to see these globally significant forests. In arid regions, even single cottonwoods or willows along the Owyhee, Malheur, or Snake provide vital ecosystem functions where diversions have not eliminated riparian life.

Plantlife far from the banks is also crucial to waterways. Tree cover on mountainsides protects soil from erosion. Where steep slopes are carelessly logged, the rain beats on the soil and washes it into streams. Furthermore, disturbed slopes lack the sponge-like qualities of native forests,

Chinook salmon jumping at Rainie Falls, Rogue River

and so runoff happens faster, crests higher, drops sooner, then dries up in summer. The altered flows play havoc with aquatic life.

For all these reasons, the health of fish populations depends on trees that grace the banks and mountainsides, on branches that shade the headwaters and tributary basins, and on roots, needles, cones, seeds, and the interwoven woodland community of microbes that protect and nourish the soil. Rivers need forests, and fish need trees.

FISH

Fish are direct indicators of river health. Oregon has 69 species and subspecies of native freshwater fishes, according to the *Oregon Native Fish Status Report*. Another 33 non-native aliens have been introduced from other parts of the country or globe and account for one-third of the state's total freshwater fish fauna. Game fish that anglers favor account for 34 species, 23 of them introduced. Common families of native fishes include lampreys, salmon, trout, minnows, sculpins, suckers, and sticklebacks (see Part II for river-by-river coverage of fish and fishing opportunities).

Nourishing the fish, an elaborate food chain begins with bacteria and fungi that decompose leaf and other organic litter. This and abundant blooms of algae create food sources. Constant current in rivers means that most algae are small and inconspicuous diatom and desmid species in the water and forming slimy mats on rocks—slippery and nutrient rich. Visible algae are filamentous and cling to the bottom with holdfasts— the waving micro-forests of "seaweed" seen at low flows. Up the trophic chain, larvae of stoneflies, mayflies, caddisflies, and dragonflies eat algae. These insects and other invertebrates become prime food for fish.

For food and places to spawn, rear, feed, and hide from predators, fish need varieties of habitats that come with channel complexity. These

Chinook salmon caught in the Sixes River

include pools along with riffles and rapids, fallen trees and logjams, back channels, sloughs, seasonally flooded riparian forests, marshes, and swamps. Healthy rivers, such as the upper McKenzie or Salmon, have a wealth of these varied habitats. Less healthy streams, such as the lower Willamette or Malheur, have been simplified into a single channel with relatively uniform banks and bed.

Anadromous fishes spawn and hatch in rivers but bide much of their lives at sea where they feed and grow larger in a greater nutrient pool. These fish are among our most valued, iconic, and ecologically important species. They include Chinook and coho salmon, steelhead, coastal cutthroat trout, lamprey, and green and white sturgeon. Anadromous fish inhabit most Oregon rivers, provided passage to sea is free of dam blockages, but every population is plagued by habitat problems, and total numbers may be as low as 3.5 percent of the historic abundance. According to *Atlas of Pacific Salmon* in 2005, 231 distinct stocks of salmon have been extirpated in the United States—mostly in the heavily dammed Columbia basin.

Chinook form the mainstay of most Oregon salmon runs, though they are the least common salmon worldwide. Fall Chinook dominate, entering the rivers in the autumn and moving upriver with the first rain and increasing river runoff. Less common, spring Chinook ("springers") enter the rivers in springtime and stay through summer. Being large and relatively plentiful in Oregon compared to other salmon species, Chinook are the basis of much of the state's recreational angling, especially along coastal streams.

Few healthy populations of coho salmon remain in Oregon, though wild coho are increasing (at this writing) in coastal rivers due to reduction in harvest and hatchery impacts. The Columbia basin has only a few wild struggling coho populations remaining, and all wild coho above Bonneville Dam are extinct. Efforts to enhance remaining coho populations guide a number of river restoration efforts. Unlike most fall Chinook, which quickly drift out to sea, coho live a full year or more in streams, where they depend on clean water, cool temperatures under the shade of riparian forests, fallen trees where they take shelter during floods, and healthy unchannelized estuaries where juveniles rear and feed. Because coho spend more time in streams, they are more vulnerable than Chinook to watershed damage from logging, making them (along with steelhead and coastal cutthroat trout) a key indicator of river health. The lake-and-stream hydrologic basins along the central coast, including Tenmile and Siltcoos, are some of the most productive coho waters remaining, owing to the lakes functioning somewhat like estuaries with shallow-water refuges and wetland-based food supplies. Chum salmon were once plentiful in Oregon but barely persist in the Tillamook and a few other northern basins, and have largely been forgotten.

Steelhead are anadromous rainbow trout that grow larger than their freshwater counterparts by migrating to the ocean's greater food source for most of their lives. Different "runs" return to their natal rivers at different times; winter runs are dominant in most coastal streams. Like coho, steelhead depend on freshwater quality and good watershed conditions—they rear one or more years before migrating to sea, and thus can be threatened in basins with heavy logging, grazing, and farming. Relatively healthy populations survive in the better-protected rivers of the Siskiyou Mountains along the south coast.

More rare, summer steelhead migrate up larger rivers east of the Cascades: Hood, Deschutes, John Day, Umatilla, and Grande Ronde. On the coast, wild "summers" are found only in the Siletz, Umpqua, and Rogue (hatchery fish return to the Tillamook and Nestucca). Unlike winter steelhead, summers haven't sexually matured when they arrive from the ocean, so they holdover for several months in freshwater and are vulnerable to pollution including high water temperatures. Those that migrate up the larger rivers encounter dams, especially in the Columbia-Snake basin.

Coastal cutthroat trout also migrate to the ocean but often stay in rivers longer after hatching—up to 8 years. When they go to sea, they don't go far, usually lingering near river mouths and remaining vulnerable to freshwater conditions. Some reside life-long as residents in upper reaches of streams separated from the ocean by waterfalls.

Sturgeon are North America's largest freshwater fish, surviving from an evolutionary history that predates nearly all other fish. They migrate from the ocean into lower reaches of Oregon's largest rivers. Also anadromous, but alien, American shad were transported from the East Coast to the Sacramento River in 1871 and soon strayed to Oregon. They move up some streams in spring and have become popular among Columbia River anglers.

Anadromous species are central to the health of entire river systems. Many animals eat salmon directly, including 41 species of mammals, 89 birds, 5 reptiles, and 2 amphibians—137 altogether, not counting a plethora of insects and invertebrates. More fundamentally, salmon bring nutrients back from the sea, where those nutrients are plentiful, to rivers, where they're limited. Thus, whole aquatic and terrestrial ecosystems have been nourished by the nutrient detritus left when these fish die after spawning. This annual nutrient exchange once entailed not hundreds but millions of salmon returning each year from the ocean. The fish likewise formed an important cog in the Northwest's economy. Though significant losses had been occurring for many decades, in the 1990s salmon fisheries still generated more than $1 billion a year in personal income and supported 60,000 jobs according to the Pacific Rivers Council, but those numbers have shrunk dramatically in recent years.

For proper functioning of the entire ecosystem and a return of the bygone economy, restoration of salmon is needed. The Wild Salmon Center's "salmon strongholds" are streams where viable populations can hopefully be maintained: the Nehalem, Tillamook, North Umpqua, Rogue, Sandy, Clackamas, and North Fork John Day, though other streams are important.

Unlike anadromous species, resident fishes live their entire lives in freshwater. Oregon's most common trout—the rainbow—thrives as a feisty game fish; both native and hatchery-based populations inhabit upper reaches of streams flowing from the Cascades and interior ranges. Other resident native fishes needing cold water include suckers, sculpins, and mountain whitefish.

Bull trout (sometimes called Dolly Varden, which is a similar species) migrate great distances in rivers and require especially cold water. These large fish once thrived through much of Oregon but survive in only 13 basins (4 percent of their original state range), mostly east of the Cascade crest. On the west side, the only remaining native bull trout linger in the McKenzie, though they've been out-planted to the Middle Fork Willamette and Clackamas. It's no coincidence that 75 percent of these threatened fish appear in roadless wild areas. Survivors face continuing risks from logging, grazing, dams, and diversions, all of which fragment habitat and isolate fish in pockets lacking connectivity needed for genetic exchange.

Columbia redband trout—a form of rainbow—evolved in the dry watersheds of eastern Oregon where they hang-on in isolated refuges, tolerating warm water better than other trout. Threatened Lahontan cutthroat trout survive in a few desert streams—vestigial habitat from the once-vast ice-age Lake Lahontan.

Whether anadromous or resident, native fishes have evolved in their home basins for millennia and are uniquely suited to natural conditions, while alien species from other parts of the country or globe pose fatal problems to native fish by preying on them, competing for food, preempting habitat, and introducing exotic diseases. Alien fishes include bass, bluegill, walleye, crappie, brown bullhead, carp, and mosquitofish. These often thrive in manipulated environments created by dams, diversions, and warm water. Non-native game fishes include shad, bass, bluegill, brown trout, brook trout, and catfish. While recognizing the appeal that some of these have to anglers, this *Field Guide* gives emphasis to native fish and the need for their protection.

Hatcheries are intended to increase the sport and commercial catch but they also affect native fish in profound ways. They add great numbers of fish to rivers where native fish are already struggling. The stocked fish compete with natives for food and habitat, introduce diseases that thrive in the feedlot-tanks of the hatcheries, stray into wild habitat on their return from the ocean, and then compromise the genetic makeup of the wild fish by interbreeding. Perhaps most important, adding large numbers of stocked fish to streams masks the decline of naturally reproducing fish, and thus the measures needed to protect them. Though popular among many anglers—and providing the bulk of fish that are caught in many rivers—the hatcheries often diminish wild stocks and may ultimately fail as their own difficulties increase and costs rise (for more on this complex topic, see *Salmon Without Rivers* by biologist James Lichatowich).

Freshwater Ecoregions of North America considers Oregon "continentally outstanding" for native fishes, yet their status here and throughout much of the West is classified as "endangered." Counting all Oregon's native fish species, 24 are listed under the Endangered Species Act as threatened or endangered, 31 are at-risk as "sensitive" species, and 9 are extinct. In another study, considering resident fishes only, the American Fisheries Society listed 25 subspecies at risk, making Oregon the fifth-worst state in the nation (this lowly rank owes in part to the fact that many native species elsewhere have been eliminated and are no longer "at risk"). One approach to part of this problem is the Department of Fish and Wildlife's designation of "Wild Trout Waters" for management to benefit native trout. Designation can mean catch-and-release requirements and no stocking of hatchery fish.

Each region of Oregon has its ichthyologic specialties. Coastal rivers are renowned for salmon and steelhead, which excel here with the greater nutrient supplies of the ocean. These species suffer, however, with habitat destruction from logging, roads, channelization of estuaries, hatcheries, and unnaturally warm water. Though badly depleted, the best native runs remain in the Nehalem, Siletz, Nestucca, Elk, Rogue, and Chetco basins. Determined efforts are being made to improve habitat in virtually all Oregon rivers, including dam removals on the Rogue and decommissioning of roads along the Siuslaw.

Streams of the Cascade region support native rainbow trout. Sport fishing is popular on the McKenzie and other west-slope streams and on the east-side Metolius, Deschutes, and Williamson. Salmon and steelhead fin their way up many Cascade rivers including the Sandy, Clackamas, and Santiam, though dams have blocked important migration routes and hatcheries have compromised native runs.

Lower-elevation rivers of the Willamette Valley were once home to many native fishes, but wetland drainage, dams, diversions, pollution, and alien species have taken a toll. Anglers today catch mostly introduced bass, catfish, and other aliens. Restoration successes throughout the Cascade region include pollution abatement in the Willamette, dam removals at the Calapooia, and watershed repair across many basins following excessive logging that will continue to degrade fisheries for decades.

In the dry-country rivers east of the Deschutes, residual salmon and steelhead runs remain where stream damage has not been egregious. Ocean-going fishes are hampered by four massive dams on the Columbia and then four more on the lower Snake, but persist in the John Day (where only two dams lie downstream), the Umatilla (where salmon were eradicated, then reinstated), and a few Snake tributaries. Dam removal on the lower Snake would bring greater returns of anadromous fish according to the Northwest Power and Conservation Council's Independent Scientific Group and others, and this may be the only way to remedy the long-term trajectory toward extinction of wild fish there (see Chapter 3).

Endemic species that live only in one stream or a limited area include the Umpqua chub and Umpqua dace (South and main Umpqua), Umpqua pikeminnow (Umpqua, Siuslaw, and Rogue, where it was accidentally introduced), Klamath Lake sculpin and slender sculpin (upper Klamath), Millicoma dace (Millicoma), and Miller Lake lamprey (Klamath basin). Willamette River dams and diversions reduced once-plentiful Oregon chubs to endangered status by 1993. Reintroductions and habitat restorations such as at the McKenzie confluence are now increasing the chub's range, and its status was downgraded to threatened in 2010. Landlocked basins of southcentral Oregon have the endemic Alvord chub, Borax Lake chub, and Warner sucker, plus a rare redband.

While many people enjoy fish by catching them, fish-watching is a delightful reward of spending time on rivers. From the front of a canoe or raft, fish can often be seen while the boat moves downriver. Sculpins can sometimes be spotted in shallow waters. To see fish better, a mask and snorkel are excellent additions to river gear. After the first good rains of autumn, salmon enter the streams of coastal Oregon and can be seen swimming upriver or spawning over beds of gravel. Good places to watch salmon or steelhead migrating upstream and jumping waterfalls in autumn are Rainie Falls on the Rogue, Fish Hatchery Park on the Applegate, Little Falls on the Illinois, Smith River Falls on the Smith, North Fork Falls on the Alsea, and Waterloo Falls on the South Santiam (see Part II).

The health of fish populations governs the lives of other wildlife that depend on them, and the conditions of rivers that determine the status of fish also affect a large suite of birds, mammals, reptiles, amphibians, and invertebrates.

WILDLIFE

Wildlife draws many of us to the outdoors. Statewide 1.7 million people participated in wildlife watching in 2008 according to the Oregon Department of Fish and Wildlife—nearly two times the number that fished and hunted, important as those activities are.

Oregon and Washington have less than 5 percent of the landmass of the forty-eight states but 37 percent of native bird species and 42 percent of mammal species. This diversity owes to the many types of habitat, and among these, biologists regard riparian areas as most important. According to the *Oregon Wildlife Diversity Plan*, the state's relatively small riparian acreage is critical to 55 percent of the state's amphibians, 66 percent of the reptiles, 40 percent of the birds, and 49 percent of the mammals. All are stressed or imperiled by an 80 percent decline in riparian habitat throughout the West. The yellow-billed cuckoo, for example, went extinct locally following the loss of forests along the Willamette and lower Columbia.

Near the base of the food chain, aquatic insects fill vital needs in the lives of fish and larger wildlife. Many eat algae, and when insect populations crash owing to pollution or siltation, the algae can multiply to stifling mats that consume oxygen when they die and rot—further degrading water quality. Crawfish, mussels, and other invertebrate species likewise play pivotal roles in river ecosystems.

Waterfowl are the most evident river-dependent wildlife. Common mergansers dive underwater and subsist largely on fish. Mallards, wood ducks, and pintails dabble and feed at the surface. Double-crested cormorants linger in lower reaches of coastal rivers.

Wading birds that spear minnows, crayfish, and other small animals include the great blue heron, snowy egret, and green heron. Emblematic of Oregon rivers, kingfishers perch on limbs above streams and catch small fish for 90 percent of their diet. Swallows and flycatchers dart above the water to snatch insects. Ospreys soar and dive from great heights for fish. Spotted sandpipers peck for insects in the sand. Less common birds dependent on riparian areas are calliope hummingbirds, which nest there, as do Veerys in the Blue Mountains. Yellow warblers, gray catbirds, MacGillivray's warblers, common yellowthroats, Wilson's warblers, yellow-breasted chats, Lincoln's sparrows, red-winged blackbirds, and willow flycatchers all depend on riparian areas.

As the quintessential river mammals, fur-bearers are capable of staying warm in cold water. Beavers build dams of sticks and mud, raising the level of small streams, which arrests streambed downcutting that comes with land disturbance, and they create wetlands benefitting many creatures. Otters live on fish, crayfish, and frogs. Much smaller, mink scurry at water's edge where they seek similar prey.

Other mammals dependent on rivers or riparian areas include the water shrew on the Cascades' east side, water vole, muskrat, Pacific jumping mouse, and mountain cottontail. Several bats thrive on rivers' insect life, including the hoary bat and little brown myotis. Terrestrial mammals, such as deer, elk, squirrels, foxes, bears, and coyotes all come to streams to drink, or for cover in the riparian zone—often the only natural habitat remaining. They use riverfronts as corridors that link otherwise fragmented natural landscapes together.

Illustrations in the next chapter identify 50 species of plants and animals commonly seen along Oregon rivers.

CHAPTER 2

FIFTY SPECIES OF RIVER AND RIPARIAN PLANTS AND ANIMALS

This chapter highlights only a sampling of what you'll see along Oregon waters but includes many of the most common or important plants and animals.

Maidenhair fern
Adiantum pedatum

Along deeply wooded streams and shaded riverbanks of the coastal mountains, Siskiyous, and Cascades, the maidenhair is recognized by its radial fan-like branching and delicate appearance. Leafstalks resemble thin black wire; Indians wove them into baskets. The vivid green pinna brighten rock gardens, spring seeps, and waterfalls.

Oregon ash
Fraxinus latifolia

This tree grows so commonly along low-elevation rivers and wetlands that it's called water ash—a mainstay of Willamette floodplains and lower tributaries. Though often stunted, it can reach 80 feet. Unlike most riparian trees, which thrive in well-drained sandy soils, these root in bottomlands where water lingers. Important for the shade it casts over streams, the foliage is savored by deer and elk.

Bigleaf maple
Acer macrophyllum

Though not confined to riverfronts, this grand tree dominates the edges of many rivers from the Cascades west. Largest American maple, its leaves can span 12 inches in order to capture spare sunlight in the Northwest's deep groves. When backlit these leaves enliven streamfronts in green domes arcing 100 feet. Squirrels devour and store the seeds. The maple hosts lichens and mosses that total four times the weight of its leaves—drapery on trunks and limbs that emblematizes deciduous old-growth and lends a rainforest-look to many riverfronts.

Vine maple

Acer circinatum

A shrubby tree west of the Cascade crest, vine maple does well on riverbanks where its delicate seven-lobed leaves appear delightfully star-like. Translucent green foliage turns to the Northwest's most dazzling yellow, orange, and red in autumn. Deer and elk browse the twigs while birds and squirrels garner seeds. Indians crafted durable baskets from vine-like branches.

Red osier dogwood

Cornus sericea

Known by its maroon stems, this shrub reaches 15 feet in tangled thickets along streambanks from high mountains to valleys. Berrylike fruits are targeted by songbirds and bears; twigs nourish deer, elk, and rabbits.

Black cottonwood

Populus trichocarpa

This is the magnificent giant of Oregon riverfronts—the tallest and girthiest broadleaf tree in the Northwest, 3 or more feet in diameter and over 100 feet high, with furrowed bark. Triangular leaves stretch longer than wide, unlike Fremont cottonwood with its wide heart-shaped leaves in drier terrain. Cottonwoods are identified from a distance by the lighter green undersides of their leaves, evident in rustling wind. They thrive on floodplains at low-medium elevations, and grow quickly with roots thickly stitched into riverbanks. This keystone species offers food and shelter for many animals, plus nesting sites for birds.

Northwest willow

Salix sessilifolia

One of three dozen Oregon willow species, this grows to 25 feet along the Willamette and south to the Siskiyou Mountains with leaves up to 4 inches long (often smaller), hairy underneath, and broadest near the middle. Other riverfront willows include Scouler (oblong leaves that diagnostically broaden toward the tips), Sitka (larger 3–5 inch leaves and satin-like hairs underneath), peachleaf (rising to 70 feet in northern/ eastern Oregon), and Geyer (reddish twigs and toothless leaves blunted at tips). Because they hybridize, many willows are difficult to identify.

Pacific willow
Salix lasiandra

Up to 60 feet tall, this has the widest range among Oregon willows, populating sandbars/riverfronts in all regions but the desert. Leaves grow to 5 inches long, 1 inch wide, finely toothed, sharply pointed, dark green above, hairless/whitish underneath, and nearly as thin as Northwest willow but more pointed. It's sometimes called black willow, which on the West Coast occurs mostly south of Oregon.

California laurel
Umbellularia californica

In Oregon this aromatic tree is proudly called "myrtle" and shades riverfronts in the southern Coast Range. Old-growth reaches 100 feet and 3 feet in diameter, often multiple stemmed. Broad but evergreen, narrow, pointed leaves are sharply pungent when crushed. Squirrels and Steller's jays eat the purple, olive-like fruits. The tree graces shaded hollows along the Rogue; other superb groves can be seen at the Chetco's Loeb State Park and Coquille Myrtle Grove State Park south of Myrtle Point. The wood is valued for crafted furnishings.

Red alder
Alnus rubra

Most common among four Oregon alders, the red grows mostly west of the Willamette, lining banks of coastal streams. Leaves are doubly toothed with margins rolled under. Though usually small, it can reach 80 feet. Nearly white bark is artfully patterned with gray and decorated with moss and lichen. Alders are so common that they're taken for granted, but their role in ecosystems is crucial, hosting nitrogen-fixing bacteria in their roots. They feed beavers, rabbits, deer, mountain beavers, moose, elk, porcupines, and grouse.

White alder inhabits high-mountain streams, and its leaf margins are not rolled under. Sitka alder, at the coast, reaches only 25 feet and has singly toothed leaves with shiny sticky undersides and unrolled edges. The shrubby thinleaf alder has flat, doubly toothed leaves.

Water birch
Betula occidentalis

This small sprawling tree features shiny whitish bark that matures to rusty brown and grows among rocks in the mountains of eastern Oregon where runoff splashes the roots. Seeds are eaten by chickadees and other small birds; grouse favor the catkins.

Poison oak
Toxicodendron diversilobum

With three shiny, irregularly lobed leaflets, poison oak grows as a shrub, occasionally to 15 feet, or as a vine in the Coast Range, Siskiyous, and low Cascades. It excels on both riparian and drier ground. Toxin in leaves and stems triggers rashes, blisters, and itching that can take 6 weeks to run their miserable course. Prompt washing can remove the oil before it takes effect. Hot compresses of concentrated saltwater temporarily relieve itching and dry the blisters.

Armenian (Himalayan) blackberry
Rubus discolor

This alien species has expanded from roadside incursions west of the Cascades and now sprawls impenetrably over riverbanks. Thorns are larger than on native blackberries. In late summer, fruits make sweet desserts on many river trips, but this invader displaces native forbs, shrubs, and trees.

Scotch broom
Cytisus scoparius

This aggressive alien shrub has stem-like evergreen foliage and yellow pea-like flowers. Invading disturbed sites, it preempts willows, cottonwoods, and alders. Though seeds remain viable 50 years, cutting or pulling broom gives native competitors an advantage; once shaded, the shrub dies.

Western pearlshell mussel
Margaritifera falcata

This is one of many freshwater mussels and clams, which are bivalves: a ligament attaches opposing shells that protect soft tissue in between. Evident in many rivers, single detached shells wash ashore after the mollusk dies. They provide food for shore birds, ducks, turtles, fish, crayfish, raccoons, muskrats, minks, and otters. Because clams and mussels are filter feeders, they are sensitive to pollution, depleted flows, and siltation. Conversely, the presence of native shellfish indicates aquatic health.

The pearlshell and other mussels (*Unionidae*) anchor in sand or gravel and use tubular siphons to draw in water and eat algae. Females release thousands of embryos that anchor to gills or scales of fish for dispersal, later falling into the streambed to grow. The pearlshell lives up to 100 years, mostly in clear waters populated by salmon or trout. It can still be found in some backwaters of the Willamette.

Crayfish   *Pacifastacus leniusculus*

Four-inch crustaceans with five pairs of legs, crayfish resemble tiny lobsters. They cling to the bottom of pools and scavenge worm, fish, and larvae carrion, and are eaten by fish and frogs. Burrowing on silty shorelines, crayfish erect hollow dirt columns of pelletized mud an inch high. Meat in the tails and claws are considered a delicacy by some people.

Mayflies   order *Ephemeroptera*

Adult mayflies flutter over the water as evanescent inch-long insects with two or three upturned tails and transparent upturned wings. They live 1 or 2 days without feeding, hovering in a mass known as a "hatch." Trout and young salmon favor them so much that fly fishermen craft countless look-alike flies. During mayflies' nymph (larval) stage, they cling to undersides of stones in moving water. Grazing on algae, they are important converters of plant nutrients to animal protein. Filling a similar ecological niche, stoneflies are nearly black and wear long translucent wings that rest against their bodies. Adults leave the water to crawl along shores. Also prime fish-food, caddisflies build larval shelters of sand particles glued together in columns, found by turning over rocks in riffles. All these insects indicate good water quality.

Blue-eyed darner dragonfly *Aeshna multicolor*

Among the largest insects, dragonflies reach 3.5 inches with bulbous compound eyes and double sets of wings. Darting over water, they prey upon flying insects including mosquitoes, and they rest with wings outstretched. Eggs hatch into larvae that eat mosquito and other larvae and in turn become food for fish, shorebirds, and waterfowl. With one of the widest ranges among Oregon's 63 dragonfly species, the blue-eyed darner male sports bright blue eyes, a blue face, and blue stripes on its thorax.

Vivid dancer damselfly

Argia vivida

Like dragonflies, damselflies have double sets of wings but are slender and shorter (1.5 inches), and most fold the wings against their bodies when resting. The vivid dancer has one of the widest ranges among Oregon's 28 species, though it avoids the coast. It has bright blue thorax, body, and eyes, with a black stripe behind the head. Other species are blue, green, or red. All prey on mosquitoes and smaller insects, while their larvae are eaten by shorebirds and waterfowl.

Water strider

family *Gerridae*

Skating on the surface of eddies and pools, striders stay afloat owing to surface tension; their feet bristle with non-wettable hairs that do not penetrate the surface film of water. When alarmed, they dive but stay dry with water-repellent scales that cover their bodies. While submerged they breathe oxygen from air bubbles trapped among tiny hairs. Less than an inch long—mostly legs—striders dart quickly across the surface several inches at once.

Similar but smaller, ripple bugs are broader at the shoulders and frequent pools in dense agitated swarms. Heavier bodied and without the striders' long legs, water boatmen swim as if randomly bouncing back and forth on the surface. All three species eat aquatic insects or flying insects that drop onto the water.

Pacific lamprey

Lampetra tridentata

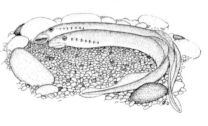

The most primitive fish, lampreys lack paired fins and scales, and have a sucking circular mouth with rasping teeth rather than jaws (eels, in contrast, have jaws). Their skeletons are not bone but cartilage. Adults excavate pits in riffles for spawning. Eggs hatch into larvae called ammocoetes, which dwell in mud or sand and filter-feed 3–8 years. Like other anadromous fishes, these lamprey (not all) migrate to sea, returning to spawn. Oregon has five other species, some with localized ranges. Once phenomenally abundant, these fishes played important but unrecognized roles in river ecosystems. All populations are now imperiled.

White sturgeon
Acipenser transmontanus

This largest North
American freshwater
fish historically
reached 20 feet
and 1,400 pounds.
Individuals can live a century, gaining weight the whole time. Ancient
species, they have cartilaginous skeletons and bony scutes—plates
showing as lumps on their back and sides. Mouths like flexible hoses
suck up bottom-dwelling invertebrates. Sturgeon inhabit estuaries and
the ocean but swim up the lower Columbia, Snake, and Rogue to spawn
and are occasionally seen rolling near the surface. Eggs are laid in deep
stony sites where they tumble in current and disperse before anchoring
to the bottom. Similar green sturgeon grow to 7 feet; in Oregon
they are found in the Columbia estuary and a few coastal rivers but
probably spawn only in the Rogue. Slow maturation makes both species
vulnerable to overharvest and poaching for caviar.

Bull trout
Salvelinus confluentus

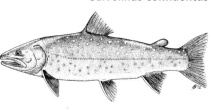

This member of the
char family has a dark
olive-brown body with
light yellow spots,
reaches 3 feet in length,
and has a broader/longer
head than other trout
and salmon. Small bull
trout look like brook trout but have no black worm-like spots on dorsal
fins. Bull trout need long reaches of clean, cold, gravel-filled rivers for
migration, spawning, and foraging on sculpins, trout, and whitefish.
Logging has eliminated essential pristine habitat through much of the
fish's range.

Brook trout
Salvelinus fontinalis

Introduced "brookies"
sport blue halos around
pink-to-red spots on
their sides. They have
worm-shaped spots
on the dorsal fins, and
the breeding male's red
underbelly blends to
yellow. Natives of the East, they favor small spring-fed streams and have
been introduced to Oregon's highcountry lakes. Some waters teem with
so many that their size is stunted at six inches and they displace native
cutthroats and rainbows.

Brown trout
Salmo trutta

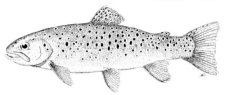

Introduced from
Europe, this trout has
black and red spots
covering most of its
body, including the
gill cover. Voracious,
they decimate juvenile
natives including rainbow trout. Browns excel in deep pools and tolerate
warmer water than other trout. Wary of anglers, they often wait to slowly
take a lure. Favored technique is to drift bait or spinners underwater
through deep pools.

Coastal cutthroat trout
Oncorhynchus clarki

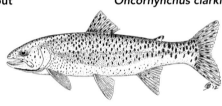

In both anadromous
and resident forms,
and in variable colors,
this beautiful trout is
distinguished by a red
line or "cut" under its
lower jaw and many
distinct black spots on its body. Its range extends throughout coastal
watersheds. Some never go to sea, particularly when above waterfalls,
and are potadromous—migrating within their river system from small
streams to large as they grow. Many occupy nearshore Pacific waters
in summer and return upriver to winter and spawn. Pure genetic
forms have been altered through hybridization with rainbow trout and
numerous developed hatchery stocks.

Rainbow trout/steelhead
Oncorhynchus mykiss

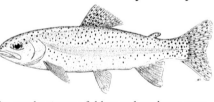

Rainbows have small
irregular spots on
their sides and a long
pinkish-red stripe. In
part owing to hatcheries,
these are Oregon's most
abundant trout, and
their range was expanded by outplantings to fishless and cutthroat trout
waters. Natives in isolated streams east of the Cascades evolved into
a subspecies, redband. All rainbows like cold riffling currents. They
position in eddies behind rocks and await prey in the drift, favoring
caddisflies, stoneflies, and mayflies. Camp Sherman on the Metolius is
an excellent place to see them.

Steelhead are anadromous rainbows that migrate to sea where they
grow to 45 inches—much larger than their freshwater cousins. After two
years they return to spawn. Coho, which enter rivers at the same time, are
similar in appearance, but steelhead generally develop less of a hooked

jaw, and are often more silvery and slender. Young steelhead and coho both thrive in small cold streams, but steelhead generally like riffles while coho prefer pools. Steelhead can return to the ocean after spawning.

Both resident rainbows and steelhead spawn in the spring; steelhead may move from the ocean into the rivers in autumn and remain there until spawning season. Unlike salmon, steelhead feed while moving upriver. This fastest freshwater fish can swim 27 feet per second and are a favorite of anglers. Wild steelhead are imperiled throughout most of their range and must be released when caught. Hatchery fish, identified by a clipped adipose fin (forward from the tail), can be kept.

Chinook (king) salmon   *Oncorhynchus tshawytscha*

Chinook salmon have distinct black spots on the back, on the adipose fin, and on both lobes of the tail fin (coho salmon have spots only on the upper tail lobe). Up to 4 feet long, Chinook grow larger than coho.

Fall Chinook spawn in coastal streams, entering with autumn rains. Others migrate far up Columbia tributaries. Eggs are laid November/December and hatch March/April. Tiny parr move downstream 3–4 weeks after hatching. Most young smolts go to sea within months, though some remain in streams for a year. "Springers" enter rivers in spring and remain through summer for autumn spawning. Once they leave the ocean, adults don't eat but subsist on body oils, a trait that makes Chinook a delicacy. Most runs are in jeopardy owing to dams, diversions, habitat loss, alien predators, hatcheries, and overharvest. Rainie Falls on the Rogue remains a good place to see them leaping upstream in October. Migrating or spawning Chinook can also be spotted in many coastal streams after the initial high waters of autumn clear.

Coho (silver) salmon   *Oncorhynchus kisutch*

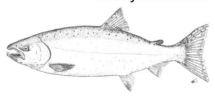

Coho are similar to Chinook but usually under 3 feet. With black spots on their backs and on the upper half of their caudal fins, they develop pink-red sides and a hooked jaw during breeding season. If you get a good look, the coho's gums are gray or white while the Chinook's are black. Young parr have a uniformly speckled adipose fin and a sickle-shaped anal fin with a white edge. Coho spawn in small streams, and the fry winter over before going to sea. Their decline can indicate stream temperatures above a fatal 77 degrees F, or silt pollution that damages the gills.

Channel catfish

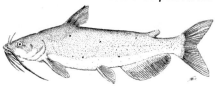

Favoring deep languid warm waters, several species of catfish were introduced here from elsewhere in the United States and have naturalized. Channel catfish have forked tails, black spots along their sides, and grow to 3 feet. They lie beneath overhanging banks and among sunken roots, tolerating brackish or polluted water. All catfish bristle four pairs of barbels—whisker-like stingers around the mouth—and have shiny gray skin lacking scales.

Riffle sculpin
Cottus gulosus

Sculpins are a delightfully distinctive native fish family with protruding eyes, large mouths, extended dorsal fins, long anal fins, and wide pectoral fins. Their flattened bodies, 2–4 inches long, are designed to lie on the bottom behind rocks where they ambush drifting insect larvae. Camouflaged, they can be seen if you look carefully in riffles and gravelly backwaters. Riffle sculpins inhabit clean cold streams through much of the Oregon coast, but not the Rogue.

Smallmouth bass
Micropterus dolomieu

This popular game fish from the East dominates many large rivers and lower elevation reservoirs. Like other sunfish, they are large-bodied with elongated dorsal fins. Smallmouth prefer warm water and gravel bottoms; largemouth favor warmer reservoirs. Opportunistic omnivores, they decimate crayfish and native fishes including young salmon.

Rough-skinned newt
Taricha granulosa

These salamanders are the most seen amphibians, 4 inches long, orange below, reddish brown above. Big eyes, soft bodies, languid movements, and cartoon-like feet endear them to many. In late winter, adults abandon underground shelters and roam the landscape without fear of predators; imbedded tetrodotoxin is powerful enough that ingestion of one newt could be fatal. Their slow pace and peregrinations endanger them at road crossings. Survivors enter streams and grow a fin for swimming. Eggs hatch into yellow larvae with gills. When 2 inches long, these "tadpoles" metamorphose, grow lungs, and exit the water to begin their terrestrial stage.

Pacific tree frog   *Pseudacris regilla*

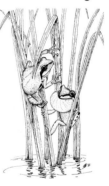

This most common West Coast frog is capable of climbing with its bulbous toes but spends more time in water than in trees. Its cricket-like call continues day and night. Females lay eggs in calm water; tadpoles hatch and small frogs swarm on gravel bars. Adults transform from brown to green and grow to 2 inches. Also in Oregon, the northern red-legged frog— up to 5 inches—is gray to reddish brown, with small dark blotches, yellow underneath, and rusty red on its rear legs and belly, found along low-elevation streams west of the Cascades but also wandering away from water. Its feeble prolonged croak contrasts with rapid patterns of the Cascades frog at higher elevations. Much larger, alien bullfrogs, with the classic "rivet," decimate native frog populations.

Western pond turtle   *Clemmys marmorata*

Olive brown or almost black on top, with yellowish tints below, this turtle reaches 5–8 inches, basks on partly submerged logs, and hibernates. It eats aquatic plants, insects, and carrion. Females lay 1–13 eggs in holes excavated on shore. Found in the Willamette and middle Rogue, just a tenth of historic numbers have survived habitat loss. Also native, the western painted turtle has yellow neck stripes. Aliens include the snapping turtle—large and stout—and the red-eared slider, with a red stripe behind its eye.

Double-crested cormorant

Most common among three Oregon cormorants, this bird frequents rivers near sea and larger streams inland, including the Snake, though they readily take to the ocean. Along tidal reaches they perch on snags and spread wings to dry after diving for fish. In the mid-1900s DDT decimated populations but they recovered to the point that some anglers consider them competition for limited fisheries (reinstatement of logs and fallen tree debris in estuaries can give fish cover from these and other predators).

Wood duck

Aix sponsa

On slow moving, tree-shaded streams, male wood ducks sport slicked-back crests of green and white with ornate patterns of blue, maroon, black, and white on their wings, breasts, and heads. Quick to flush at the approach of a boat, they fly with a distinct squeaking sound. Dependent on cavities in large trees for nesting, they eat seeds, acorns, and vegetation. Market hunters drove these colorful ducks nearly to extinction in the early 1900s. They've recovered along wooded shorelines, including Willamette tributaries, yet remain vulnerable to loss of riparian forests.

Mallard

Anas platyrhynchos

Everyday resident of city parks, mallards are also among the most common ducks on rivers. Males shine with iridescent green heads and maroon breasts; females are mottled brown. They dip their heads and tip their bodies forward to pluck aquatic vegetation, and leap into flight without running across the water's surface.

Common merganser

Mergus merganser

This is the most common duck on rivers in summer. The female's red head feathers sweep back into a sleek crest. Adult males show a striking green head with white-and-black body. Diving ducks, they swim underwater snagging sculpins, suckers, and other fish with their serrated beaks. In early summer females tend three to seven chicks; the very young scamper onto mother's back for travel. Mergansers are a sign of good fish populations and healthy aquatic ecosystems.

Great blue heron
Ardea herodias

Statuesque, these largest birds of Oregon rivers stand 46 inches. With stilted legs for wading, long necks, and dagger-like beaks for spearing fish, crayfish, frogs, and snakes, they wait at waterline for prey. Building sizable nests of sticks in cottonwoods, herons sometimes group up in rookeries. When disturbed, they croak in a raspy voice and fly with elegantly slow wingbeats.

Bald eagle
Haliaeetus leucocephalus

The national bird made a comeback from threatened status after DDT was banned in 1973. In 2012 nearly 600 nested in Oregon; many more come for winter. The Klamath basin alone gets 1,000. Singles or pairs can be seen along rivers, eating fish acquired dead or alive. They spend most of their time along large waterways, and need tall trees for building nests of sticks.

Osprey
Pandion haliaetus

This fish hawk is the principal raptor of riverscapes, with mottled wings that angle back at the wrist (looks like an elbow) and can span 5 feet. They call in a piercing whistle, especially if you approach their nests—hemispheres of sticks atop tall snags. Ospreys perch on limbs with good vantage to water, or soar until they spot prey, then dive, snatch fish in their talons, and return to their nests to feed their chicks.

Spotted sandpiper

Actitis macularia

With a gray-brown back and white breast—spotted in breeding season—this most-common shorebird along rivers scurries plucking caddisfly and dragonfly nymphs, beetles, and ants at water's edge, tail-bobbing the whole time. It flies with double wing-beats while letting out a shrill cry.

Belted kingfisher

Megaceryle alcyon

This charismatic 12-inch, blue-and-white bird has an impressive crown of head-feathers and powerful beak. With gliding dipping flight it cries in a rattling chattering voice. Kingfishers perch on overhanging limbs or rocks and dive for small fish, occasionally submerging themselves. To nest they dig burrows 3–6 feet deep into sandy banks.

Cliff swallow

Petrochelidon pyrrhonota

The cliff swallow has a squared-off tail and blue cap, and builds a mud-dabbed, gourd-shaped nest in colonies under shelter of overhanging bridges or rocks—basalt columns work well. Five species of swallows collectively rank first in numbers of birds along Oregon rivers. All zoom in acrobatic flight as they catch insects. Tree swallows—green-backed—nest in tree cavities. Similar violet-green

swallows have white underbelly markings that nearly meet on the back behind the wings. The bank swallow is brown with a white chin, white breast, and brown breast band below the chin. Riparian specialist, it nests in holes excavated in banks. The rough-winged swallow looks much like a bank swallow but lacks the brown breast band.

American dipper (water ouzel)   *Cinclus mexicanus*

This 6-inch, slate gray songbird is the star of
mountain streams. Bobbing at the edge of
rapids and in the spray of waterfalls, it plucks
insects from rocks and dives to swim or walk
on the bottom, snagging larvae sometimes 20
feet deep. Its chatter occasionally bursts forth
with a melody of trills. Dippers are the only
songbirds that winter over at unfrozen spots
along mountain streams.

Canyon wren   *Catherpes mexicanus*

Dwelling along canyon riverfronts of eastern
Oregon, this 5-inch wren has a rusty back, white
upper breast, and long down-turned yellow bill
that probes for insects among rocks. It's best
identified by a delightful descending trill that
becomes slower at the end.

Beaver   *Castor canadensis*

Oregon's official state
animal is America's largest
rodent, reaching 60 pounds
and living in streams up to
7,000 feet. Beavers prefer
twigs and bark of willows,
aspens, cottonwoods,
and alders. Bacteria and
protozoa in their stomachs
digest cellulose; scat
resembles coarse sawdust.
Occasionally seen in
daylight, beavers are chiefly

nocturnal; staccato slaps of their tails can be heard from river campsites.
Evidence is often seen in cut stumps and limbs, large webbed tracks,
and drag-lines of branches in sand. In Oregon they inhabit riverbank
dens rather than the classic lodges of conical stick-piles seen in
northern ponds. In smaller streams they construct low dams that retard
flows, reverse erosive downcutting, raise water tables, foster riparian
communities, and enhance fish habitat.

River otter
Lontra canadensis

Quintessential river mammals, otters are playful swimmers and aquatic acrobats. Among the largest members of the weasel family, they reach 30 inches. Their size and furry tails set them apart from minks and muskrats, which also swim and scurry at water's edge. Distinctive tracks show 5 toes. A porpoise-like roll in the water might be all you see, but occasionally whiskered heads surface, stare curiously, and hiss. On shore, families romp and lie together in a pile. Though populations were decimated by trapping, numbers have increased and otters again range throughout much of Oregon, even visiting saltwater where they're mistaken for sea otters, which do not occur in Oregon. Scat is an unshaped mass of bone and shell fragments. They eat crayfish, frogs, shellfish, and slow fish such as carp and suckers.

Mink
Mustela vison

Smaller and more terrestrial than otters, mink reach 17 inches and hurry along riverbanks, slipping into water when threatened. They eat mostly invertebrates such as crayfish, plus frogs, but also fish, and occasionally kill muskrats, which are comparable in size but have furless tails and prefer grassy banks.

CHAPTER 3

PROBLEMS, PROTECTION, AND RESTORATION

Oregon rivers serve our needs for water, recreation, and beauty, and they provide for fish and wildlife. But most of the streams have been severely diminished from what nature once offered. The problems for rivers today are water pollution, dams, diversions for water supply and hydroelectric power, floodplain development, invasive species, channelization along with levees and riprap, climate change, and population growth—a fundamental source of many of the other problems. This chapter presents an overview of these difficulties and describes protection and restoration strategies, with attention to places where both troubles and solutions can be seen on the ground (see Part II for river-by-river sites). Here and in later chapters I touch upon Oregon's rich history of river conservation—a topic that deserves an entire book of its own.

WATER POLLUTION

Through a citizen's initiative in 1938, communities built sewage treatment plants along Oregon rivers, but the remedies were far from complete. Increased efforts after a stronger state law in 1967 and the federal Clean Water Act of 1972 brought much of the wastes of towns and cities under control, and the severely polluted Willamette became a community asset and exemplar of industrial and municipal cleanup. Yet problems remain. The *Oregon*

Algae at Keno Dam, Klamath River

Water Quality Index reports that quality is excellent in most of the Cascades region; fair in the Coast Range and Blue Mountains; and poor in the Klamath, Willamette Valley, and eastern basins. According to the Department of Environmental Quality, 26 percent of surveyed miles are impaired with serious problems, and the number rises to 71 percent when additional standards for temperature and biological diversity are considered.

State and federal data indicate that agricultural runoff is the leading culprit. Up to 80 percent of the Willamette's pollution now comes from farm runoff—a problem also seen in the Malheur, Klamath, and estuaries of Tillamook Bay. Evading regulations aimed at the pipe-discharges of cities and industries, farm runoff carries feedlot waste, pesticides, chemical fertilizers, and silt into rivers. Heavy grazing along watercourses causes erosion, compaction of soil, bank collapse from unrestricted cow access, fecal contamination, and downcutting of streams with related losses of groundwater. Recommended practices to avoid pollution include reducing pesticides, increasing water efficiency, shunting surface water around feedlots instead of through them, establishing riparian buffers that allow silt to settle before reaching the river, effective rotation of cattle to prevent overgrazing, fencing livestock from streams, and—most effective of all— organic farming. Many farmers are pursuing these reforms and making headway. For example, with help from the South Coast Watershed Council, some cranberry farmers are starting integrated pest management approaches to reduce pesticide use along salmon bearing rivers.

Polluted runoff is also caused by logging and especially clearcutting that exposes soil to erosion and destabilizes steep slopes. Use of heavy equipment compacts the soil and causes increased runoff. Roads associated with logging cause the worst problems; they sluice water away from

Eroding channel and landslide beginning at a clearcut below a logging road, Lobster Creek, Rogue River watershed

Landslide that extends from a timber sale boundary into the South Fork Coquille

its natural sheet-flow across the land and subsequent percolation into the ground, and instead channel it into ditches, where it scours and triggers landslides. Culverts plug with debris when not maintained, causing water to back up and then overflow across the road, erode it, and cause cave-ins. In Siuslaw National Forest, a single rainstorm in 1975 triggered 245 landslides; all but 27 were traceable to clearcut logging and road building. Following heavy storms in February 1996, Pacific Watershed Associates found that 71 percent of 610 landslides in western Oregon/Washington occurred on relatively bare and recently logged sites.

In contrast, mature forests shelter the soil, provide a thick layer of organic duff that's sponge-like when it rains, and stabilize slopes with networks of roots. Rain and snowmelt consequently soak deep, recharge groundwater, then seep out slowly in dry months. But among forestlands statewide, only about 10 percent remain uncut; in the Coast Range, only 1–6 percent have survived according to *Oregon's Living Landscape* and other sources. Often hidden from highways by a thin "beauty strip," clearcuts and resulting erosion are evident if you fly over Oregon.

To reserve and reestablish undisturbed forests is a critical need for the health of rivers; to improve logging practices where they occur near riverfronts and on steep slopes is another. The Northwest Forest Plan of 1994 improved regulation of logging on National Forest and federal BLM land west of the Cascade crest. But cutting on timber industry property—blanketing 57 percent of the Coast Range and large tracts in the lower Cascades and Blue Mountains—is subject only to state rules that allow unrestricted cutting on steep slopes, in riparian areas down to a 100-foot setback (even there logging of large conifers is permitted), and with no buffers along small streams where fish are absent (both California and Washington require better streamside protection). Being too thin, some

Silt discharge into the South Fork Coquille directly below a clearcut and landslide

buffers are blown down once the adjacent forest is cut—a problem evident on the upper Siuslaw and elsewhere. On the South Fork Coquille a massive mudslide extending the entire way from a harvest boundary into the river downstream from Baker Creek is just one example that raises questions about the adequacy of Oregon's state law to protect water quality and salmon-spawning habitat. Washington state law, in contrast, mandates a risk assessment and larger buffers in areas prone to sliding.

In periods of low flow, the state's overall water quality assessment is "poor to very poor," according to *Oregon State of the Environment Report*. Unnatural warming of water is the most common violation of standards. Stream temperatures have increased by up to 10 degrees in the Rogue basin. Warmed water kills or inhibits health and reproduction of native fish and other life, and reduces water's capacity to hold oxygen. When water temperatures exceed 70 degrees F, trout and salmon face disease, stunted growth, and reproductive difficulty; sustained warmth at that temperature kills salmon and trout because pools and cold-water refuges disappear.

Warmed water results where shade is eliminated by clearcutting, overgrazing, farming, paving, and urban development, and also where the flatwater of reservoirs warms in the sun. Watershed disturbance that depletes groundwater recharge further warms streams because they lack input of cold springflows during dry months. In a lawsuit brought by Northwest Environmental Advocates, a U.S. District Court in 2012 ruled that federal agencies had inadequately reviewed Oregon's water standards for temperature. This finding may hasten long-evaded solutions to ubiquitous warm-water problems.

Industrial waste and toxic spills also cause traumatic effects on rivers. Many of Oregon's 17 Superfund toxic sites are located near rivers, including nerve gas lagoons at Hermiston, railroad tie–treating facilities near the Columbia, and many sites in the Willamette Valley and especially in the Portland Harbor area contaminated with dioxin, pesticides, chromium, PCBs, and mercury. Much has been done to clean up waste from industries such as pulp mills, but residual toxins linger in sediment, pollution seeps from unmonitored sources, and new chemicals constantly add to the toxic brew that affects rivers.

Mining is another pollution problem, especially in southwestern and northeastern Oregon. Rivers are still recovering from past abuse, but dozens of new cyanide heap-leach gold mines threatening toxic runoff have been proposed in the Owyhee and Malheur basins. In the salmon-rich Rogue basin, gold miners excavate the riverbed with suction hoses and then run water through the diggings to expose gold—in the process damaging spawning gravels, destabilizing riverbeds and shores, and destroying invertebrate life among the gravel and rocks.

On lower reaches of many rivers, gravel mining without proper care can degrade estuaries, eliminate riparian habitat, and affect the morphology or shape of riverbeds. Oregon's Removal-Fill Law requires a permit for gravel mines of 50 acres or more, or for any mining on State Scenic Waterways and critical salmon-spawning streams. Army Corps of Engineers "404" permits are also required, yet violations are common.

DAMS

Pollution degrades rivers, but dams bury them completely under reservoirs. In Oregon, 1,100 dams rise over 25 feet or contain reservoirs of 50 acre-feet or more, according to the *Atlas of Oregon*. Some of these have provided water, power, and flood control but in the process all have eliminated the rivers' current, gravel beds, and floodplains by permanently flooding them. Dams halt or restrict the migration of fish, including some of the finest salmon and steelhead runs in the Willamette, Clackamas, Santiam, Metolius, Deschutes, Rogue, Klamath, and Snake Rivers. Below the dams, water is often depleted and temperatures heightened. The new conditions aid alien species, which displace natives. Dams also capture silt and gravel that would otherwise be washed downstream, thus withholding deposits from floodplains on the insides of bends where the sediment would naturally and beneficially accumulate. Degrading or entrenched riverbeds result.

Dams built for flood control may lessen or eliminate many floods, but not the largest. When a dam is most needed—after prolonged and intense storms—its reservoir might already be filled, requiring that the full force of floodwaters be released. This occurred in 1996 with the Willamette River floods—unanticipated by people who had come to expect full control by the Army Corps of Engineers and who had proceeded to develop on the floodplain.

Dams also manipulate flows in unnatural ways. Even releases that might appear beneficial, such as in the Rogue below Lost Creek Dam, have been altered, causing harm to native life. Natural rivers run high in winter,

Lost Creek Dam and drawn-down reservoir, Rogue River

spring, and early summer, but dam releases are often low in spring and then high in summer. The inverted schedules wreak havoc on streamlife that evolved under natural conditions, such as native salmon and steelhead needing high rainy-season flows. The Snake River in Hells Canyon offers an extreme example of dam-altered flows: Idaho Power Company generates peaking power upstream, releasing heavily in the afternoon and then holding water back after demand slackens. The resulting daily flush erodes once-expansive sandy beaches, eliminates wildlife and fish habitat at the river's edge, and destroys banks by undercutting them.

Oregon's largest reservoirs are Brownlee on the Snake, McNary on the Columbia, Owyhee on the Owyhee, Link on the Klamath, Round Butte on the Deschutes, John Day on the Columbia, and Lost Creek on the Rogue. In the Willamette basin, 13 sizable dams store 2.3 million acre-feet of water.

In 1976 the Bureau of Reclamation listed 30 "potential" new dam sites in Oregon. Some of these had been authorized but were never constructed, including Days Creek on the South Umpqua, Grande Ronde above La Grande, Catherine Creek on a Grande Ronde tributary, Holley on the Calapooia, and Gate Creek in the McKenzie basin. One of the last big dams to be built was on the Applegate River after an intense campaign to stop it in the late 1970s. But because dams were already constructed on the most economical sites, and because remaining proposals faced growing opposition, the big-dam construction era in the United States ended in the 1980s. A sign of the times, Elk Creek Dam in the Rogue basin was begun but stopped as the tide of public opinion turned. The uncompleted but substantial structure was breached in 2008 to restore salmon runs. Large new dams are seldom discussed today, though proposals may arise again as water and power demands increase with a growing population.

DIVERSIONS

Many Oregon rivers flowing to farms or cities suffer from the diversion of water into canals, ditches, and pipelines. Even in high mountains, streams such as the North Umpqua are modified for hydropower. The U.S. Geological Survey in 2011 found that 90 percent of the mileage of major streams in the United States were degraded from diversions. The diminished flows fail to provide enough water for fish and wildlife, cause temperatures to climb, lessen the ability of streams to maintain their channels through periodic flooding, destroy fishes' spawning habitat, favor alien species such as carp that tolerate low flows, concentrate pollutants, eliminate recreation opportunities, and make less water available for people downstream. Canal headgates, unscreened ditches, and pumps can entrain, trap, and funnel fish into turbines and irrigated fields. Half of Oregon's cropland is irrigated, which accounts for 88 percent of the state's total water diversions. Cattle alone account for 70 percent of this amount, according to *The Oregon Water Handbook*.

A complex convention of water rights governs diversions, determined by who claimed the water first and having little to do with the amount of water needed for the life of the river or for other uses. According to the Department of Water Resources' *Integrated Water Resources Strategy* of 2012, the state has typically over-appropriated streams throughout Oregon—more water is permitted for withdrawal than exists during low-flow periods. Agricultural diversions create problems for fish in the Deschutes, Powder, Klamath, Crooked, John Day, Umatilla, Wallowa, and Owyhee. Municipal withdrawal plans have threatened the Clackamas, McKenzie, Row, and Kilchis. *WaterWatch* monitors allocation and advocates for instream flows.

The depleted Powder River is at the left; a ditch carrying most of the water is at the right

Efficient irrigation can solve some diversion problems. Savings result from laser-leveling of fields, conversion from flood to sprinkler or drip facilities, and monitoring to avoid overwatering. Screens built on ditches can prevent fish entrapment. In cities and homes, residents can fix leaks, install water-saving shower heads and low-flush toilets, and avoid waste when washing cars and sprinkling lawns. Owing to conservation measures, urban water use per capita in many cities has decreased in recent years.

State laws long enabled water users to claim and extract water with little concern for the streams, but in 1987 the legislature established a reservation system for instream flows benefitting fish and wildlife. With a good record compared to the rest of the West, Oregon now has 1,500 instream rights specified for protection. However, "minimum" prescribed flows here are far from optimum, they are typically junior water rights subordinate to established users, and they lack adequate monitoring.

FLOODPLAIN DEVELOPMENT AND LOSS OF RIPARIAN HABITAT

Flowing water is only part of a river. Floodplains and riparian habitat form the rest. No less important to the health of the river system, these lowlands constitute 15 percent of the state and are vulnerable to loss from development. Attractive to settlers and farmers, riverfronts were among the first lands to be claimed by homesteaders and the timber industry, setting the stage for flood damage and habitat loss. For example, the most crucial areas for threatened coho salmon are wide valleys with low stream gradient near the ocean, but 90 percent of those are now private and half have been developed or recently logged.

Delineation for floodplain zoning depends on hydrologic analysis, but a simple informed view can reveal much. The floodplains lie next to

Floodplain development, lower McKenzie River

the water, and the riparian zone includes plantlife that depends on the stream or related groundwater. Development in zones subject to powerful flood-flows leads to hazards and costly losses, but building in any riparian habitat degrades natural river values.

Many counties and communities have adopted floodplain regulations, but most reflect only minimum standards to make subsidized federal flood insurance available to residents. This program requires communities to zone the floodplain for open space, but loopholes for flood "proofing" of buildings are exploited, and structures are permitted in flood areas if the first floor is elevated. Testament to its failure at preventing future losses, the insurance program's greatest costs go for damage where homes or businesses flood repeatedly. Losses from the February 1996 flood in the Portland region alone cost $60 million when 202 homes were inundated. With climate change, the likelihood of far greater "megafloods" is high, according to a January 2013 *Scientific American* article, and the damages will be extreme.

Because of floodplain development combined with logging, farming, and grazing, the *Oregon State of the Environment Report* concluded, "Riparian conditions are typically poor or very poor across the state, with the exception of some high mountain streams." Acreage of bottomland forests in the Western Cascades region, including the Willamette Valley, has declined by more than 95 percent. East of the Cascades, the results are also grim. Acquisition of floodplain property or of easements for safeguarding by land trusts or agencies costs more than zoning but offers more complete protection and does not require regulation.

CHANNELIZATION, LEVEES, AND RIPRAP

Stream straightening, building levees close to rivers, and lining banks with rock or construction debris (riprap) are activities intended to protect land from floods and bank erosion, but they destroy riparian habitat and bottomlife in streams, eliminate natural meanders along with pool-and-riffle patterns, warm the water by removing trees and vegetation, halt interactions between the river and its floodplain/groundwater, increase flooding and erosion in nearby areas, and in many cases aggravate problems they aim to solve. What was once a biological bonanza of streamfront forest becomes a lifeless embankment of rock or concrete. Fish, including young salmon, need periodically flooded vegetation for cover, feeding, or spawning, but all of that is eliminated by riprap and levees built too close to rivers.

When floodplain forests are cut and river corridors narrowed through channelization or levees, the current moves faster but flood capacity overall is reduced because the area being flooded is dramatically reduced. High waters that once spread out across miles of width—dissipating the flow, delaying the crest, and recharging the groundwater table—have been concentrated in man-made sluiceways. Floods in channelized streams now overflow their banks less often but—rising higher between levees than they rose in the natural system—they pack more destructive punch

Riprap along the Willamette River below the Long Tom confluence

because large storms can still overflow or rupture the levees. The specter of extreme damage is even greater now because people have developed or farmed up to the levees' edges with a false sense of security, believing that their lowlands would never again be flooded. Yet levee failures occur nearly every year somewhere in America. Worsening a bad situation, riverbeds between levees often aggrade, or rise with deposition of bedload gravel and sediment, forcing flood flows higher up the sides of the levees.

Effects of riprap and other channel narrowing and simplification are seen along much of the Willamette below Harrisburg and on low-elevation rivers through farm and ranchland statewide, including recreational rivers such as the lower McKenzie. Channelizing for development, farming, dredging, and instream gravel mining have also altered crucial estuarine habitat at the lower ends of coastal streams including the Coquille, Chetco, and Umpqua.

INVASIVE SPECIES

Alien or invasive species eliminate native animals and plants through competition, predation, disease, habitat changes, and hybridization. The majority of fish in many streams are now aliens introduced deliberately as game fish or from ballast water, bait cans, and motorboat washing. Aliens total 60 percent of all the fish fauna in the lower Willamette. New Zealand mud snails have appeared in Tillamook Bay, the Sixes River, and other coastal streams, and can multiply to phenomenal densities harming native mollusks. The mitten crab with its hairy claws has entered the Columbia River. Zebra mussels can devastate local mussels and ecological balance, and have been intercepted at boat-checking stations on highways entering the state. Half the riparian zone of the lower Willamette is cluttered with alien plants.

The poisoning of noxious fauna is sometimes the only way to reinstate native species and ecological balance. Anglers and boaters should inspect their boots and gear for hitchhiking snails (pebble-like, and often less than a quarter-inch long) and clean equipment to avoid spreading exotics, especially when entering another stream within a week.

Though unwanted weeds regrow by sprouts or seeds, pulling or cutting them can give native plants a competitive advantage. Hand-pulling of aliens has become a part of most of my river visits as I paddle downstream or walk along the water. Though the effort might seem futile, pulling invasive weeds is satisfying because you immediately see results of your work.

CLIMATE CHANGE

The weather of course changes annually, but our climate is warming at an alarming rate. The 14 warmest years on record worldwide occurred in the 16 years from 1997 to 2012. In 2012, heat records in the United States were surpassed by a full degree F—a huge jump statistically. On Mount Hood, six of eleven glaciers have receded 61 percent in the past century. These are a few among many indicators of global warming and climate change occurring because of increased carbon dioxide and methane in the atmosphere.

The *Oregon State of the Environment Report 2000* indicated that climate change models predicted a 10–25 percent reduction in summer runoff in coming decades with consequences for irrigation, water supplies, and streams. The Climate Impacts Group at the University of Washington in 2004 reported that temperatures in the Northwest are expected to climb 4.1 degrees F by 2040 while precipitation increases 5 percent. The Institute for Sustainable Environment at the University of Oregon reported that temperatures in the Rogue basin could increase a searing 15 degrees by 2080. The Cascades snowpack is expected to diminish by 50 percent by 2050. By late in the century, the typical snowpack on March 1 will likely resemble what we now see in June.

Global warming will affect rivers in egregious ways. The reduction in snowpack will mean higher floods, more runoff in winter, intensified droughts, and less runoff in summer. Sea-level rise will degrade estuaries and lower reaches of Oregon's ocean-bound rivers. Species already stressed by warm water and low runoff, including salmon and trout, will be pushed toward extinction. The *Proceedings of the National Academy of Sciences* reported in August 2011 that trout habitat in the West could decline 50 percent by 2080 because of global warming. Forest and chaparral fires will increase, along with intensified erosion in their aftermaths, more sediment clogging rivers, and heated runoff from burned land. Owing to hotter temperatures, demand for electricity will rise in summer. Meanwhile, owing to the loss of snowpack, hydroelectric production will be curtailed; more power will be needed but less will be available, and new hydro-dam proposals may surface as people scramble for ways to maintain energy use and reduce the portion coming from fossil fuels. Streams reliant on low-elevation snowpack (such as the South Umpqua) will be affected the most; those dependent on high elevation snow and groundwater (North Umpqua) will be affected less.

To cut the rate of warming by reducing both fossil fuel burning and deforestation is the first climate-change challenge in regard to rivers, and a large burden of this solution lies in the United States, where 4 percent of the world's population creates 29 percent of the global-warming gasses, according to the World Resources Institute.

The second challenge is to address the inevitable by helping river ecosystems be resilient. Reserving adequate stream flows will be more important because stream flows will be lower and warmer than they already are. Riparian habitat will be more necessary as a refuge for native life and as a buffer from warming fields and cities. Flows that deliver cold runoff from high elevations, north sides of mountain peaks, and groundwater springs will become more crucial. Larger areas of floodplains will have to be protected from development because the floods are going to get worse. In short, everything river conservationists have been trying to do for the past half-century will have to be done more, better, and faster.

POPULATION GROWTH

At recent rates of growth reported by the Census Bureau, the U.S. population will double in roughly 60 years. Oregon's rate of growth has been greater than the national average, and in the long-term will continue as people migrate to avoid the overheated, drought-stressed conditions that climate change is bringing to the interior West, California, and the world. State population grew 150 percent since 1950. The 3.8 million people in 2012 are expected to increase to 5.4 million by 2040.

A growing population will tend to neutralize efforts for greater energy efficiency aimed at combating global warming, and will negate other essential reforms relating to rivers. For example, even if per capita use of water is halved, the savings merely keeps pace when population doubles, leaving the next generation in the same position of needing to sacrifice qualities and amenities of our rivers, environment, and communities to accommodate more people. Stabilizing population is the only long-term option to avoid unending diminishment of our rivers and natural environment. According to Census Bureau data, most American population growth now owes to immigration—a topic beyond the scope of this modest guidebook. I encourage readers to investigate this difficult subject and to engage in open dialogue about it.

PROTECTING OREGON'S RIVERS

Protection programs seek to safeguard what remains of value along Oregon's rivers and to prevent problems from getting worse. One key tool for protecting natural streams is Wild and Scenic River designation under national or state laws. National status is conferred by Congress, or by the Secretary of the Interior or Agriculture at the request of a governor. The act bans new dams or other projects that are harmful to rivers or that require federal funds or licensing, including hydroelectric withdrawals.

On federal land, designated river reaches must be safeguarded from damaging activities, which can include logging within a quarter mile of the banks. For private land, the program encourages but does not require zoning by local governments.

Not counting small tributaries, Oregon has more rivers designated in the National Wild and Scenic system than any other state (though Alaska and California have more mileage). Statewide, about 1,900 miles on 70 rivers and tributaries of all sizes have been included. The Rogue was among the initial 12 rivers and tributaries protected nationwide in the 1968 Wild and Scenic Act. Many others were designated in 1988 (see Appendix). Yet protected mileage totals only 1.5 percent of total Oregon stream miles. For comparison, 4 percent of the state landmass is designated as wilderness (far less than in neighboring states).

The Oregon State Scenic Waterways program is similar, with a ban on dams, placer mining, and most diversions on 1,100 miles of streams. The state, however, cannot clearly limit federal actions such as hydropower licenses, and the program is constrained by tight budgeting and staffing.

In another important protection program, the Northwest Forest Plan of 1994 designated federal lands in 164 key watersheds west of the Cascade crest in Oregon, Washington, and northern California for protection from riparian clearcutting, and mandates buffers along the Forest Service and BLM streamfronts. This administrative fix, however, is vulnerable to political change.

According to *Atlas of Oregon*, 15 percent of the state is protected in the combined acreage of wilderness, national/state parks, and the Northwest Forest Plan—not a large amount considering that ecologists Reed Noss and Allen Cooperrider in *Saving Nature's Legacy* indicate that 50 percent may be necessary for the proper functioning of natural ecosystems.

Moreover, existing programs have not protected a full spectrum of native fish habitat, and most of the state Department of Fish and Wildlife's attention has gone to game fish. To address this inequity, the American Fisheries Society proposed a system of Aquatic Diversity Management Areas where essential habitat for all native fishes would be managed for biological value. Likewise, the Wild Salmon Center has identified a few key "Salmon Strongholds" for protection. However, no action program for either initiative has been launched as of this writing.

Another important protection technique is acquisition of riverfront land or conservation easements. Public agencies and land trusts have done much to safeguard natural assets along rivers by buying private property, including tracts along the Sandy, Deschutes, Elk, Willamette, Chetco, and other streams. The Western Rivers Conservancy acquired 16,000 acres along the John Day that will become a state park. Gains such as this are significant but, as with Wild and Scenic Rivers, the areas protected by acquisition remain a tiny percentage of critical acreage.

Because the Siskiyou Mountain region sustains a concentration of still-wild, biologically important streams, conservation groups there have sought to gain federally protected status for the suite of rivers from the North Fork Smith at the California border northward through the Chetco, Illinois, Rogue, Elk, and South Fork Coquille. Targeted efforts are underway to designate wilderness along Rogue tributaries and to protect the Chetco, Baldface Creek, Rough and Ready Creek, and Hunter Creek from increased mining. Headwaters and north-side tributaries of the Elk River have been safeguarded as wilderness, but south-side streams, including some of the best salmon-spawning habitat, remain vulnerable to logging. Friends of Elk River and Kalmiopsis Audubon Society propose a Salmon Emphasis Area where federal policy would favor management for the stream's native fish over logging and mining when conflicts arise.

Land use regulation through floodplain zoning is one of few measures affecting private riverfronts and could become the most important of all protection techniques in the future. Though largely ignored by conservation organizations, better floodplain regulation has potential to safeguard the greatest mileage of riverfront at the least cost. The importance of this task will become increasingly evident with intensified flooding that climate change will bring.

RESTORATION

Though it's harder and more expensive to restore a river that has been damaged than to stop damage before it occurs, people and governments are often more willing to fix problems, spend money, and reclaim values of the past than to halt new development or resource extraction—in other words, to remedy the problems created by inadequate protection measures.

Restoration of rivers entails repairing damage of the past and reinstating native fish and wildlife, natural runoff cycles, water quality, and undeveloped shorelines. Full restoration is rarely possible, but even partial success can improve the qualities of rivers. For example, the entire floodplain and riparian corridor are important, but 2-year floodplains nearest the river are the most essential as habitat. Inundation at that frequency benefits fish the most, since the 2-year rhythm is within most fishes' life cycles. Studies by stream ecologist Stan Gregory and others at Oregon State University seek to identify areas such as this where restoration would yield the greatest return.

Portland, Eugene, and a number of other Oregon cities have restored streams and riverfronts by reinstating riparian open space, daylighting creeks previously buried in culverts, and eliminating salmon barriers such as poorly placed culverts. Though the affected mileage may be small, these high-profile sites in urban areas now offer a more natural riverscape to many people.

The most dramatic restoration efforts have involved the removal of antiquated, unsafe, harmful dams. Dams have been removed on the Calapooia and Sprague Rivers. The 47-foot Marmot Dam on the Sandy River was dismantled in 2009, allowing more salmon to reach spawning areas. Likewise, the removal of Savage Rapids, Gold Hill, and Gold Ray Dams on the Rogue opened 50 miles of stream to additional salmon and

Elk Creek Dam, partly constructed in the Rogue basin and later breached

steelhead spawning. A consortium of conservation groups, tribes, and water users have proposed the largest river restoration in history on the upper Klamath, where four dams would be eliminated.

One of the most intensive efforts for dam removal anywhere has focused on the lower Snake River, where four dams built in the 1960s and 70s extract a heavy toll on salmon migrating to Oregon and Idaho tributaries. Only 4 percent of the Northwest's electric power comes from the four dams, and can be replaced with efficiency improvements. Irrigation intakes can easily be extended to tap a dam-free river, and barge traffic heavily subsidized on federal reservoirs can economically be replaced by rail. The Save Our Wild Salmon Coalition argues for removal, while barge companies, utilities, agribusinesses, and the Bonneville Power Administration argue for continued maintenance of the taxpayer-subsidized dams (see Chapter 13).

As another restoration opportunity, Federal Energy Regulatory Commission licenses for private hydropower dams must be renewed every 50 years on the basis of current laws, including environmental reforms, and better flows below many dams have resulted. Relicensing of North Umpqua dams, for example, led to improved instream flows.

Correcting problems caused by logging is another restoration approach. After the logging boom of the 1980s, Siuslaw National Forest officials launched initiatives aimed at closing unneeded roads and protecting streamside buffers, and turned that heavily cut forest into a budding model of reform-in-progress (business-as-usual continues on many forest industry lands, which are affected only by state regulations).

To fund restoration of native salmon, state legislation in 1995 established the Watershed Enhancement Board as a path-breaking effort unique to Oregon. The state likewise encouraged formation of 90

Watershed Councils of diverse "stakeholders" to restore streams. Many have replanted riparian corridors, eliminated migration blockages such as culverts, and helped farmers and ranchers upgrade land management.

GET INVOLVED

As part of your own exploration and enjoyment of Oregon waterways, inquire about what's being done to safeguard or improve your stream. Fishing organizations such as Trout Unlimited do excellent work while advocacy groups, watershed councils, and land trusts are active on many rivers. County and local planning commissions welcome citizen involvement, or at least they should, and positions on these important councils are often available for the asking.

Anyone interested in the future and fate of a favorite stream can learn about it through local groups or agencies, by searching on the Internet and at the library, and by simply going to the river and taking time to look. Use this knowledge to engage others. Teach children, and encourage schools to become involved with nearby streams. Join groups that are undertaking good work. Become politically active by supporting better care for our streams and electing politicians who will do the job. The fate of Oregon's rivers depends on people who take responsibility for the future of our streams.

Facing page: West Fork Wallowa River, lower gorge
Following spread: Salt Creek Falls

As the heart of this book, Part II offers profiles of 120 waterways and mentions many others. Streams were selected based on importance, size, biological significance, and appeal for hiking, fishing, and non-motorized boating. For each river, notes about geography, geology, ecology, fish, and conservation are followed by a section on how to see and enjoy the stream. For quick reference these tips are keyed by icons for access and hiking, fishing, and boating.

SAFETY FIRST

When you're out, keep in mind that conditions change, and watch for hazards not identified here. I find surprises all the time related not only to the vagaries of weather and water level but also to landslides, fallen trees, and people's varying assessment of danger. I've personally visited most of the streams and paddled my canoe or rowed my raft on many, but not all, and so I've drawn from other guidebooks, especially for difficult Class 4–5 whitewater. Read the disclaimer at the opening of this book; if you're boating, see American Whitewater's *Safety Code* and follow it.

Logs across streams can create extreme hazards and are common on most of Oregon's smaller waterways. Though always vigilant, I find streams of 50-foot width or less especially prone to blockages. A lesser but common hazard, poison oak in the west and poison ivy in the east grow along many of Oregon's low-elevation rivers. Toxic blue-green algae now infests some warm-water rivers in summer; if you see bright green scum (the Klamath and South Umpqua have been infected), avoid swimming and keep dogs out. Also, rattlesnakes might be seen along dryland rivers. Encountering dozens over the years, I conclude that rarely would one strike if I didn't step on it. So don't! When in buzz-tail country I keep my eyes on the trail, and if brush occludes the view, I slow to a moderate pace, which gives most of the reptiles time to move, and I use my basketless ski poles to thump the trail ahead of me if I can't see the ground.

ACCESS: HIKING, FISHING, AND BOATING

Under each river's description I include practical tips for access by driving to the river and then hiking, plus the occasional chance to take a bike for a riverfront spin, followed by tips for fishing and boating. Directions to anglers' and boaters' access points are often covered under the first icon addressing hiking access. Keep in mind there are multiple ways to get to places, and that space doesn't permit me to list all access areas.

I generally limit my discussion of fishing to identifying the species of game fish present, plus seasonal notes. Boating information that follows the fishing tips might be helpful to anglers because much of the best fishing is done from a boat, and access areas for launching are sometimes the only places where you can legally fish from shore. I expect that most boaters here will be independent rafters, kayakers, and canoeists. For guided trips, search the Internet for outfitters.

Landowners reasonably restrict use on private property. For access, public land is usually needed, which can include thin streamfront rights-of-way at bridges or directly next to roads. In Oregon, the right to walk on the streambed up to the "line of ordinary high water" is established on 12 "navigable" rivers: Chetco, Columbia, Coos, Coquille, John Day, Klamath, McKenzie, Rogue, Sandy, Snake, Umpqua, and Willamette. For others, the State Attorney General reported that people have a right to use the streambed if the river carries enough water for a boat to "make progress on it," but warns that you might be challenged. Personally I've never encountered this problem floating on a river of any size, provided I don't land. On small ranchland streams, barbed wire might be strung across the water, creating a serious hazard; avoid these streams or carefully pass through or around fences, which are often difficult to see when approaching in the current.

SEASONS AND FLOW LEVELS

Each month has its specialties, but May and June are great times to tour many of Oregon's rivers. The wet and cold weather that continues through spring has warmed, yet flows are still up on many streams that later drop to unboatable levels if not to a trickle. Summer is delightful for boating on larger rivers and hiking along mountain streams. Rivers in winter and spring always amaze me with their high flows. See each chapter introduction in Part II for seasonal highlights by basin.

Difficulty in boating on rivers changes dramatically with water level. My recommendations for paddling are most relevant for boatable flows at the low-medium level. As water rises, hazards increase. Simply choosing the proper season for boating on a particular river is sometimes an adequate strategy, but it's often necessary to know the specific level of flow, especially in the high-water season and after storms, which can peak radically, especially on coastal streams. Beware of launching on any rising river or during winter rains. Notations about boatable volumes of flow in cubic feet per second (cfs) are usually taken from Oregon's principal whitewater guidebooks, *Soggy Sneakers* and *Paddling Oregon*. These levels are not necessarily recommended but represent flows that those authors considered runnable by competent boaters. I usually prefer the lower end of their ranges, especially when canoeing.

Levels can most easily be checked on the Internet from Dreamflows; the past 3 days are listed. The Northwest River Forecast Center provides data on current and predicted runoff for 3 days ahead. For flows coupled with boating difficulty ratings, see the Willamette Kayak and Canoe Club's website, which also lists reported log blockages on popular streams. For the largest selection of rivers and immediate flow levels, go to the agency that does the measurements: U.S. Geological Survey (Oregon river flows).

For the ultimate test, eyeball your flow at the put-in. More than once I've cancelled trips because I've found levels too low, or too high for safe boating. Never be too committed. It's good to have in mind a backup river or reach nearby that's either larger or smaller, and safer.

Just as the revolution in self-bailing rafts expanded upward the flow-levels that people can raft, the use of inflatable kayaks expanded opportunities for low-water paddling—virtually a new sport. Dozens of rivers long-regarded as too low in summer are now delightfully runnable with small inflatables and frequent dragging. While low-water hazards (foot entrapment in rocks, walking/falling injuries, and rocky swims) replace big-water hazards (hypothermia, log entrapment, and long swims), the low-water experience for the physically fit usually makes more deliberation and carefulness possible.

WHITEWATER DIFFICULTY

Paddling or rowing is rated Class 1–5 according to the International Scale of River Difficulty. Ratings cited in this *Field Guide* are largely taken from other guidebooks. In the past few decades, some boaters have downgraded ratings owing to refined equipment and rising skill levels; I tend not to do that, and in some cases may report ratings slightly higher than what appear in other guides. In Oregon, even Class 1 boating can present challenges to beginning paddlers owing to log hazards and swift currents against brushy banks. So, even for Class 1, boaters should have proper training and some experience. Here are the standard difficulty ratings, as abridged by the Bureau of Land Management:

Class 1: Small waves, passages clear, no serious obstacles.

Class 2: Medium sized regular waves, passages clear, some maneuvering required.

Class 3: Waves numerous high and irregular, rocks, eddies, narrow passages, scouting usually required.

Class 4: Powerful irregular waves, boiling eddies, dangerous rocks, congested passages, precise maneuvering required, scouting mandatory.

Class 5: Exceedingly difficult, violent rapids often following each other without interruption, big drops, violent current, scouting mandatory but often difficult.

ALIEN SPECIES

A curse of globalizing times is that precautions must be taken to not spread alien or invasive species of animals and plants from one stream to another on boating and fishing gear. If there's any chance of encountering the exotic quagga mussels, New Zealand mud snails, or other alien species (often the case in low-elevation waters), wash your gear (especially waders and shoes) thoroughly before going to another stream, especially if your turn-around time is within 2 days. To fund alien-species work, the state requires permits even for non-motorized boats (www.boatoregon.com). I wash mud from my footgear and dispose of weed seeds after hiking.

MILEAGE AND DATA SOURCES

Many of the road mileages given here were clocked on my odometer, but some were scaled from maps, and some are rounded to the mile. Keep your eyes peeled for the prize, as your drive might be a bit shorter or longer than my numbers indicate.

Statistics for river length, volume, and watershed area—listed at the beginning of each river description—are elsewhere surprisingly difficult to find. No official gazetteer of such information exists. Other published data, even from reputable sources, vary widely, so don't be surprised if you've seen different numbers. The figures I've listed were calculated through GIS and related computer systems by GIS-trained specialists of the consulting firm Conservation Geography. Lengths were taken from the USGS National Hydrography Dataset (high resolution 1:24,000). For specific reaches covered in paddling guidebooks, I often use their mileages to avoid confusion. Some rivers' names begin with the confluence of two tributaries; when that happens I also note the mileage of the combined main stem and its extension up the largest headwater tributary (same river with another name).

The size of a river ("second-largest") refers to amount of flow—not length—and I use mean (average) cubic feet per second (cfs). Some of this data was collected by the Conservation Geography analysts using a Unit Runoff Method (MAFLOWU as a component of dataset NHDPlus, established for modeling by the USGS and Environmental Protection Agency), though in most cases where USGS gauge numbers were available I used those (but many streams do not have gauges). Volume varies radically by season; I cite the average so one stream can be compared to another. Watershed area in square miles was derived from a GIS program, CUMDRAINAG (component of NHDPlus).

When collecting field information, I do not use a GPS device, as I do not assume my readers will have one. Plus, I dislike dependency on battery power and all it entails, and quite frankly, I still enjoy the challenges and skills of old-school navigation techniques.

MAPS

Maps at the outset of each regional chapter locate featured rivers; I wrote directions in the text to minimize the need for detailed maps. But anyone going out will want a state highway map and probably coverage such as the *DeLorme Atlas* of Oregon—the most information for the least cost. National forest maps are excellent, especially for hiking, and U.S. Geological Survey topographic maps offer detail. These can all be found in outdoor stores or on the Internet.

ADDITIONAL INFORMATION

I'm indebted to the authors of *Soggy Sneakers: A Guide to Oregon Rivers* and to Robb Keller for *Paddling Oregon*; see those guides especially for difficult whitewater. The Willamette Kayak and Canoe Club and American Whitewater provide Internet boating information. If you're interested in the outer edge of what may be possible (but by no means recommended) by a select group of expert paddlers, see Oregon Kayaking (www.oregonkayaking.net).

"Water Trails" have thus far been designated for the Alsea, Siuslaw estuary, Rogue, Willamette, lower Columbia, Sandy, and Deschutes; maps identify access and camping sites (search for Oregon Water Trails on the Internet).

See *Fishing Oregon* and *Oregon River Maps & Fishing Guide* for details about angling. Oregon Department of Fish and Wildlife's *Recreation Reports* website offers timely fishing tips. Angling restrictions are by necessity detailed, complex, and timely; always see *Oregon Sport Fishing Regulations* for specific rivers, game fish, and schedules.

In text that follows, BLM means federal Bureau of Land Management, and FR indicates Forest Road (U.S. Forest Service). "River-right" means the right side when facing downriver.

CHAPTER 4

COASTAL RIVERS

Coastal mountains blanket the state's 310-mile western border and send 26 rivers and hundreds of tributaries to the Pacific. With tremendous rainfall and a rugged landscape giving rise to waterways in every fold of topography, the density of rivers here may be greater than anywhere in America; a major stream pours into the ocean on average once every 10 miles. It's a river aficionado's paradise, especially in winter.

Even without the Columbia, Umpqua, and Rogue basins—covered separately in this book because they flow from the Cascade Mountains as well—coastal rivers, according to *The Oregon Water Handbook*, account for 9 percent of Oregon's land but 30 percent of its runoff, which occurs at an extremely high rate of 4 cfs per square mile (some desert basins generate 0.1 cfs per square mile).

From the Columbia south through the lower Coquille, streams drain the Coast Range; south of there the mountains are considered part of the "greater" Coast Range but most land is actually in the Siskiyou Range— geologically older, higher, and more erosion-resistant. The only rivers to completely cross the Coast Range are the Columbia in its wide gap, the Umpqua, and the Rogue, though by headwall erosion the Nehalem and Siuslaw extend far eastward.

Though the region has been heavily logged, with roads and some development, enchanting green gorges remain. Much of the Coast Range consists of sandstone layered on top of oceanic basalt, and both surface at rapids and shorelines. Spanning the central Coast, Tyee sandstone forms distinctive ledge-type rapids such as Smith River Falls.

Estuarine reaches from the Columbia south to the Coquille are the West Coast's only set of extended tidal rivers with passages that wind, fjord-like, far inland (true fjords are formed by glaciers). Farther south, the Sixes, Elk, Pistol, and Winchuck are among few major streams with only short estuaries. In the ice ages, the ocean dropped 300 feet lower than now, allowing rivers to cut deeper at the continent's edge. When the ice melted and the sea rose, lower canyons were flooded to become today's ocean trenches and estuaries. As streams now approach an even faster-rising sea level, silt is deposited where we see flat floodplains and broad bench-lands both above and below the upriver extent of tides.

Sand delivered by the rivers (along with some Pacific shoreline erosion) has created the longest coastal dune complex in North America along Oregon's central coast. Rivers there become pinned by the drifting sand into lowland lakes—a unique collection of ponded waters at

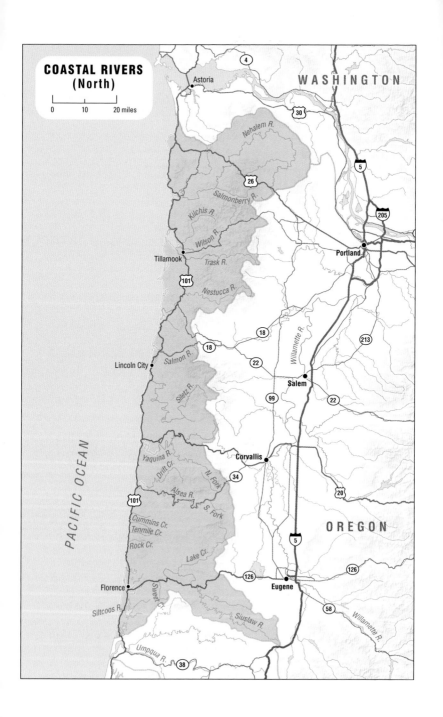

COASTAL RIVERS
(North)

0   10   20 miles

WASHINGTON

Astoria

Nehalem R.

Salmonberry R.

Kilchis R.

Wilson R.

Tillamook

Trask R.

Nestucca R.

Portland

Willamette R.

Lincoln City

Salmon R.

Siletz R.

Salem

Yaquina R.

Drift Cr.

N. Fork

Corvallis

Alsea R.

S. Fork

Cummins Cr.

Tenmile Cr.

Rock Cr.

Lake Cr.

PACIFIC OCEAN

OREGON

Florence

Sweet Cr.

Siltcoos R.

Siuslaw R.

Eugene

Umpqua R.

Willamette R.

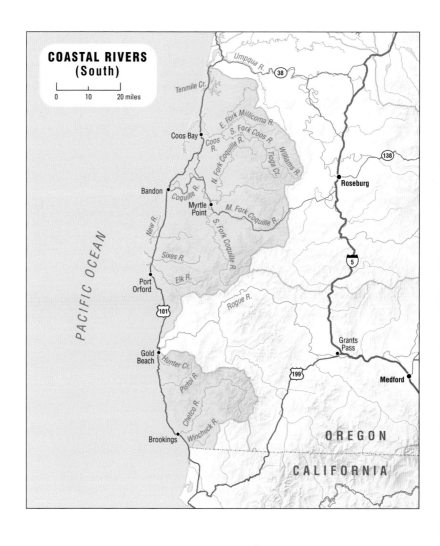

COASTAL RIVERS
(South)

0   10   20 miles

Umpqua R.

Tenmile Cr.

38

138

E. Fork Millicoma R.

S. Fork Coos R.

Coos Bay

Coos R.

Williams R.

Tioga Cr.

N. Fork Coquille R.

Roseburg

Bandon

Coquille R.

Myrtle
Point

M. Fork Coquille R.

New R.

S. Fork Coquille R.

PACIFIC OCEAN

Sixes R.

Elk R.

Port
Orford

5

Rogue R.

101

Grants
Pass

Gold
Beach

Hunter Cr.

199

Medford

Pistol R.

Chetco R.

Brookings

Winchuck R.

OREGON

CALIFORNIA

the base of coastal mountains—choice rearing habitat for young salmon before they head out to sea.

Coast Range streams remain largely free of the dams which diminish nature on virtually all other major rivers nationwide. Furthermore, these waterways flow through no cities except at the seashore. Logging has taken a toll everywhere, but forests are recovering—to a degree—from past abuse. Thus, Oregon's suite of coastal streams constitutes one of the finest relatively natural river regions in America, though it's seldom recognized as such.

Coastal rivers are legendary for salmon and steelhead, which dominate fish fauna. Though populations are greatly diminished by various problems, the coastal streams offer some of the best habitat remaining on the West Coast. In nearly all the once-similar rivers of northern California, salmon are threatened, endangered, or extinct.

Other native fishes include sculpins, dace, suckers, and pikeminnows. However, in a curious and unexplained anomaly, few of these natives are found from the Trask south through the Alsea, and also from the Elk through Winchuck (natives do populate a mid-section from the Siuslaw through Sixes and resume in the Klamath of northern California).

Coastal waterways flush high with rain in autumn, winter, and spring, then drop because their elevations lack snow and its steadying influence on runoff. Aggravating natural low flows, watershed damage has crippled the recharge of groundwater, which used to sink in and later seep out slowly to feed the rivers in summer. With improved timber management, regeneration of forests in riparian and steep-slope areas, and reinstatement of large fallen trees in streambeds, these rivers could once again become a truly magnificent asset to Oregon and the nation.

While coastal rivers are delightful any time of year, the opportunity to enjoy them expands if you're prepared for the cool, short, wet days of winter; that's the fishing season when most salmon and steelhead enter from the ocean, and that's when the rain brings levels up for canoeing, kayaking, and rafting. Hazardous peak flows occur after storms; 1–3 weeks later the rivers are often at good levels for boating. If one prepares with warm, stormproof gear, the rewards of seeing these streams during winter and spring are rich.

Virtually all the major rivers have paved roads up their valleys, offering the unusual opportunity for easy access on otherwise semi-wild rivers and serving anglers in winter, paddlers in spring, and campers and swimmers in the low-water months. With little traffic, some of these roads make the best riverfront bike paths one might imagine.

Whitewater rapids typically lie in upper reaches. Logjams there on streams less than 50 feet wide (and often more) should be expected, sometimes requiring arduous and careful dragging of boats (actual portage around logjams is often nearly impossible because of brush, banks, and steep slopes). In mid- and lower-river reaches, frequent accesses make dozens of day trips possible for paddlers and drift boaters. In addition to the lower Umpqua, Rogue, and Chetco, which are excellent for overnight camping, the Nehalem, Siletz, Alsea, and Siuslaw offer tempting reaches for overnight river trips in springtime. On these rivers, occasional remote gravel bars and flats are inviting, however, adequate campsites are often restricted by steep silty banks, heavy brush, backyards or farmed fields along lower reaches, and limited public land.

NEHALEM RIVER

Length: 128 miles
Average flow: 2,660 cfs
Watershed: 852 square miles

As Oregon's longest and second-largest river that's fed entirely by coastal mountains, the Nehalem wraps circuitously west, nearly transecting the range (only the Coquille is larger). It begins northwest of Portland and ends in Nehalem Bay—the first sizable estuary south of the Columbia. No dams have been built here, and only two other Oregon streams emptying directly into the Pacific have longer free-flowing mileage: the Umpqua and Rogue. Unlike other regional rivers, except the Siuslaw, the Nehalem begins in gentle interior plateaus seldom found elsewhere in the Coast Range and runs muddy when high with runoff from farmland, rural development, eroding banks, and soft siltstone. Along the resoundingly wilder lower river, mountains soar 1,200 feet. The watershed has been thoroughly logged, and roads parallel the entire length, but most sit back from the water.

In winter the Nehalem can become a high-volume artery roaring to 30,000 cfs or more, providing a rare chance to see mega-water comparable to the Colorado River in the Grand Canyon but from a watershed that reaches barely 40 miles inland. Tides penetrate upstream 15 miles from Nehalem Bay.

The American Fisheries Society listed the Nehalem among Oregon's top rivers for aquatic diversity, and the Wild Salmon Center gave it the

Nehalem River above Nehalem Falls

highest rating of any Oregon stream. Productive habitat supports summer Chinook, winter steelhead, cutthroat, and lamprey. The North Fork has a hatchery, but the main stem and its Salmonberry River are managed as wild fisheries. Chinook dominate, entering the estuary July–November, moving up with autumn rains. Cutthroat enter in early fall, coho in late autumn, and steelhead through winter. Uncommon in Oregon, chum salmon appear here and south through Tillamook Bay but rarely beyond that.

Tillamook State Forest blankets much of the lower basin. Here, several conservation groups strive toward a modest yet challenging goal of reserving 15 percent of the land for watershed protection where logging has long dominated under state policy. With its public land and surviving anadromous runs, the Nehalem has high restoration potential and could again become one of the truly great rivers of the West Coast.

A major tributary, the North Fork, has a hatchery and a popular sport fishery. Tides encroach to Aldervale Bridge, 7 miles above the main stem confluence. Upper reaches, along with tributary Soapstone Creek, pass through deep rainforest gorges.

Just to the north, the Necanicum is the only river flowing directly into the Pacific between the Nehalem and Columbia. Its 20 miles offer a full suite of salmon/steelhead and, unlike the Nehalem, clear quickly for good fishing after rains. Drift boaters float lower reaches. At Klootchy Creek County Park, 5 miles up Hwy 26 from Seaside, the world's largest Sitka spruce grew along Necanicum banks since before Columbus. But shorn of thick surrounding forests that had shielded it from wind, the 200-foot tree blew down in 2007. Remains can be seen.

 From Hwy 101 at Garibaldi drive north to Nehalem Bay, go east on Hwy 53 for 1 mile, turn right on Miami-Foley Road for 1 mile, then left on Foss Road. This leads upriver 100 miles, variously known as Lower River Road, Hwy 103, Fishhawk Falls Hwy, Hwy 202, Hwy 47, Nehalem Hwy, and Timber Road. Good access in the lower third serves summer swimming and winter steelhead fishing in Clatsop and Tillamook State Forests. Nehalem Falls Park lies 7 miles up from Hwy 53, with a path to the turbulent drop. For the next 7 miles up to the Salmonberry confluence, the gravel road is good for mountain biking, with a few pullouts and paths to the water. Spruce Run Park is another 8 miles up (to get there from Portland, take Hwy 26 west to Elsie, turn south on Lower Nehalem Road, and go 6 miles). Upstream from Spruce Run, roads parallel the rural river but offer few access points. North (downstream) of Vernonia 8 miles, Big Eddy Park has access, and Vernonia has access and camping at Anderson Park.

 The lower Nehalem is famous for Chinook, August–October. Steelhead peak February–March. Anglers use drift boats below Nehalem Falls. This is one of few Oregon streams with a coho season; North Fork hatchery stock are fished August–October. Anglers catch sea-run cutthroat below the Salmonberry, July–September, and resident cutthroat above, catch-and-release. The North Fork is popular for Chinook/steelhead above and below the hatchery (below the Hwy 53 bridge).

Paddling Oregon reports Class 1–2 boating with log hazards likely for 80 miles of the upper river down to the Salmon-berry—one of the longest boatable reaches in the Coast Range—though only on high muddy water of winter/spring. The rural stream is wilder below its second crossing of Hwy 26. For uppermost river access from Portland, drive Hwy 26 west, take Hwy 47 north almost to Vernonia, then west on Timber Road 7 miles to a bridge and USGS gauge. Below there, Vernonia and Big Eddy Park have access (see above), followed by a long farming valley.

For a deeper canyon outing, start at the beautiful Spruce Run Camp-ground and paddle 7 miles to Morrison Eddy Campground. In another mile a Class 4 rapid lies below the Salmonberry confluence (scout/por-tage right), followed by 8 miles of Class 2–3, plus Nehalem Falls and its takeout or portage. Downstream, another rapid is followed by the Foss Road bridge with an access path on river-right. Runnable into summer, Class 2 water continues 8 forested miles to Roy Creek ramp. A final 7 miles, mostly tidal, ends at Nehalem's city dock.

SALMONBERRY RIVER

Length: 20 miles
Average flow: 350 cfs
Watershed: 71 square miles

One of the wildest sizable Coast Range streams, the Salmonberry begins near the Nehalem's source but flows directly west through Tillamook State Forest. This remote, clear-water gem foams with Class 3–4 boulder-drops through green canyons. Seeing the beauti-ful but little-known Nehalem tributary at springtime flows could be on every Oregon river enthusiast's to-do list, remote as the stream is. The wild winter run of large steelhead remains one of the coast's finest, though at

Salmonberry River 1 mile above the Nehalem confluence

one-third historic abundance. The river is recognized as a Salmon Strong-hold by the Wild Salmon Center, a Core Area by the Department of Fish and Wildlife, and a Salmon Anchor area by the Department of Forestry.

The watershed was logged and then burned but illustrates how recovery is possible if even part of the forest is left alone. A Port of Tillamook Bay railroad, severely damaged and closed in 2007, follows the river 14 miles and is proposed for reopening, though no work is scheduled. Because of erodible slopes, chronic flooding, frequent landslides, and encroachment on the river, the Wild Salmon Center and a conservation coalition urge abandonment of the line.

 From Hwy 101 at Nehalem Bay turn east on 53, go 1 mile, turn right on Miami-Foley Road for 1 mile, left on Foss Road, continue 15 miles to the Nehalem-Salmonberry confluence, cross the bridge, and hike up the railroad tracks. Weathered ties here are not as annoying to walk on as most; the entire reach makes a good backpack trip.

 Anglers hike in for wild steelhead, catch-and-release. Competent kayakers and rafters occasionally run 9 miles of Class 3–4 from Beaver Slide Road to the Nehalem in winter/spring (3,000 cfs on the Wilson River at Tillamook). To put in, *Soggy Sneakers* says take Hwy 26 west a few miles from the Timber Road intersection and turn south on Salmonberry Road (before Sunset Highway Rest Area), in 1.2 miles go straight at a 4-way, at 4.4 miles angle left on a sharp turn, at 8.5 miles turn left at a 3-way, then 1 mile farther descend the muddy 4-wheel-drive Beaver Slide Road 1.5 miles. Take a map! An easier drive but shorter float is possible via Salmonberry and North Fork Roads—long shuttle either way.

KILCHIS RIVER

| Length: 18 miles, 27 with NF |
| Average flow: 422 cfs |
| Watershed: 63 square miles |

Exquisite, the Kilchis' narrow, deeply wooded canyon with crystal clear water ends in north Tillamook Bay, where tides lap 1 mile upstream of Hwy 101. For its small size, this is among the most productive salmon rivers on the north coast, and the most-natural of six streams southward through the Little Nestucca, collectively ranking as Oregon's top cluster of high-quality, fall-run Chinook waterways. Upper reaches lie in Tillamook State Forest; lower sections are private and farmed. Thoroughly logged decades ago, the basin now exemplifies ecosystem recovery, though new logging threatens and municipal withdrawals by coastal cities have been considered. With proper care and restoration, this basin could become a model of nearly pristine conditions.

North of the Kilchis, the smaller Miami River flows 15 miles as the northernmost Tillamook Bay source. A lower reach can be seen from Miami River Road east of Garibaldi; restored estuarine channels lie above 101.

 To reach the Kilchis, go 2 miles north of Tillamook on Hwy 101, turn east on Alderbrook Loop, and immediately left to tide-line access. Continue east on Alderbrook 1 mile and

Kilchis River at Kilchis County Park

go right, then 4 miles to Kilchis Park/Campground (fee) on the north side. A 1-mile trail leads to a 7-foot-diameter Sitka spruce and other old-growth—rare in the Coast Range. To drive farther upriver, backtrack on Kilchis River Road 3 miles, turn south, cross the bridge to Mapes access (fee), and continue on the potholed road (good mountain biking) upstream 2 miles to the Little South Fork and a path to the river. Upstream, occasional 4-wheel lanes and paths reach the water, including easy access in 6.5 miles along a side-road bridge.

 Chinook peak in October, hatchery steelhead in late December, wild steelhead March–April. Cutthroat migrate in the lower river spring and fall. Drift boaters float from Kilchis Park to Mapes or Alderbrook ramps.

 This enchanting stream is a favorite Class 3+ run of kayakers in the rainy season (down to 1,100 cfs on the Wilson River gauge). From the south side of Mapes Bridge drive upstream to turn-offs at 4.8, 6.5, or 8.5 miles. Take out at Little South Fork or Mapes. If you want an easier run, as I did on a very wintry day, a Class 1–2 reach extends 3 miles from the county park to Mapes Bridge, and onward to Alderbrook.

WILSON RIVER

Length: 24 miles, 36 with SF
Average flow: 1,173 cfs
Watershed: 194 square miles

This river features a spectacular forested canyon with signature blue-green water. Unlike many other north coast rivers that have farmland and light development in extended lower reaches, the Wilson becomes abruptly wild above its canyon mouth; most of the river's length is rugged and wooded, though Hwy 6 here is the busiest road spanning the northern Coast Range.

Wilson River and tributary (on left) below Kansas Creek Road

The Wilson is the principal source of Tillamook Bay—Oregon's second-largest estuary south of the Columbia, fed also by the Miami, Kilchis, Trask, and Tillamook. Among the region's best steelhead and Chinook fisheries—and stocked from hatcheries—the Wilson also has one of the southernmost runs of chum salmon. Tides penetrate 8 miles to Hwy 101. Most of the basin lies in Tillamook State Forest.

The Tillamook Bay dairy region houses 25,000 cows, with water quality problems contaminating shellfish, according to Department of Environmental Quality reports. Adding to its problems, the river lacks large woody debris necessary for excellent fish habitat and channel complexity, and dikes for farming have made much of the estuary unavailable to coho and other fish needing wetlands to spawn and rear. The Tillamook Estuaries Partnership works to curb pollution and restore habitat.

 Several county boat ramps serve the lower river from Hwy 6 east of Tillamook. After entering the canyon, eastbound 6 has frequent pullouts/paths to sparkling waters, immense cobble bars at lower flows, steep rapids, and deep pools. For a spectacular view, go 12 miles east of Tillamook (but still west of Kansas Creek Road) to a small anglers' trail sign leading to a narrow chute. Upstream, Keenig Campground lies 18 miles from Tillamook; Jones Creek Park is 5 miles farther east where Wilson River Trail, with river views in its upper half, leads downstream 4 miles to a lower trailhead.

The highway continues eastward up the South Fork and then up Devil's Lake Fork toward Portland; smaller gravel roads climb the wilder North Fork and upper South Fork.

 Anglers flock to the Wilson for hatchery steelhead, which can be kept and are a big draw all winter, peaking in December. Wild steelhead (catch-and-release) peak March–April. The

estuary is famous for large Chinook, spring and fall. Spring Chinook peak in early June; summer steelhead in July and again with autumn rains. Cutthroat migrate early spring and early fall.

 With a longer season than most coastal rivers, and only an hour from Portland, the Wilson is the Coast Range's most popular whitewater north of the Rogue. Several Class 3–4 upper reaches offer challenging ledges, emerald gorges, and possible logjams. Rain can spike to raging flows. Below milepost 15, steep Class 2 drops become turbulent Class 3 when high and continue to Vanderzanden boat-slide access, marked by a small sign 10 miles east of Tillamook. From there a pleasant 9-mile Class 2 run ends at Sollie Smith Bridge ramp; to reach it from Tillamook, go 2 miles east on Hwy 6, then north on Wilson Loop Road.

TRASK RIVER

Deeply wooded in upper sections, and clear, the Trask enters its estuary south of Tillamook. Tides lap 9 miles to the

> Length: 19 miles, 31 with NF
> Average flow: 977 cfs
> Watershed: 174 square miles

ramp just east of Hwy 101. Among just a few interbasin transfers in the Coast Range, upper Trask water is pumped to the Tualatin watershed from Barney Reservoir, built in 1998. Though the Trask has good habitat, the popular fishery is hatchery-stocked.

To the south, the smaller Tillamook River winds through farmland and riparian thickets, seen at the Hwy 101 roadside rest 4 miles south of Tillamook. Tributary Munson Creek has Oregon's second-tallest waterfall, dropping 319 feet amid hoary old-growth that the Western Rivers Conservancy bought in 1998—now Munson Creek Falls State Park. From Tillamook, take 101 south 7 miles and turn east at the sign.

Trask River and red alders below Loren's access

Tillamook River at roadside rest south of Tillamook

 For a scenic view of the Trask, take 101 south from Tillamook 2 miles, go east on Long Prairie Road 3 miles, right on Trask River Road for 5 miles to a pullout, and walk to bedrock shelves at "Dam Drop." Another mile leads to Peninsula County Park's 1-mile trail. Upstream another 4 miles, Trask Park's campground/access lie at the North/South Forks confluence. Above there, the potholed North and South Fork Roads have riverfront pullouts.

 The Trask is known for spring Chinook, May–June; fall Chinook in October; wild winter steelhead, January–March; and hatchery coho, September–November. Cutthroat migrate upstream in late summer. Drift boaters row the lower river below Cedar Creek boat-slide or Loren's ramp.

Soggy Sneakers reports a rainy season, mostly Class 3 North Fork run plus the Class 5 Crawdad Hole, seen at a pullout 0.5 miles above Trask Park. The main stem from Trask Park down to Upper Peninsula ramp is 8 miles (4 via road), Class 3, often runnable until June.

Below Upper Peninsula, several Class 3 drops lead in 1 mile to the Class 3–4 Dam Drop (scout/portage right). To miss it, put in at Cedar Creek boat slide, 2.5 road miles below Upper Peninsula. For an easier 5-mile Class 1–2 through farmland and riparian forest, put in 2 miles lower on the south-side at Loren's ramp; from 101 take Long Prairie Road 2 miles east, turn right and go 2 miles, and turn left. To take out, drive to the south side of the 101 bridge, go east on Long Prairie Road, and at a small sign turn north on gravel.

NESTUCCA RIVER

Length: 57 miles
Average flow: 1,050 cfs
Watershed: 255 square miles

This queen of North Coast streams has enticing forested canyons and good whitewater followed by an easy run out to the scenic estuary at Pacific City. With more public land than most other coastal rivers, it's a productive salmon and steelhead fishery. Upper reaches are proposed for wilderness on the northern flanks of Mount Hebo—at 3,154 feet the second-highest peak in the Oregon Coast Range north of the Siskiyou Mountains. At headwaters, McGuire Dam diverts water east to McMinnville.

The upper 12 miles through BLM land are an Area of Critical Environmental Concern where "adaptive management" tests strategies for restoring old-growth forests and fisheries. Then the river runs through Siuslaw National Forest as one of the most delightful Coast Range streams. However, much of the basin has been heavily logged while dairy farms, roads, and some homes populate lower miles. Though stocked with hatchery fish, the river has wild salmon habitat and is being improved by restoration projects. Tides creep 9 miles up from Nestucca Bay. The upper river along with tributary Walker Creek is a State Scenic Waterway—the Coast Range's only designated State or National Wild and Scenic River north of the Elk.

Entering from the south, Niagara Creek and its tributary Pheasant Creek have impressive adjacent waterfalls, 107 and 112 feet. From 101 at Beaver take Blaine Road east 13 miles up the Nestucca, turn south on Niagara Road, climb 4 miles, and go right for 0.7 miles to the 1-mile trail. Another tributary—Three Rivers—enters the lower Nestucca at Hebo; its Forest Service campground with access lies 5 miles southeast of 101 along Hwy 22. The 23-mile Little Nestucca is the major tributary at the estuary's

Nestucca River below Rocky Bend Campground

Niagara Creek Falls

south end; from Hwy 101, Little Nestucca Road leads upstream 3 miles to an abandoned county park and a path, followed by 7 miles with pullouts for bushwhacking to the shore.

 The lower Nestucca, west of Hwy 101, is reached at Woods Park, just above Nestucca Bay (north of Pacific City). To reach the middle/upper river, take 101 south from Tillamook 16 miles to Beaver and turn east on Blaine Road. The charming byway wends 36 miles with many paths and five campgrounds beginning at Rocky Bend, 14 miles from 101. Excellent for biking, this is one of the least traveled paved roads along a Coast Range river. Another 3 miles up, Alder Glen may be the region's most beautiful riverfront campground; at high flows a tributary waterfall spills into the Nestucca amid old-growth. Another 5 miles up, a massive logjam—once common in Coast Range rivers and now rare but ecologically important—can be seen from the road.

 A fine coastal sport fishery, the Nestucca has hatchery and wild Chinook. The spring run peaks May–mid-June, with the fall run in October, principally fished in the bay. Steelhead—mostly hatchery fish—are in the river year-round; the winter run peaks in December, the summer run in July. Fly fishing for stocked and wild cutthroat is best in spring and late summer. Drift boaters work lower reaches from Fourth Bridge (3 miles east of 101) to Three Rivers ramp north of Cloverdale. Areas upstream of Fourth Bridge are fished from the banks; no angling is allowed above Elk Creek.

 The temptingly beautiful upper river is fraught with access problems and unpredictability. It can be reached at the mouth of Elk Creek; logjams lie above there and are likely below. Downstream from Rocky Bend a steep canyon was blocked with an impassible log when I last looked, and a must-do portage is aggressively posted. Avoid this and put in from pullouts starting at milepost 12 above Blaine. Downstream, a Class 3+ run awaits at milepost 9.5. Turbulent water follows (1,500 cfs) down to Sixth Bridge access. Powerful Class 2 continues to Fourth Bridge (3 road miles east of 101). Class 2 water follows to First Bridge, just east of 101. Then the lower Nestucca is mostly riffles for 5 more miles to Three Rivers ramp. To drive there from Cloverdale go 2 miles north on 101 and turn west on Hansen Road. At the estuary, a mountainous Sitka spruce forest rises at Bob Straub State Park, across from Pacific City. The park is named for the Oregon state treasurer and governor who championed a campaign to halt freeway construction along the seashore here and elsewhere.

SALMON RIVER

Length:	26 miles
Average flow:	339 cfs
Watershed:	75 square miles

North of Lincoln City, the mouth of the Salmon is seen from dramatic overlooks on Cascade Head—the highest mountain rising directly from sea on the Oregon coast, protected with money raised by volunteers in 1966 and deeded to the Nature Conservancy.

For the Cascade Head hike and bird's-eye view to the Salmon's mouth, take Hwy 101 north from Lincoln City to the Salmon River bridge, continue 3 miles, and turn west on Cascade Head Road. To go upriver, take 101 north of Lincoln City, turn east on Hwy 18, go 1.4 miles, left on Old 101 for 0.3 miles, right on North Bank Road, and continue 4 miles to a bridge/pullout at a great cliff. Farther east on 18, H.B. Van Duzer State Park features a path to splendid old Sitka spruce along the beautifully clear stream.

Salmon River at H.B. Van Duzer State Park

Peaking with autumn rains, stocked Chinook and coho are caught just below a hatchery; from Old 101 turn east on North Bank Road and go 0.5 miles to the hatchery sign.

 For tidal boating at Knight Park ramp, take Hwy 101 north from the 101/18 intersection 0.5 miles and turn west on Three Rocks Road to the ramp. Paddle upstream or down and stop at a spit near the ocean (avoid outgoing tide).

SILETZ RIVER

Length: 69 miles, 84 with SF
Average flow: 1,520 cfs
Watershed: 304 square miles

This major coastal river begins with its North and South Forks and continues to Siletz Bay, south of Lincoln City. It's known for great whitewater in upper reaches and—though a ghost of its past—good summer steelhead. One of the more diverse fisheries on the coast survives here with coho, spring Chinook, and winter steelhead, mostly hatchery-based. There's little public land except Moonshine County Park and isolated ramps.

Polk County has proposed a new dam near an abandoned dam on the South Fork at Valsetz and would transfer flows to the Willamette Valley. WaterWatch opposed this withdrawal in 2009, pointing to fishery values and a lack of demonstrated need.

Entering the Siletz near its mouth, Drift Creek has a challenging springtime whitewater run and a 1.5-mile trail crossing a dizzying suspension bridge to 75-foot Drift Creek Falls; south of Lincoln and Cutler Cities turn east on Drift Creek Road, right on South Drift Creek Road for a quarter mile, left on FR 17, then 10 miles (fee).

Siletz River upstream of Moonshine Park

To see the Siletz, take Hwy 101 south from Lincoln City, turn east on 229, pass several commercial ramps, and drive to tide-line 19 miles up. The road continues past other ramps to the town of Siletz. East of it, Upper Siletz Road winds 15 miles through one of the most wonderfully pastoral Coast Range valleys to Moonshine Park (fee), then becomes a gravel timber industry road open only on weekends and not at all in the summer–fall fire season. If you time it right, magnificent Class 4 rapids 4 miles above Moonshine are worth the drive.

 On the popular mid- and lower river, summer steelhead peak June–July; winter runs February–March. Spring Chinook peak June–July; fall runs September–October. Before the rains begin, fall Chinook are caught in the lower 10 miles of tidewater. Because of private land throughout, fishing is mostly by drift boat below Moonshine or, with easier rapids, below Twin Bridges (east of Siletz). Moonshine and smaller access areas have bank fishing.

 According to guidebooks, the upper Siletz from Elk Creek to Buck Creek offers Class 3 rainy season whitewater for a scenic 5 miles on weekends when the road is open. From Siletz, drive east to Moonshine Park, continue 4 miles, cross the river, go 2 miles, and take the right fork to Buck Creek takeout. For the put-in, return to the road's fork, turn right, and go 6 miles to Elk Creek Bridge (the unrunnable 70-foot Valsetz Falls lies 1 mile upstream). Below Buck Creek, a notorious Class 4 run ends at Moonshine, with its campground, rapid, surfing hole, and tributary waterfall spraying into the river.

Below Moonshine the river runs Class 2+ for 5 miles to the Logsden Bridge; one powerful drop lies just below the park. Flows are often boat-able into early summer. From Logsden down, easier Class 1–2 water extends 30 river miles to Strome access (fee), with 5 ramps along the way. This is the best canoe trip on the North Coast that's both long and easy—doable in a day at medium-high flows. Though it is possible, and tempting, canoe-camping is difficult because of the river's entrenchment within high banks, private land, and rules against camping at access parks. Logsden store arranges shuttles.

If you want a tidal-river tour by canoe or ocean kayak, paddle 19 miles from Strome to Siletz Bay. Even with homes and farms, most of this narrow corridor is wooded until near the sea.

YAQUINA RIVER

Length: 59 miles	
Average flow: 248 cfs	
Watershed: 252 square miles	

This small stream is principally known for its 18-mile estuary and broad salt-water bay at Newport. The river supports Chinook, steelhead, and cutthroat.

 From Hwy 101 in Newport take Hwy 20 east, turn south to Toledo, cross the river, and turn left (upstream) on Elk City Road. This later rejoins Hwy 20, which continues eastward following the diminutive river to Eddyville.

Fall Chinook move upriver September–November, caught mostly in the bay.

Tidal water is accessible at 8 ramps from Elk City down.

ALSEA RIVER

Length: 48 miles, 64 with NF
Average flow: 1,468 cfs
Watershed: 471 square miles

The Alsea gathers runoff from its North and South Forks and reaches the central coast at Waldport. Though the basin largely lies in Siuslaw National Forest, river frontage is mostly private.

Unlike many estuaries, the Alsea still has wetlands, salt marshes, eelgrass, and side channels with woody debris—all essential to young coho, cutthroat, and Chinook. This was once considered the best coho stream on the Oregon coast. Here and along lower Drift Creek land trusts are acquiring estuarine property and restoring wetlands for threatened fish.

Hwy 34 follows the main stem but in places leaves the river isolated. Many of the 10 public access areas are beautifully wooded.

At North Fork Falls, below the former hatchery, salmon can sometimes be seen jumping in autumn; take Hwy 34 west from Corvallis, and 3 miles east of Alsea village turn right on North Fork Road.

For the South Fork's Alsea Falls—impressive at high flows—take Hwy 34 to Alsea, turn south on Alsea-Deadwood Highway for 1 mile, and go left on South Fork Road 9 miles. For a 2-mile round-trip hike, start at the falls, cross via footbridge to the north side, walk down the South Fork through old-growth forest showing what much of the Alsea basin once resembled, then climb tributary Peak Creek to 50-foot Green Peak Falls.

Alsea River above Salmonberry Road

Drift boaters ply the lower Alsea, especially from Blackberry Park downstream 7 miles to tidewater. Hatchery winter steelhead peak December–January; wild fish come later. Coho survive, and cutthroat migrate to sea. Fall Chinook are mainly caught in tidewater and peak in the river September–October.

 The main stem flows 33 miles through Class 1–2 rapids to tidewater—an excellent rainy season canoe trip, often lasting through spring (3 feet minimum at tidewater). For access go 1 mile west of Alsea to Mill Creek Park, then 6 road miles downstream at Salmonberry Road, 2 road miles farther at Missouri Bend, 8 more to River Edge, 4 more to Walters ramp, 2 more to Blackberry Campground, and another 1 to Beaver Wayside (river distances are longer). The largest rapid (milepost 14.9) lies 2 more miles downstream with paths above and below the drop. Tidal flows begin 3 miles farther and run 12 miles to Waldport's city dock on the south side of the wide bay, reached via Broadway.

DRIFT CREEK

Length: 30 miles	
Average flow: 116 cfs	
Watershed: 69 square miles	

This Alsea tributary ends in the river's estuary near Waldport. Ancient Sitka spruce, western hemlock, and Douglas-fir reach 3–7 feet in diameter in the 5,800-acre Drift Creek Wilderness—one of the finest (of few) near the Oregon coast. Upstream and down from the wilderness the creek traverses heavily cut National Forest and private land. Native Chinook, coho, steelhead, and cutthroat spawn here; hatchery fish have never been stocked. Valuable tidal habitat near the mouth has been protected for coho and other fish.

Drift Creek in the Drift Creek Wilderness

Fine trails drop to this wild stream but none parallel it. From Waldport take Hwy 34 east 7 miles, cross the Alsea, turn left on FR 3446, and left on 346 to Harris Ranch Trailhead and the steep path.

 The creek's excellent 20 miles of whitewater offer a rare opportunity to paddle through a wilderness rainforest (a more difficult Drift Creek lies north in the Siletz basin). During winter flows, usually ending in March (5.5 feet at Alsea), the run includes continuous Class 2 rock dodging and a few Class 3 drops. Brushy banks make landing difficult; logs and collapsed bridges may require portages.

From Hwy 101 north of Alsea Bay turn east on North Bayview Road for 2.4 miles, left on South Beaver Creek Road for 5.2 miles, right on North Beaver Creek Road for 10.7 miles, right on 1000 Line Road, stay right at 3.2 miles, then stay left at a fork to the put-in bridge.

Take out in Alsea Bay at commercial accesses along Hwy 34 across and west from the Drift Creek confluence, or paddle west (often windy) to Waldport's city dock. For a shorter trip without the estuary crossing, take 101 from Waldport to the north end of Alsea Bridge, turn east on North Bayview Road for 6.7 miles, right on May Road for 2.7 miles to the takeout across the bridge.

CUMMINS, ROCK, AND TENMILE CREEKS

Cummins and Rock Creeks are the only two sizable streams entering the Pacific with no valley roads or development of any kind (except Hwy 101 bridges).

> Length: Cummins, 7 miles; Rock, 6 miles; Tenmile, 12 miles

Cummins Creek upstream of Hwy 101

Yachats River in its tidal reach

Both basins are National Forest wilderness totaling 16,700 acres. Tenmile Creek sits between the two (another Tenmile appears south of the Umpqua). South of Rock Creek, and similar, Big Creek is mostly wild. Next southward, Cape Creek flows from Siuslaw National Forest, has only a narrow road up its valley, and runs clear as a coho haven with flooded back channels, logjams, and gravel flats (a smaller Cape Creek reaches the ocean northward at Cape Perpetua).

This is the Coast's finest suite of small adjacent creeks supporting native runs of salmon, steelhead, and cutthroat. Along with upper Elk River on the south coast, they illustrate stream quality that's possible if watersheds are simply left alone. A National Audubon Society sanctuary, 5 miles east of 101 and mostly unsigned, harbors the largest stand of Sitka spruce/western hemlock rainforest south of the Olympic Mountains. Tenmile and Cape are examples of logging-road decommissioning to restore water quality.

Not much larger than these, the Yachats River lies just north with its enchanting woods-and-water interface. Its lower valley is privately owned, but much of the upper watershed is in Siuslaw National Forest.

See Cummins Creek at the ocean 4 miles south of Yachats at Neptune State Park; from the parking lot walk under the 101 bridge. The misnamed Cummins Creek Trail, off 101 just north of Neptune, offers no creek views, but 200 yards up the path an unmarked spur heads downhill through Sitka spruce to the stream.

South of Cummins 3 miles, the gravel Tenmile Creek Road follows that stream through private land, but a National Forest campground lies 6 miles east of 101. Rock Creek is 3 more miles south—wild but accessible at the ocean and a campground. Gravel roads up Tenmile, Rock, and Cape Creeks are excellent for mountain biking. To see one of the largest Sitka spruces, go to "North" Cape Creek at Cape Perpetua, turn east from 101 toward the campground, and walk, drive, or bike a mile upstream.

SIUSLAW RIVER

Between the Nehalem and Umpqua, the Siuslaw takes the longest route to the Pacific, and lacking dams, it's one of the

Length: 109 miles	
Average flow: 2,285 cfs	
Watershed: 773 square miles	

more significant free-flowing rivers on the West Coast. Headwaters lie only 2 miles west of the Coast Fork Willamette where that stream passes through Cottage Grove; the Siuslaw nearly transects the entire Coast Range. Excellent for sea-run cutthroat, it also supports Chinook and winter steelhead.

Below the river's headwater meanderings through rural ranchland, scattered groves of big trees survive on floodplains for 55 miles from Siuslaw Falls down to Hwy 126. The next 15 miles to Swisshome have a railroad and gravel byway alongside but feel remote. Swelling half again in volume with Lake Creek, the Siuslaw drops 7 more miles to tide-line (1 mile upstream of Mapleton), then ebbs and flows 15 miles to Florence. In final estuarine bends, the river cuts through tall dunes to its bay.

Through the last century this and many coastal rivers suffered not only clearcut logging and removal of logjams from the channels, but also splash dams. Temporary reservoirs were filled with logs, then blown up sequentially, sending their cargo downstream like thousands of battering-rams scouring the riverbed and banks. Done repeatedly, this excavated the stream to bedrock, obliterating flats, floodplains, gravel bars, and wet-lands needed by coho and other fish. Evidence of the dams is long-gone except for the scoured channel. In a restoration effort, BLM has created 1- to 4-foot drops by installing rock rubble across the channel in about 20 locations through the 40-mile section above Whittaker Creek. Minor pools above these are intended to trap spawning gravels hospitable to fish. At most of these partial check-dams, enough water sieves between boulders to slip a canoe through, though at low water the passages tighten or close.

Most of the basin's remaining old-growth forest was cut in the 1980s, but after the Northwest Forest Plan of 1994, Siuslaw National Forest re-invented itself as a restoration model-in-progress. With involvement by the Siuslaw Stewardship Group of local stakeholders, further logging of old-growth was halted, plantations thinned, and habitat improved.

Entering from the south at Mapleton, Knowles Creek once sent 100,000 coho to sea but less than 1,700 as of the early 2000s. Habitat had disappeared with the loss of logjams, which had caused water to overflow onto floodplains rather than downcut. In a pioneering effort to reinstate channel complexity, the Pacific Rivers Council, John Hancock Company, and Siuslaw National Forest in 1992 experimentally placed large logs at strategic locations. Monitoring confirmed the importance of woody de-bris and that restoration through log placement is possible.

Siuslaw River and logjam above Clay Creek

From 101 in Florence turn east on Hwy 126 for 14 miles to Mapleton's boat ramp. Continue going straight and upriver (now Hwy 36) to ramps in 2 miles, then in 6 miles at Tide (misnamed, it's above tide-line). Lake Creek's confluence at Swisshome is another 3 miles upstream. To ascend the Siuslaw rather than Lake Creek, turn right at Swisshome on Stagecoach Road (paved, then gravel), go about 12 miles, turn right and cross the bridge, turn left on Hwy 126, then left into Richardson access. To shortcut from Mapleton, take Hwy 126 directly east 9.8 miles to Richardson.

To proceed upstream, cross the Siuslaw on 126, turn right on Siuslaw River Road, and enjoy 70 miles to headwaters. This wonderfully remote byway, mostly along riverfront, sees little traffic. It's one of Oregon's finest riverfront bike routes for 16 miles from 126 up to Clay Creek Campground (good swimming), then 10 miles beyond to where the road bends away (later returning to the river).

Siuslaw tidewater is popular for Chinook, arriving in August and moving up with the first rain. Native steelhead, in the river much of the year but peaking February–March, are fished from Whittaker access (above the 126/Siuslaw River Road intersection) down to Tide, with heavy shore angling and drift boating for 6 miles below Whittaker. Most take out at Richardson access (rapids below!). Lake Creek's hatchery produces winter steelhead and cutthroat.

A 97-mile canoe trip is possible from near Siuslaw Falls to Florence—an epic Oregon river adventure in winter/spring, though few will actually want to do it. I portaged 18 logjams here in 2012. Some were just a one-trunk drag, but many were difficult, including one at Clay Creek as big as a house (gone as of this writing). Thick thorny brush often prevents carrying on shore. Plus, a few among the many rock barriers installed by BLM require scouting and lining. I recommend 300 cfs at upper reaches (the gauge at Mapleton read 2,800). The deeply wooded upper river winds 34 miles from Siuslaw Falls to Clay Creek recreation site, with Siuslaw River Road clinging closely to the river half that distance.

More sensibly, put in at Clay Creek for a pleasant Class 1–2 paddle with few obstructions (though some logs are likely) for 26 miles to Richardson access. From headwaters down, old-growth on floodplains alternates with clearcuts that barely stop at the state-required 100-foot buffer and sometimes don't.

The 12 miles from Richardson to Lake Creek flow adequately for paddling into summer and present three powerful Class 2–3 rapids at 1,000–2,000 cfs. Scout the first two at railroad bridges; the third and sketchier lies just below a lower railroad bridge (onerous portage up and down steep banks on the right).

Below Lake Creek, 8 miles of heavy Class 2–3 swell following winter storms—one of Oregon's wider reaches of turbulent water. Tidal currents at Mapleton lag 2 hours behind Florence.

LAKE CREEK

Length: 40 miles	
Average flow: 706 cfs	
Watershed: 223 square miles	

Really a river, Lake Creek carries a third of the lower Siuslaw's volume and in winter can pump massively. Headwaters not far from Eugene drop west to Triangle Lake, which is skirted by Hwy 36. Then the stream tumbles to the Siuslaw at Swisshome.

 For a turbulent view, take Hwy 36 east of Swisshome 0.6 miles to a pullout overlooking the Horn. At super-high flows this drop has the awesome hydraulics of a gnarly rapid in the Grand Canyon. Another half mile upstream, a large pullout

Lake Creek at high flow below the Horn, upstream of Swisshome

accommodates parking and camping space. Farther up are accesses at Schindler (Indiola), Green Creek, and Deadwood Creek (5 miles above Swisshome). Farther upstream, and 0.5 miles south of Triangle Lake, an interpretive path leads to Lake Creek Falls, where a fish ladder installed in 1989 opened 110 stream miles to coho and Chinook.

 Below Lake Creek Falls the river drops 8 miles through Class 2+ rapids with brush and logs likely to Deadwood access, according to *Paddling Oregon*. Farther downstream is "Oregon's premier whitewater surf" when the Siuslaw runs 1,000–3,000 cfs at Mapleton. Ledges create ideal play-boating waves and holes, Class 2+ at low flows, harder when higher. From Deadwood to Schindler is 3 miles, followed by the Class 3–4 Horn. Below the Siuslaw confluence, a Class 2–3 run continues 3 miles to Tide.

SWEET CREEK

| Length: 13 miles |
| Average flow: 96 cfs |
| Watershed: 25 square miles |

This Siuslaw tributary enters tidewater from the south through a rainforest canyon. In high water, its linked chain of waterfalls left me spellbound.

From Hwy 36 in Mapleton turn east on 126, cross the bridge, go right on Sweet Creek Road 10 miles to Homestead Trailhead, and walk a mile upriver past 15 waterfalls, 3–50 feet high.

SILTCOOS RIVER

| Length: 4 miles |
| Average flow: 278 cfs |
| Watershed: 71 square miles |

The unusual Siltcoos eases from dune-barrier lakes and through Oregon Dunes National Recreation Area to the sea.

Sweet Creek above Homestead Trailhead

Siltcoos River entering the Pacific Ocean on the right

 Drive south from Florence 7 miles on 101, turn west at the Oregon Dunes sign, cross two bridges, and walk the Waxmyrtle Trail 1 mile downriver to the beach. To spare threatened snowy plovers, avoid dry sand March 15–September 15.

 South of Florence 6 miles turn east on Pacific Avenue to Siltcoos Lake (fee), then paddle south shortly to the lake's obscure outlet and a 3-mile drift downriver to sea, including an easy drag over a dam. Or stay on 101 another mile south, turn west at the Oregon Dunes sign, and launch at Lodgepole picnic area for a 1.5-mile paddle. Stop before the last bend, which sucks swiftly to sea at low tide. With little current at high tide it's easy to paddle back upstream; low or outgoing tides make the return difficult.

SMITH RIVER

The Smith is an undiscovered gem, and even with a valley-length paved road, the river's sharply meandering route ranks among the wildest in the Coast Range. The corridor has been heavily logged but suffers no dams and virtually no development until near tide-line. Substantial old-growth remains with BLM and the Forest Service, however, much of the main stem watershed is industrially owned. Fall Chinook, winter steelhead, and coho migrate here, aided by the Smith River Falls fish ladder. If a restoration program with road decommissioning, riparian protection, and steep slope stabilization were launched, the basin could become a model of recovery. The Smith's lower 21 tidal miles through farmland are entrenched within eroding banks of flood-borne silt. Hydrologically, this stream lies in the

| Length: 91 miles |
| Average flow: 735 cfs |
| Watershed: 352 square miles |

Umpqua basin, but barely so, joining just before the lower estuary meets the ocean.

An exceptional tributary, 18-mile Wassen Creek hides on the south side in Siuslaw National Forest, plunging over waterfalls and through one of the Coast Range's larger tracts of ancient forest. Four runs of anadromous fish, including threatened coho and resident cutthroat, thrive in this region otherwise heavily logged. To visit requires bushwhacking 8 infamous miles through steep thick cover. Designation of a 27,000-acre wilderness here and a 7-mile reach of National Wild and Scenic River were pending in 2014.

Cars and log trucks scarcely appear on Smith River Road, making it one of Oregon's premier riverfront biking opportunities for 80 miles, headwaters to Reedsport. To reach the top, drive 2 miles north from Drain on Hwy 99, turn north on Smith River Road, and climb 8 miles to the Umpqua/Smith divide. From there I've enjoyed biking 53 miles to Smith River Falls and even onward for the length of the basin (a shuttle car can take Hwy 38 to Reedsport). After an initial steep descent the road tracks the stream corridor with some views to the water, especially in mid/lower reaches. Bikers can camp at remote sites or BLM campgrounds at Smith River Falls and Vincent Creek—25 and 30 miles east of Hwy 101.

An attraction in its own right, Smith River Falls drops 6 feet within an ornate complex of sandstone ledges and pour-overs, dominated on the north side by a concrete fish ladder. It's one of the largest waterfalls (by volume) in the coastal mountains—spectacular in rainy months when steelhead jump. For several miles above and below, river-wide sandstone ledges distinguish this stream.

To reach the Smith from the bottom, take Hwy 101 north from Reedsport, and at the end of the Umpqua bridge turn east. The broad tidal river is reached at Noel Ranch ramp, 9 miles up.

Smith River and canoe below Big Creek

Some anglers come for winter steelhead, but wild fish must be released (no hatchery here). Fall Chinook enter August–October and move up with autumn rain, but are not fished above the estuary.

 Though not mentioned in paddling guidebooks, the Smith is a premier Class 2 canoeing stream for 43 miles in the rainy season, from Yellow Creek to Smith River Falls (low but adequate flow when the much larger Siuslaw at Mapleton ran 2,100 cfs). In winter the stream remains floatable far up because the bed narrows as volume decreases. I've started at Yellow Creek Bridge (47 road miles east of Hwy 101) for 3 days of boating. However, a massive logjam must be portaged below the put-in or avoided with a brushy launch at the second bridge below Yellow Creek. The upper Smith features a surprising amount of old-growth BLM forest for 12 miles to an easy portage at a low-water bridge 3 miles above Big Creek, also reached via the 13-mile gravel Weatherly Road (from Scottsburg take 38 east 7 miles and turn north). Another scenic 15-mile reach of Class 2 winds from the low-water bridge to Twin Sisters Creek, followed by 16 miles ending with a mandatory takeout above Smith River Falls Campground. New logjams can appear at any time, especially above Twin Sisters.

If the weather cooperates and you accommodate the chill of winter/ spring and the possibility of logjams, the Smith makes for excellent day-trips or a 3-day expedition with rocky rapids, old-growth forest, towering sandstone cliffs dressed in ferns and saxifrage, and dozens of tributaries hosting spawning habitat. Camping is mostly limited to brushy sites or micro-bars at low flows.

NORTH FORK SMITH RIVER

Length: 34 miles
Average flow: 214 cfs
Watershed: 69 square miles

This superb isolated stream supports native fish and flows through some of the finest old-growth forest along a coastal river. It meets the main stem Smith several miles below tide-line.

From Reedsport go north on 101, cross the Umpqua, turn east on Smith River Road for 15 miles, left on North Fork Road, and after 6 miles of farmland enter a narrow valley with riparian old-growth. The potholed road soon improves, reverts to pavement, and makes for excellent biking. Ten miles up from the main stem Smith River Road turn right on FR 23 and go 5 miles to North Fork Smith Trailhead. Here a 9-mile path ascends North Fork Canyon—one of the finest old-growth riverfront hikes in the Coast Range. In summer you can trek the whole way to a North Fork waterfall and two other 100-foot cataracts on tributary Kentucky Creek, then exit via Kentucky Falls Trailhead. To start there, continue driving from the lower trailhead on FR 23 for 5.7 miles, turn left, go 3 miles, then hike down Kentucky Creek to the two falls in 0.8 and 2.2 miles. During high water, choose either the upper or lower parts of North Fork Trail to avoid two fords. If this path

North Fork Smith River above Paxton Creek

were continued downstream along the North Fork to the National Forest boundary, it would be one of the state's premier extended river hikes.

 Wild steelhead must be released; Chinook spawn but cannot be fished.

 Seldom run, the North Fork makes a fine Class 2 rocky canoe run in the rainy season (I've found nice low flows when the Siuslaw at Mapleton ran 3000 cfs), with easy portage at a 5-foot waterfall. The 12-mile run passes under eight bridges. Beware of rebar in the stream. To put in, drive 13 miles above the intersection of the North Fork and main stem roads to a lane on the left that ends at a charming campsite. Take out at a publicly used lane 6 miles upstream from the Smith River Road intersection. Though the old-growth corridor is narrow and discontinuous, and the boating season short, this is some of the Coast Range's finest Class 2 paddling through relatively intact forest.

UMPQUA RIVER (see Chapter 5)

TENMILE CREEK

Length: 8 miles
Average flow: 338 cfs
Watershed: 89 square miles

The southerly of two Tenmiles, this one cuts through shifting sand below Tenmile Lake and emerges at one of the coast's wildest stream mouths—no road, development, jetty, or dredging. Even Hwy 101 sits far eastward. The creek supports threatened coho, as do other lake-studded watersheds along the central coast where dunes have blocked the creeks' direct paths to sea. Upstream, industrial property and Elliott State Forest are heavily cut.

Tenmile Creek at Oregon Dunes south of Reedsport

From Reedsport drive 12 miles south on 101, then south of Tugman picnic area turn west to Spinreel ramp.

Rarely paddled, the intimate Tenmile is my favorite estuary for canoeing. Float 2 flatwater miles to tour a suite of plantlife in succession: bare sand to aging Sitka spruce. I prefer this to the similar and more visited Siltcoos River because it cuts directly through tall dunes. This is also a great place to paddle close to the ocean; incoming tides can send small surfable waves into the lower river. Summer's northerly winds hamper the return, but more important, avoid low and outgoing tides. ATVs are banned for 1 mile north and south of Tenmile, making this outlet a pristine reminder of what was once the norm at our continent's edge.

COOS RIVER

Length: 20 miles, 73 with SF and Williams River	
Average flow: 1,441 cfs	
Watershed: 408 square miles	

Coos Bay is the largest estuary between the Columbia and California's Humboldt Bay, with sloughs fingering out. Lowlands here must have been one of the West Coast's richest wetlands, but 3,500 acres were filled. South Slough—Oregon's only National Estuarine Research Reserve—is an essentially natural bay, fed by Winchester Creek.

Wide and tidal for all 20 miles, the Coos River's main stem forms where the Millicoma River joins the South Fork Coos (tides continue 6 miles up each). For navigation, the estuary was dredged to the confluence in the early 1900s. Upriver, and underlain by erosive sandstone and mudstone, the Coos basin has virtually all been clearcut. Weyerhaeuser owns most of the South Fork watershed, though some public land remains as a checkerboard of BLM acreage.

South Fork Coos River and tributary waterfall 3 miles below Williams River

The South Fork is logged and roaded but has no houses or development. Improving management, Weyerhaeuser has upgraded roads to reduce sediment and has fixed thousands of culverts to avoid blowouts and open fish passage at tributaries. With the Coos Watershed Association the company has placed logs in the river to increase fish productivity. Furthermore, Weyerhaeuser's habitat conservation plan for spotted owls in many places requires wider riparian buffers than are mandated under the State Forest Practices Act, and the company's risk-assessment process adds to the otherwise nominal width of state-required buffers in areas prone to sliding.

 From Hwy 101 at the southern end of Coos Bay turn east at the sign for Allegany, join Coos River Road, stay on the south side where "Coos River Highway" crosses to the north, and continue to Dellwood and Weyerhaeuser's gate—open only on Saturday and Sunday, November–May (closed entirely in fire season, which is typically mid-June–October). However, permits for fishing (usable for boating) are available for weekdays, November–April, by calling 888-741-5403. Camping is not permitted by Weyerhaeuser but is on BLM parcels; see Siskiyou National Forest (Coos Bay District) or BLM maps.

The confluence of Tioga Creek and Williams River forms the South Fork Coos 22 miles above Dellwood. Access downstream appears at mile markers 12.2, 6.2, and 1 (numbered from Dellwood up).

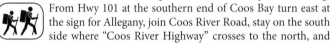 Anglers fish the South Fork up to Williams River for hatchery steelhead, peaking in January, and the tidal Coos for Chinook, August–October. Cutthroat remain in tributaries above and below waterfall barriers. Steep slopes, brush, and limited parking deter access.

 I've found 18 miles of the South Fork a little-known delight of technical sandstone-ledge and rock-garden Class 2–3 canoeing in winter/spring at relatively low flows (500 cfs in the

Coquille at Powers). Start on Williams River 2 miles above the Tioga confluence. A Class 2 run with a handful of Class 3 drops extends 12 miles to takeout at mile marker 12.2 (not all rapids are seen from the road). From there down to marker 6.2 easier Class 2 rapids prevail with a pair of Class 3 drops. The tidal river creeps 1 mile above Dellwood and is reached there and at a tidal ramp 4 miles west of Dellwood.

MILLICOMA RIVER

Length: 9 miles, 45 with WF	
Average flow: 518 cfs	
Watershed: 149 square miles	

The Millicoma is the "North Fork" Coos. Industrial forests drain into its 24-mile East Fork. After Glenn Creek enters, the stream jogs south and the 36-mile West Fork joins to form the main stem. A hatchery 9 miles up the West Fork produces steelhead and Chinook; wild runs also survive along with coho in Elliott State Forest.

 From Hwy 101 at the south end of Coos Bay, follow signs east for Allegany, cross to the north side of the Coos on "Coos River Highway," and drive up the Millicoma. Rooke-Higgins County Park, 10 miles from 101, offers camping at upper tidewater (its ramp at this writing is "closed" for liability reasons). In another 4 miles, West Fork Bridge (Allegany) lies just above the inaccessible East Fork confluence. Weyerhaeuser's road going far up the southeast side of the East Fork is open only on weekends, winter–spring. A shorter public road continues up the west side, where Nesika Park (10 miles above Rooke-Higgins) offers access, camping, and a path through a myrtlewood forest—best place to see this pretty stream. Continue another 3 miles to the Glenn Creek confluence. Here a 2-mile gravel road leads north to a state park at Golden and Silver Falls, 200 and 160 feet high respectively—splendid at winter flows.

West Fork Millicoma River 8 miles above the East Fork confluence

The lower West Fork is somewhat gentrified along its paved/gravel road, then wild up to the hatchery, 9 miles above Allegany. See this beautiful stream at a pullout and ledge-drop 1 mile below the hatchery. In Elliott State Forest the upper West Fork is reached via back roads beyond a high divide.

 The lower Millicoma is visited by tidal craft launching from Doris Ramp on Coos River Highway below the South Fork/ Millicoma confluence. Hatchery winter steelhead draw anglers to the East Fork, with access at Nesika, plus pullouts. The West Fork has steelhead angling above and below the hatchery.

 The East Fork offers a seldom paddled 3-mile canoe reach, Class 2 with a pair of 2+ drops, good at low winter flows when the South Fork Coquille runs 500 cfs at Powers. Start at a pullout 2 miles above Nesika and go to a 4-foot ledge along the road 1 mile below Nesika. Further boating lacks sanctioned access until far below tide-line at Doris ramp.

West Fork paddling from the hatchery to Rooke-Higgins is reportedly 12 miles of rainy season Class 2 and 3 rapids, plus tidal water with log hazards possible. Isolated loops hide drops not seen from the road; I haven't done this tempting but difficult-to-schedule run yet.

COQUILLE RIVER

Like the Coos River, the Coquille empties into a vast sea-level estuary—once among the West Coast's prime wetlands.

| Length: 36 miles, 100 with SF |
| Average flow: 4,526 cfs |
| Watershed: 1,053 square miles |

Remnants remain, which make this basin one of the finer coho refuges.

Fingering inland 30 miles to Myrtle Point, the Coquille has the longest tidal reach in Oregon next to the Columbia. This owes to the Coquille's

South Fork Coquille River above South Fork Falls

lobe of mountainous terrain jutting up west of the principal Coast Range axis and forcing the middle river north rather than letting it flow directly out to sea. The configuration makes this watershed the state's largest lying entirely in the Coast Range (the Nehalem runs longer, but its basin is smaller in area).

A highlight here, the upper South Fork Coquille carves one of Oregon's more remarkable rainforest canyons. The 40-mile Middle Fork joins the South Fork downstream of Myrtle Point, and then the estuarine main stem starts at the confluence of the North Fork—53 miles long with its own Middle and East Forks.

Noted for fall Chinook, the Coquille also has an uncommon residual run of spring Chinook that enter May–July. Cutthroat survive in less disturbed enclaves, few as they are. Coho persist in the long estuary with the cover and food it provides to rearing fish.

The largest Port Orford cedars grow in the South Fork basin; four giants have escaped the deadly fungus that is spread through water—including mud in tires—along and downslope of roads. A National Forest Natural Area designation protects the South Fork's Coquille River Falls, and some old-growth remains along the stream's narrow "beauty-strip" south of Powers.

Though most BLM and Siskiyou National Forest land has been logged, and over half the watershed is industry owned, the basin has been the focus of important restoration efforts. At Bandon Marsh National Wildlife Refuge, dikes that for decades benefitted cattle pasture were removed in 2011, reclaiming 420 acres of tidal floodlands for coho plus Chinook, cutthroat, steelhead, marine fishes, waterfowl, and shorebirds. Amid local controversy, additional restoration of 510 acres upstream is planned by the Nature Conservancy (more than 4,600 private acres of tidal lowlands will remain channelized and diked). Upstream, the Coquille Watershed Association and Forest Service have replaced fish-blocking culverts. Mixed private and public ownership along the upper South Fork adjoins protected areas extending to the Rogue and Elk Rivers and onward to the Illinois and Chetco; restoration of the upper South Fork could create the state's most significant reserve in the otherwise heavily logged coastal mountains.

To visit the wide mouth of this river, go to Coquille River Lighthouse; on Hwy 101 north of the Coquille bridge turn west. The tidal river and its wharf highlight downtown Bandon. To see the estuarine reach of drained and pastured wetlands, take 101 to north Bandon, turn east on 42, go 3 miles and turn north to the Judah Parker access, or go another 8 miles to Riverton ramp. Just west of the town of Coquille, Sturdivant Park offers access and camping, and in downtown a "Riverwalk" is being developed along the tidal frontage. Northward, the East Fork of the North Fork's Brewster Canyon and its elegant forested waterfall can be seen on the Myrtle Point-Sitkum Road northeast of Myrtle Point. The Middle Fork is easily seen from pulloffs along busy Hwy 42.

For South Fork access at tide-line, take Hwy 42 to Myrtle Point and turn west on Spruce Street to the boat ramp. To drive up the South Fork, head 2 miles south of Myrtle Point on 42 and right on 242. In 9 miles the Coquille Myrtle Grove Natural Area has access. Another 5 miles south, Baker Road turns west to an access at the bridge. Just north of Powers and the 242 bridge, the river is reached by turning east on Woodward Road and using a lane on the right. South (upstream) of Powers 2 miles, Orchard City Park has riverfront camping.

At the National Forest boundary 4 miles south of Powers, the exquisite South Fork canyon begins; the road upstream leads to enticing pullouts and campgrounds. Little known, this is one of the most awesome whitewater river canyons in Oregon. During high flows, steep gradient and massive rockpiles in the wild setting are spectacular. A path to the river lies 100 hundred yards south of the National Forest boundary sign. Drive 2 mile ssouth for a short trail to tributary Elk Creek's picturesque 60-foot falls; the path also loops uphill 2 miles to the champion Port Orford cedar.

South of Powers 18 miles, stay left on FR 3348 and go 1.5 miles to Coquille River Falls Natural Area where a 0.5-mile trail drops to an ornate waterfall shrouded with ancient forest. Upstream (east), a paved road follows the bubbling upper South Fork to campgrounds. The entire byway makes a superb riverfront bicycle journey; late spring is stunning in this brilliant green canyon.

 The lower Coquille is popular for fall Chinook and winter steelhead. Chinook are caught below tide-line, peaking August–October. Steelhead peak January–February. Hatchery coho can be fished August–October along 9 miles from Hwy 101 up to Bear Creek access. Nearly all fishing in the tidal, pastured, private-land river is by boats from Myrtle Point down.

The Middle Fork has occasional bank access for steelhead off Hwy 42. The South Fork offers hatchery steelhead in a popular drift-boat reach from Baker Creek to Myrtle Grove State Park, and is closed to fishing above the National Forest boundary.

 The South Fork canyon is a Class 4–5 kayak run with portages during the rainy season and "some of the finest technical whitewater in Oregon" according to *Soggy Sneakers*, which notes 300–3,000 cfs at Powers (3,000 is *big*). But this run is riddled with dangerously undercut boulders that should give pause even to the best experts. Intense rapids can be seen at an 8-foot drop below Daphne Grove Campground, at Roadside Narrows below Myrtle Grove Campground, and other pullouts. Guidebooks list a 4-mile Class 2–3 inclusion, Kelly Creek to Myrtle Grove Campground, but I found a formidably boulder-congested rapid midway and a final drop that's too tight to fit a boat at lower flows.

At the lower National Forest boundary you can carry your boat down the arduous put-in trail and paddle 8 miles of Class 2 water to Woodward Road access (upstream from Powers' northern Hwy 242 bridge), runnable down to 250 cfs (Powers gauge). Soft eroded shale of the Coast Range dominates in contrast to harder rocks of the Siskiyou Mountain province armoring the riverbed upstream—one of the best places to see the difference between these two geologic provinces.

Below Powers' northernmost bridge, the 2-mile Powers Gorge features a Class 4 10-foot drop. Then Baker Creek Road access opens a 7-mile Class 2 run to Coquille Myrtle Grove State Park, including a tight rapid with monumental boulders. Weathering December's chill, I've enjoyed some of my best salmon-viewing in Oregon on this reach—hundreds of Chinook in late-stages of spawning, bald eagles and vultures eyeballing the carcasses. The salmon spawning could be at risk; 2 miles below Baker Creek a massive landslide has been intermittently active for years, but in 2011 the forest above was clearcut and the entire "buffer strip" promptly liquefied into the river, creating one of the worst slides I've seen along a major stream (see Chapter 3 photos). Below Myrtle Grove State Park, gradient eases to Class 1–2 for 19 miles to Myrtle Point; from there to Bandon tidal water ebbs through the farmed estuary.

NEW RIVER

The New is an unusual coastal stream. This entire sea-level, dune-barrier river is separated from the ocean merely by a

> Length: 8 miles
> Average flow: 350 cfs
> Watershed: 126 square miles

sand bar. Strangest of all, its outlet occurs midway, where a northbound arm of the river meets head-on with a southbound arm and together they cut out to sea.

The southern source is Floras Lake; its outlet creek meanders through marsh grass and soon joins 21-mile-long Floras Creek. The flood of 1890 rearranged outflow here and established a "new" channel parallel to the Pacific. European dunegrass, planted in the early 1900s, stabilized sand

New River north of Floras Lake

and pinned the river in place but introduced ecological catastrophe as the grass spread up and down the coast, displacing native plants such as sand verbena and arresting the natural progression of sand migration on which threatened snowy plovers and others depended.

Ranchers occasionally bulldoze the outlet through the bar to avoid rising water in streamside pastures when drifting sand blocks the mouth. BLM has bulldozed swaths of its land to remove exotic beachgrass and increase habitat for snowy plovers.

Once superb for coho, tidal marshlands still provide some rearing habitat, and grasses here feed formerly threatened Aleutian Canada Geese, which flock to riverfront fields when staging for their epic flight to Alaska. An industrial-scale wind farm was proposed here but dropped (for now). Swamp and forest land to the south of Floras Lake, owned by Curry County, has been threatened by proposals for golf courses.

 The source of this beautiful, tidal, annually morphing hydro-logic system can be seen at Floras Lake; from Bandon take Hwy 101 south 15 miles and turn west at the Boice-Cope Park sign.

 Put in at Floras Lake's outlet and paddle the outgoing tide north in a serpentine channel that widens with Floras Creek's inflow. At 3 miles the New veers treacherously to an angry ocean; stay right and now paddle northward *against* the outgoing tide through good birding areas for 4 miles, including narrow channels and a lake (avoid eastern sloughs), ending at Croft ramp. To drive there, go 9 miles south of Bandon, turn west on Croft Lake Road, and wind 2 miles to BLM's trail/ramp. Do this trip between winter storms, because March 15–September 15 the road is gated 0.5 miles from the water with closure of sandy areas for snowy plover nesting. In those months, paddle north from Floras Lake and back on the fulcrum of outgoing/incoming tides. South-blowing winds on most summer afternoons and periodic north-blowing gales in winter make this outing impossible.

SIXES RIVER

Length: 33 miles
Average flow: 752 cfs
Watershed: 134 square miles

With headwaters in timber industry and ranch land, the Sixes flows through the isolated Coquille lobe of coastal moun-tains west of Powers. Downstream from a deep gorge, the South Fork joins for another 18 miles running to a perfectly natural mouth—one of few sizable West Coast streams without a jetty, harbor, or channelized outlet, and also peaceably removed from Hwy 101 by 4 miles.

Most of this basin is logged on short rotations with resulting land-slides, erosion, and siltation (see the contrast with the Elk River imme-diately south). Wilder, the South Fork flows through Siskiyou National Forest with some unlogged areas, though a few gold miners have claimed key tracts and live along the remote stream. In the lower basin, Dry Creek, draining Grassy Knob Wilderness, is an outstanding tributary and ac-counts for much of the remaining Sixes fishery.

Sixes River Gorge downstream of Sixes River Campground

 The mouth of the Sixes is a stunning meeting place of river and ocean—river slicing through sand bars, jagged sea stacks, seals, sea birds, mountain views, turbulent surf, and exhilarating wind; from Port Orford take 101 north 5 miles, turn west on Cape Blanco Road, park near the lighthouse, and at low tide walk the beach 1 mile north. Or, from the historic Hughes House a path (soggy at high tide) leads to the mouth. Cape Blanco has some of America's highest winds; in summer expect a stiff northern blow; in winter storms rage from the south at 70–100 mph—hurricanes elsewhere but here simply called "wind."

Upstream, BLM has 2 riverfront campgrounds; from Port Orford take 101 north 6 miles, turn east on Sixes River Road, and go 4 and 11 miles. Six miles farther, industrial timber owners gate the headwaters road.

 The river is open to salmon fishing below the South Fork and draws anglers for fall Chinook, peaking in November. Wild winter steelhead peak in January; cutthroat can be caught in summer. Drift boaters put in at the lower BLM campground once autumn rains begin. Many regard the Sixes as backup when the Elk is crowded.

Virtually unknown to boaters, the Sixes offers a rainforest gorge of Class 3+ challenges plus a significant Class 5 rapid in the rainy season, reached from the gravel road upstream of Sixes Campground. From the campground downstream, a charming Class 2+ gorge extends 2 miles followed by 4 easier miles to the Edson Campground takeout. Though short, this is one of the most convenient rainforest gorges for paddling. Another 8 miles riffle to Hughes House. To reach this tidal takeout, follow Cape Blanco Road and turn right at the sign. Levels are good when the Elk runs 4–5 feet; call ODFW, 541-332-0405 in winter.

ELK RIVER

Length: 25 miles, 31 with NF	
Average flow: 716 cfs	
Watershed: 91 square miles	

An Oregon gem, the Elk is the best-protected sizable basin in the coastal region and has some of the clearest water, largest old-growth forest, and most challenging rapids. Some fisheries biologists regard this as the finest Chinook and steelhead stream of its size on our coast. Like the Sixes, the Elk's mouth is unaffected by jetties or dredging, but quite different, it cuts behind a barrier bar and carves a dramatic sand cliff before jutting to sea. With the Sixes and South Fork Coquille, the Elk basin lies at the northwestern end of the Siskiyous on the geological bridge where those mountains merge with the Coast Range; harder rocks of the upper canyon yield to softer strata in lower miles.

Upper reaches are wild or only slightly affected by logging roads. Rainfall there tops 200 inches—comparable to the wettest mountains of Oregon's north coast. The main stem churns 14 miles through a rugged forest canyon of outstanding whitewater, then the lower river meanders 11 miles through ranchland to its wild beach.

Fall Chinook, coho, winter steelhead, and sea-run cutthroat all thrive here. Forest Service biologists stated that the Elk has "one of the few remaining healthy populations of coastal anadromous cutthroat trout," that "wild steelhead trout population levels are high," and that "wild Chinook juveniles are equaled by few other coastal watersheds" south of Canada. This river's contribution to Oregon's maritime commercial fishery is disproportionately high. Chinook returning to the Elk's hatchery underpin the fishery but also stray into tributaries for unwanted genetic exchange with wild fish, raising important and unresolved dilemmas about hatchery management. Coho densities are relatively good but still at "high risk" for extinction.

Elk River Gorge below Bald Mountain Creek

Most of Oregon's wild fall Chinook smolts leave freshwater within 5 months at most, though a small percentage linger a year in freshwater as a genetic hedge against conditions that may favor this. But in the Elk, up to 18 percent have this often-superior yearling life-history—larger and more capable when going to sea, and larger, older, and more fecund when returning.

Natural production of coho and steelhead is driven by spawning availability in tributaries. Chinook return November–January, somewhat later than most coastal streams owing to lower flows that persist into autumn on the south coast. The Elk is also a rare coastal stream with resident rainbow trout—testament to its colder flows.

Bordering the north bank for 10 miles, the 17,200-acre Grassy Knob Wilderness is Oregon's largest wilderness near the ocean. Adjoining it upstream, the 13,700-acre Copper-Salmon Wilderness was designated in 2009, blanketing the north side with a combined 30,900 acres of wilderness but leaving the National Forest south of the river vulnerable to logging. The Elk is also a National Wild and Scenic River down to the hatchery. Because these protected lands result in better spawning and rearing habitat for fish, efforts are underway to also safeguard non-wilderness drainages south of the river through a proposed "Salmon Emphasis Area."

Through the lower 11 miles of lightly developed private land, some ranchers are striving for greater river and open space protection. Acreage here is plagued with one of the Coast's worst infestations of gorse—a thorny alien shrub that invades once-farmed or logged tracts. Short of shading it out with trees, little can be done to eradicate it on lands that are not intensively managed.

As the upriver extension of the main stem, the North Fork is the best spawning tributary. Exquisite Panther Creek, entering the main stem

Panther Creek above its confluence with the Elk River

from the south, is next-best. Both contain "flats"—terraced interludes of gentler gradient and winding channels formed by outcrops or historic logjams, all resulting in buildup of salmon-spawning gravels. Productive flats are typically found in unlogged or lightly cut basins. In contrast, cut-over areas can become either highly aggraded (overfilled with gravel and silt) or scoured and downcut, according to *Forest and Stream Management in the Oregon Coast Range*. Wild tributaries Red Cedar and Anvil Creeks support threatened coho.

 The undeveloped mouth can be seen with a 1-mile walk south from Cape Blanco; from Port Orford take Hwy 101 north 5 miles, turn west to Cape Blanco State Park, drive to the end, and walk south. At this thrilling continental edge I've seen whales, bald eagles, ospreys, seals, and sea lions all at once.

To reach the river upstream, drive 3 miles north from Port Orford on 101 and turn east on Elk River Road. In 0.8 miles turn left for access, or continue 8 miles to the hatchery. Upriver from there, transparent green pools offer excellent swimming and a few riverfront camp spots (busy in summer) along the 11-mile paved road to Butler Bar Campground—a prime coastal-canyon biking route. Panther Creek has one of few trails; 9.5 miles above the hatchery take an unmarked lane to a 1.2-mile path through mossy forest and old-growth. In winter's high water, two Panther Creek fords a mile up halt walking to old-growth at the trail's end.

 Anglers flock here for Chinook in November and steelhead all winter. Salmon fishing is not allowed above Bald Mountain Creek—2 miles above the hatchery. Private land lies below the hatchery, so drift boats are the craft of choice, with access at the hatchery (square up and push through a steep drop just below at the weir).

The upper river from Butler Bar down to the hatchery offers Class 4+ rainy season whitewater with log hazards. An easier window to this enchanting rainforest canyon can be seen in an obscure 3-mile section of Class 2+; put in from a path at milepost 9 above the hatchery; take out above major rapids at Slate Creek Bar, 6.3 miles above the hatchery, best at low winter flows of 3 feet (541-332-7025).

From the hatchery down to the access above 101 is an 8-mile Class 1–2 run with a steep weir-drop just below the put-in (portage left) and swift currents through forest and ranchland. Flag the takeout—you won't see your car from the river—or get out at the 101 bridge and its steep bank.

ROGUE RIVER (see Chapter 6)

HUNTER CREEK

One mile south of Gold Beach, Hunter Creek is a small stream with road access at its lower end. Upper reaches are wilder, with an unlogged 4,000 acres proposed as the Veva Stansell

Length: 20 miles
Average flow: 319 cfs
Watershed: 44 square miles

Hunter Creek 5 miles upstream from the mouth

Botanical Area and an adjacent mountaintop threatened, at this writing, by a proposed nickel mine.

 The spectacular mouth is reached along Hwy 101 a mile south of Gold Beach. Park at the Half Dome–like rock south of the bridge. Farther south on 101, turn east on Hunter Creek Road to informal access at 1.3 and 1.7 miles. At 5 miles, cross the bridge and scramble down to an excellent pool with a massive rock-maze just above.

 For a Class 2 springtime paddle, put in at the bridge 5 miles up and take out at 101. Just above the put-in, a long Class 5 rapid at wintertime flows has pinning points and log possibilities. Other intense whitewater, with portages, lies upstream.

PISTOL RIVER

This stream flows from wild headwaters in Siskiyou National Forest down to timber industry/ranch lands. Though

Length: 21 miles
Average flow: 736 cfs
Watershed: 102 square miles

much has been clearcut, the river hosts a steelhead run and is known for large Chinook.

 The tidal reach flows along Hwy 101 behind a remarkable barrier bar. North of Brookings 17 miles, park south of the 101 bridge for a mile of beach strolling on the exposed outer peninsula created by the river (avoid high tide and storm surges).

 Few people paddle the Pistol's mostly Class 2+ run, possible from a pullout along Pistol River Road about 5 miles up from 101 but with an onerous portage around a Class 5 rapid (poison oak!).

Pistol River estuary at the Pacific

CHETCO RIVER

Length: 57 miles
Average flow: 2,244 cfs
Watershed: 353 square miles

This outstanding, important salmon and steelhead stream with pristine water flows through the heart of the Siskiyou Range and to the ocean at Brookings. Seventh-largest river on Oregon's coast, it's also one of the flashiest statewide. Winter discharges 50 times those of summer can spike from 1,000 to 60,000 cfs in a few days. A hydrologic phenomenon, the small watershed can briefly produce as much water as a high-flowing Willamette or Snake. This is also the wildest major river on the West Coast south of the Olympic Mountains, with no dams, towns, development, or roads along its upper 30 miles, and little below that until near sea level (even the Illinois River has towns above its wilderness canyon). Half the length lies in the Kalmiopsis Wilderness and its distinctive, real-life museum of geology and plants. Below, the road-accessible reach is one of the finest for summertime recreation.

Unlike most rivers, which flow somewhat directly out of their mountains, the Chetco wanders its forbidding topography, first north, then west, south, and again west. In the Chetco Gorge, 3 miles above the South Fork, chert boulders were formed undersea from skeletons of microscopic radiolaria, now stunningly striped in earthy tones of red, white, and gray. At the South Fork the valley broadens with spacious blue-gray gravel bars along jade-green water. The world's northernmost naturally growing redwoods tower at Loeb State Park.

Cutthroat thrive throughout, steelhead migrate to upper reaches, coho survive in one of their more southerly enclaves, and Chinook are a storied fishery with occasional 60-pounders and some of Oregon's highest smolt returns.

Chetco River at Loeb State Park

For three-quarters of its length, down to the Siskiyou National Forest boundary, the Chetco is a National Wild and Scenic River. Headwaters include the longest reach through a designated wilderness on the West Coast. This river and the neighboring Illinois also have the greatest undammed vertical drop among Oregon's coastal streams. In short, the little-known Chetco is an exceptional river.

The lower 7 miles flow through private land near Brookings and face development pressure; municipal water demands for a new 1,000-home subdivision north of town could overtax summertime flows. Upstream, a gold mining proposal jeopardizes 15 miles in the Wild and Scenic reach; applications in 2011 sought to expand from 4- to 8-inch gasoline-powered dredges—a vast increase in material extracted and then flushed back as silt, which can destabilize the riverbed and destroy invertebrate communities elemental in the food chain. Conservation groups strive to limit the mining and declare new claims off-limits through a congressional bill pending in 2014.

 From Hwy 101 in south Brookings turn east on North Shore Road. Loeb State Park, 7 miles up, offers access and a 1-mile trail along the Chetco through a fine myrtle grove. The Redwood Nature Trail lies 0.5 miles farther.

Turnoffs for excellent gravel-bar recreation sites and camping are 2.6 miles above Loeb at Miller Bar, 0.3 miles farther at Nook Bar, and 1.4 miles further at Redwood Bar. These all offer dreamy summertime swimming, and the snorkeling may be Oregon's best with clear, warm water and a rocky bottom. The South Fork access is 3 miles farther. Then 1 mile above South Fork Bridge, turn left on gravel FR 1407 to Low Water Crossing, where in summer the river can be waded to the west-side Chetco Gorge Trail. This runs 2 miles upstream to Eagle Creek's confluence, just below the formidable boulder garden of Chetco Gorge (volunteer trail maintenance needed!).

More remote, the upper river can nominally be reached by a rougher road: cross South Fork Bridge and stay left, go nearly 1 mile, turn right on FR 1917, in another 2.8 miles go left on unsigned FR 060, after 4.4 more miles go left on unsigned dirt 067 and drop 1 mile (high clearance) to south bank access. Avoid Tolman Ranch on the other side.

Farther up, the Chetco is best reached by arduous hiking from the east side of the Siskiyou Mountains. Since the widespread 2002 Biscuit Fire, trails have been in disrepair, but the Siskiyou Mountain Club is upgrading these. Take Hwy 199 north from Cave Junction 5 miles, turn west on Eight Dollar Mountain Road (later FR 4201), in 2.8 miles cross to the west side of the Illinois River, and (if the gate's open) go another 12 steep miles to road's end at Onion Camp. Here the Babyfoot Lake/Bailey Mountain/ Chetco River Trail leads southwest 9 miles to the canyon bottom: take the trail on the right, in a quarter mile go left (the right branch is a longer alternate), and in 3 miles switchback right at a junction with the Canyon Peak Trail. In another mile or so, in an open area above an old mine, take the fork leading uphill, continue to the shoulder of Bailey Mountain (mile 7), and drop to the river (see *California Creeks* website). A shorter trail may open in summer from Chetco Pass, though brush may be thick: from Hwy 199 in Selma turn west on Illinois River Road, go about 12 miles, park at the trailhead if further mileage is gated, cross the Illinois, walk or drive the jeep road 5 miles up to Chetco Pass, then hike 3 steep miles down to the river at Slide Creek. Take a map!

 Fishing for fall Chinook begins in the tidal reach in September and peaks in November. Winter steelhead below the South Fork peak January–February. Drift boats ply from the South Fork down and use eight access areas, which also offer bank fishing. The river above tide-line is closed to summer fishing.

 The upper Chetco through Kalmiopsis Wilderness is Oregon's ultimate epic river adventure for ultra-fit paddlers. It features crystalline water and pristine wilderness as remote as anywhere in the state. After the rigorous hike and boat-carry from the east side (see above), paddle 3–5 days in Class 3–5 rapids plus portages. Avoid high or rising water. Flows are hazardously erratic until late spring (200–400 at Brookings suits some paddlers), and hundreds of boulders define the word "undercut." In summer, a low-water trip with inflatable kayaks, frequent dragging, and challenging boulder scrambling is a remarkable athletic experience and river adventure on as little as 80 cfs at Brookings.

For a more accessible but still jaw-dropping upper Chetco outing, put in at Tolman (see above) and paddle 6 miles to Steel Bridge (for this takeout, drive 3 miles north from the South Fork on FR 1376, cross the Chetco, and turn left), or continue paddling 8 more miles through the lower gorge. This geologically wondrous wild-river extravaganza includes a tumult of Class 4–5 drops. Radiolaria is a colossal blockage of massive boulders requiring a rigorous carry (the name refers to undersea protozoa

Chetco River portage downstream of Boulder Creek

whose metamorphosed skeletons form the striped, candy cane–like rock). Soon after, two pointed monoliths mark Conehead, where the river collides into boulders and logs—line and drag with care.

The reach from Low Water Crossing to Brookings Harbor is a superb 20-mile Class 1–2 run on riffles with multiple accesses—an excellent trip for early to intermediate paddlers. After winter storms clear, the water turns turquoise-blue. Expansive gravel bars offer fine campsites on this seldom run overnighter—a miniature lower Rogue without the jet boat roar. Expect headwinds, especially on summer afternoons. Take out at Loeb, or tide-line's Social Security Bar (3.2 miles east of Hwy 101), or go to Brookings harbor. Flows of 2,000 or more feel big; low flows enchant with carefree clarity. All summer the stream is day-trip boatable with depthless pools and tight gravel riffles that channelize as flows drop; 200 cfs at Brookings is good, but with minor dragging I've enjoyed paddling on as little as 80. Fallen trees, however, pose serious hazards, especially to beginners who might be tempted by the apparent carefree nature of this float; get out and wade or drag on shore wherever trees cross the stream! Boaters must register at a roadside stop near the Redwood Bar turnoff. I do not leave my vehicle overnight at the South Fork's weekend-rowdy campsite.

WINCHUCK RIVER

Length: 10 miles, 19 with EF
Average flow: 494 cfs
Watershed: 71 square miles

Southernmost river to enter the ocean in Oregon, the Winchuck begins near the Kalmiopsis Wilderness and ends half a mile north of California. The East Fork and its tributary, Fourth of July Creek, are largely roadless, while tributary Wheeler Creek flows through a Forest Service Research Natural Area. The river supports Chinook,

East Fork Winchuck River above main stem confluence

coho, steelhead, and cutthroat. In Wheeler and Elk Creeks the Forest Service and South Coast Watersheds Council in 2012 reinstated large logs to improve habitat.

 The surf-pounded Winchuck mouth can be enjoyed at Crissey Field State Park visitor center south of the 101 bridge. A path through Sitka spruce leads to the tidal river, to dunes formed from Winchuck-borne sand, and to the wave-tossed mouth. To go upstream from 101, turn east on Hwy 896 and drive 8 miles to Winchuck picnic area. The road continues 3 miles to the East Fork and its wild streamfront trail.

 Though fished for Chinook, steelhead, and cutthroat, the river sees little angling because of limited access: the lower 8 miles are private, and fishing is not allowed from boats or above Wheeler Creek (1 mile above Winchuck picnic area).

 On high springflows, nice Class 2 water runs from Winchuck picnic area to the visitor center.

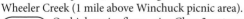

SMITH RIVER, NORTH FORK (tributary to California's Smith River)

Length: 28 miles (14 in OR)
Average flow: 942 cfs
Watershed: 158 square miles

The Smith ranks as a premier river of the West Coast, and while the main stem is Californian, the North Fork starts in Oregon. From Chetco Peak in the Kalmiopsis Wilderness it flows 12 miles to the border and another 16 to the Middle Fork at Gasquet.

This is the Smith's wildest fork, with exceptionally clear water. Much of the basin has lateritic soils, which lack calcium, nitrogen, sodium, and potassium needed by trees and most plants. Furthermore, minerals here such as nickel, chromium, and cobalt stunt growth. As a result, little timber harvest (and related road building/erosion) has occurred, so deep pools have not become filled with silt and gravel, as they are elsewhere. The North Fork's clarity and pools illustrate this critical relationship between watershed conditions, streambed morphology, and logging. And because of the strange soil chemistry, an unusual assortment of forbs, shrubs, and carnivorous plants excel for a botanist's holiday.

Exquisite Baldface Creek enters 2 miles north of the California boundary. Nickel mining claims there threaten excellent anadromous habitat and the health of the legendary main stem Smith—the finest salmon stream and arguably most pristine river left in California.

No roads follow the North Fork, and trails are few. To reach the lower river in California, take Hwy 199 to Gasquet, turn left on Middle Fork Road, cross the Middle Fork, turn left on FR 318, go to the end and hike up the trail. For the middle river, take Hwy 101 north from Crescent City, turn east on Hwy 197, go north on Low Divide Road (FR 305) for 9 miles, angle sharp right where Rowdy Creek Road joins, and continue 13 miles on Low Divide (Wimer Road) to North Fork Bridge—21 slow miles of dirt road in all. To see the remote Baldface Creek in Oregon, go to North Fork Bridge, proceed east 3 miles, turn left at FR 206 (closed until summer), and continue 6 miles. For the upper river in Oregon, take Hwy 101 south from Brookings 4 miles, turn east on Winchuck River Road (896), go 8 miles, turn right on FR 1107, and continue about 18 miles to the Horse Creek turnoff near the river.

California Whitewater calls the North Fork reach "one of the loveliest wilderness whitewater runs in the country." The stream receives light use owing to remoteness, difficulty, and a short, flashy winter/spring season. The 13-mile, continuous Class 3–4 raft or kayak run begins just south of Oregon and ends at Gasquet. The rarely paddled upper North Fork and its wilderness can be reached from Horse Creek (see above) for Class 3–4 kayaking with logs, called "ultra-classic" by local paddler J.R. Weir.

CHAPTER 5

UMPQUA

Like coastal streams, the Umpqua swells with winter rains, which bring salmon and steelhead home, but it also enjoys healthy year-round flows and remarkable headwaters at the snowy Cascade crest, making it the fifth-largest river in Oregon and second-largest entirely in-state. Fishable, boatable water runs all through summer and a glorious autumn. This basin offers some of the most diverse angling opportunities in the West and a premier long-distance canoe journey. One of two principal tributaries, the North Umpqua is perhaps the most legendary steelhead stream anywhere.

UMPQUA RIVER

Beginning at the confluence of the North and South Umpqua northwest of Roseburg, the main stem flows to

Length: 108 miles, 226 with SF and Castle Rock Fork
Average flow: 7,729 cfs
Watershed: 4,668 square miles

the Pacific at Reedsport. Next to the Columbia, this is the largest Oregon river emptying into the sea. Unique on the Pacific Coast south of Canada, it's also the largest river lacking dams. The combined main stem/South Umpqua/Castle Rock Fork flows dam-free 226 miles—second only to the John Day with its North Fork for free-flowing mileage statewide.

Umpqua River and drift boat above Osprey access

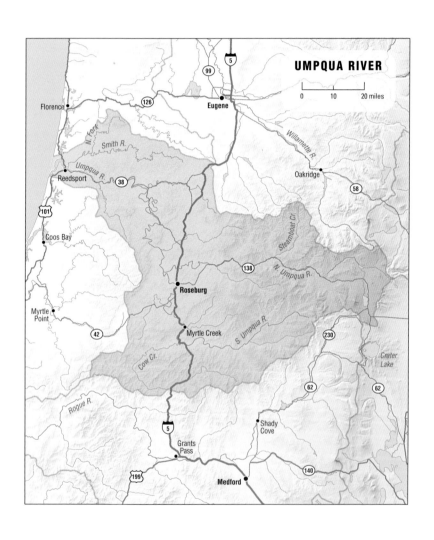

UMPQUA RIVER

0   10   20 miles

Florence

Eugene

99

5

126

Willamette R.

Oakridge

58

N. Fork

Smith R.

Umpqua R.

Reedsport

38

101

Coos Bay

Steamboat Cr.

138

N. Umpqua R.

Roseburg

Myrtle
Point

42

Myrtle Creek

S. Umpqua R.

230

Cow Cr.

Crater
Lake

62

62

Rogue R.

5

Grants
Pass

Shady
Cove

199

Medford

140

Umpqua River and sandstone 2 miles below Kellogg Bridge

The Umpqua negotiates hundreds of riffles and rapids interspersed with placid pools. As it transects the Coast Range it cuts through strikingly unusual drops: river-wide bedrock slabs of sandstone have eroded like washboards turned sideways with water running not across but through the grooves.

Unlike the Rogue and Klamath, which are the only other rivers similarly crossing the Coast Range where mountains rise high, the Umpqua's course is gentler and its valley wider and more accessible through uplifted Tyee sandstone. Its riverfront is settled with occasional homesites in a ranch and forest mosaic. BLM parcels scattered between Roseburg and tidewater harbor the only old-growth forest remaining in the lower basin, where the timber industry owns much of the land. Willows and cottonwoods line the shores. Testament to its fishery, ospreys can be seen almost continuously in spring and summer; bald eagles are common.

The basin supports an unusual variety of fishes. This is one of few West Coast rivers with a healthy summer steelhead run (headed for the cool North Umpqua). Winter steelhead and spring and fall Chinook are also highlights, and the river is an important refuge for threatened coho. Endemics found nowhere else include the small secretive Umpqua chub in the South Fork and upper main stem, plus the rare Umpqua dace in backwaters possibly down to the estuary. The locally abundant Umpqua pikeminnow lives only here and in the Siuslaw and Rogue. Introduced smallmouth bass prey heavily on natives but make for great angling and eating. *Freshwater Ecoregions of North America* lists the Umpqua among six Oregon regions exceptionally important for aquatic biodiversity.

While water quality generally looks good in summer, the main stem fails standards for temperature and bacteria and suffers occasional blooms of toxic blue-green algae. The warm water reflects deforestation, development, and withdrawals. Even so, the river's size, free-flowing length, and habitat diversity make it exceptional in Oregon and the West.

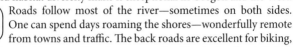 Roads follow most of the river—sometimes on both sides. One can spend days roaming the shores—wonderfully remote from towns and traffic. The back roads are excellent for biking, and there's no better tour of the Oregon countryside via riverfront. Swimming's good in the hot summers that are typical east of the cool coastal breeze that wafts to Elkton.

For the North/South Umpqua confluence, take I-5 exit 125 at Roseburg, go north on Garden Valley Boulevard 6 miles, turn left after the North Umpqua bridge, and continue 2 miles to River Forks Park. Cleveland Rapids Park is another 3 miles downstream on Hwy 6; Umpqua Landing another 6 miles. Then Hwy 33 continues 8 miles to James Wood access. Another 8 miles downstream is Osprey access, followed in 7 miles by Tyee ramp/campground. Here the busier Hwy 138 joins the valley. Another 3 miles lead to Yellow Creek ramp, then an RV park and popular beach 4 miles below. From there to Elkton, 30 miles of idyllic riverscape have relatively little road access.

From Elkton west, Hwy 38 follows the lower valley. To easily explore what's uniquely Umpqua, turn south off 38 in Elkton, go to the western end of town, and stroll downstream across the expansive pothole-riddled bedrock (summer/fall; flooded in spring!). An access lies 6 miles west of Elkton. The next appears in 7 more miles, followed by Sawyer's Rapids—a private campground with access to a turbulent bedrock ledge—the sharpest drop on the main stem. Tidewater stretches 27 miles up from sea to Scottsburg, and another ramp lies 1 mile west. From there down the river resembles a majestic fjord. East of Reedsport 4 miles on Hwy 38, the Dean Creek Wayside offers the best Roosevelt elk viewing in Oregon. Downtown Reedsport has Rainbow Plaza access east of Hwy 101. To see the Umpqua's broad sand-blown Pacific outlet, take 101 south of Reedsport 3 miles to Winchester Bay, turn west, and follow Salmon Harbor Drive to the jetty.

 Oregon Fishing Guide boldly states, "The Umpqua offers the widest variety of world-class fishing opportunities of any river in the Northwest." Chinook and summer/winter steelhead seasons span the year. Starting in July, fall Chinook run throughout the main stem. Spring Chinook peak in April in the lower river and continue into May to River Forks. Winter steelhead are sought January–March, often caught between River Forks and Osprey ramps, and at Sawyer's. Summer steelhead peak May–July. Smallmouth bass make for excellent angling and are easily caught, especially from Tyee to Elkton in August. Next to the Columbia, the state's largest run of introduced shad appear May–June and ascend to River Forks.

 Though virtually unknown as such, the main stem is not just a great Oregon canoe trip, but a great American canoe trip. The 100-mile reach from the confluence to Reedsport makes a superb weeklong expedition with quiet pools, hundreds of riffles, many Class 2 drops, and several Class 3 challenges. Put in 7 miles up the

North Umpqua at Hwy 99 for a 107-mile trip to Reedsport (windy estuary below). Too easy for most kayakers, and too flat and windy for most rafters, the river is ideal for experienced canoeists. I first did the trip in 1977 when I recognized this was one of few long river voyages possible without dams on the West Coast. It flows adequately all summer and fall (1,000–3,000 cfs at Elkton). Summer is hot and easy; autumn is crisp and beautiful. Avoid winter-spring floods, which reach a whopping 50,000 cfs. By combining the main stem and South Umpqua directly above, an early-summer expedition of 176 miles (with a few portages) offers the third-longest dam-free expedition in Oregon.

Rapids challenging for paddlers with laden canoes come as scattered surprises throughout. The largest lie in the relatively inaccessible Umpqua Loop area: Brad's Creek Rapid is 8 miles below the Route 138 bridge at Kellogg (by road, this is the second bridge south of Elkton). Smith Ferry Rapids is a larger Class 3 drop 12 miles below the same bridge (within sight of a lower 138 bridge). Both can be carried. The jet-flume of Sawyer's Rapid, 10 miles below Elkton, is easily portaged left.

While roads follow most of the corridor's length, sizable bends lack intrusion and feel remote; the best make a 34-mile loop-sojourn from Yellow Creek access to Elkton. Unlike popular whitewater rivers including the Rogue, the Umpqua offers many miles where you won't see another boat in summer. Yet plentiful ramps make trips of any length possible.

NORTH UMPQUA RIVER

From the Cascade crest this stream plunges west to its confluence with the South Umpqua near Roseburg. Jade-green water whitened in rapids over black basalt is a world-renowned

Length: 106 miles
Average flow: 3,705 cfs
Watershed: 1,356 square miles

North Umpqua River downstream of Deadline Falls

steelhead fishery and perhaps the most revered river in the Oregon Cascades. Considering its rapids, conifers, great summertime weather (not too hot), and clear water for 100 recreational miles, I'm hard pressed to name a better road-accessible river in the West for a weeklong river vacation. With excellent canoeing, rafting, kayaking, fishing, mountain biking, and running, make that 3 weeks! Healthy flows continue through summer owing to 9,182-foot Mount Thielsen's snowpack and to groundwater stored in volcanic rock of the high Cascades. The trail here is also the longest nearly full-basin tour in Oregon—snowcapped headwaters to lowlands.

The upper North Umpqua plus Fish Creek and Clearwater River are dammed eight times and diverted by PacifiCorp for hydropower, however, most of this waterworks is upstream of anadromous habitat. New passage facilities at the lowest dam—Soda Springs—will return spawners to Fish Creek, above the reservoir.

Below Soda Springs Dam, the middle river drops through magnificent rapids and deep pools to Glide while Hwy 138 curves alongside. Then, with just a few accesses, the lower river enters oak-savanna foothills. Below Winchester Dam the final 7 miles tour cottonwood floodplains to the main stem, which continues dam-free to sea.

The North Umpqua upstream of Rock Creek and its hatchery (above Glide) is managed as a wild trout and salmon fishery, though hatchery escapement and straying occurs. Tributaries Steamboat and Canton Creeks are top spawning areas for wild fish. With special regulations dating to 1923 and fly-fishing only, the North Umpqua became one of America's first fish refuges. In spite of such care, the watershed was ravaged by aggressive logging and road building from the 1950s to 90s (canoeing in 1987, I counted log trucks barreling down the highway—no kidding—every 20 seconds). But now the river is slowly recovering. In ranking streams for anadromous qualities, the Wild Salmon Center reported that the North Umpqua and upper Rogue were tied for second place statewide (Nehalem was first). From Soda Springs Powerhouse to Rock Creek, 34 miles are a National Wild and Scenic River.

TRIBUTARIES

Small Watson Creek, in the upper basin, has one of Oregon's tallest waterfalls, 293 feet over Toketee basalt; from Toketee Reservoir take Hwy 138 east 2.2 miles and turn south on FR 37.

Boulder Creek is an excellent example of a pristine Cascade Mountain stream as it plummets 8 miles through Boulder Creek Wilderness. A trail climbs high, then follows the creek for 3 miles; take Hwy 138 west of Toketee 6 miles, turn north on Medicine Creek Road, cross the river, and go 1.2 miles to the trailhead.

Little River enters the North Umpqua at Glide. On tributary Wolf Creek, a 75-foot waterfall, best in winter/spring, is reached by a 1-mile trail; drive south from Glide on Little River Road 11 miles.

You can reach the lower North Umpqua from the south side of the Hwy 99 bridge, north of Roseburg. From there up to Glide, the land is mostly private. For access, go to Whistlers Park on the south side; take 138 east of Roseburg 12 miles and turn north on Whistlers Lane. Another 4.5 miles east, at Glide, the turbulent confluence of Little River is the centerpiece of Colliding Rivers viewpoint.

Upstream from Glide, many campgrounds, recreation sites, and river accesses appear through BLM and then National Forest land. Paths reach turbulent flumes at The Narrows, 3.6 miles east of Glide. Just above Rock Creek, steelhead and spring Chinook can sometimes be seen jumping Deadline Falls, May–October; 4.3 miles east of Glide turn south, cross Swiftwater Bridge, and stroll upstream to the falls. Baker Falls (rapid) highlights a picnic area 2 miles above Deadline. Another 4.4 miles up, Susan Creek access has a path running upstream to a campground. Below the Steamboat Creek confluence, Steamboat Inn is perhaps Oregon's most classic river resort and you can get a flavor for the state's rich angling history just by pausing for breakfast.

Farther upriver, Toketee Falls' two-tiered plunge showers over perfect hexagonal basalt; at milepost 59 (from Roseburg) turn north on FR 34, cross the bridge, go left, and hike 0.5 miles. Hwy 138 continues eastward up tributary Clearwater River—hidden in its gorge just north of the road.

One of Oregon's longest and premier river hikes, the 79-mile North Umpqua Trail starts at Deadline and climbs to Maidu Lake with 12 National Forest trailheads along Hwy 138 (see *North Umpqua Trail*). This is the longest of Oregon's extended riverfront trails, though the road on the opposite side is more evident than on other routes. Backpack for a week or enjoy day hikes. After the first old-growth stroll to Deadline Falls, the lower 16 miles up to Wright Creek are mostly set back from the river. The next five trail sections upriver are 4–6 miles each. I especially like reaches above and below Mott Bridge (above Steamboat Creek). Upstream, at Apple Creek Campground, turn south on FR 4714 to a trailhead and walk west into old-growth, which is also found east of Calf Creek Trailhead (from 138 turn south on FR 4750).

The premier trail section is along the upper river—13 miles from Umpqua Hot Springs (above Toketee Reservoir) up to White Mule Trailhead (west of Lemolo Reservoir). With impressive old-growth, gushing crystalline springs, splendid wildness far from roads, and constant river views, this is the best river trail in Oregon. Near the upper end, Lemolo Falls is fabulous. For the lower trailhead, turn north off 138 on FR 34 at Toketee Reservoir, in 2.2 miles bear right on FR 3401, go 2 miles to the Hot Springs parking lot (fee) or roadside, and hike upstream. For the upper trailhead, take 138 east from Toketee 13.8 miles, turn north on FR 2610 toward Lemolo Reservoir, go 5.1 miles, turn left, cross the aqueduct, and immediately park at the trailhead.

The river's Maidu Lake source in Mount Thielsen Wilderness is reached by a 9-mile hike through Rocky Mountain–like lodgepole pine forest; on 138 about 6 miles north of Diamond Lake turn northeast on FR 60, go

4 miles to a trailhead on the south side of the river, and hike up (mosquitoes!). For the top of the watershed, hike to Mount Thielsen and its Matterhorn-like view, reached by a separate trail from the north end of Diamond Lake.

The entire North Umpqua Trail is considered one of Oregon's top destinations for advanced mountain bikers.

 Many anglers regard the North Umpqua as the state's premier summer steelhead stream. *Oregon Fishing Guide* boasts it "may be the most legendary steelhead river in the world." Chinook, coho, rainbow, cutthroat, and brown trout do well, and the river retains its full complement of native fishes, even with the Rock Creek hatchery. The combination of large fish, clear water, steep banks, and slippery drop-offs challenge the most expert anglers. On the lower river, winter steelhead peak in February. Owing to private shorelines, lower-river fishing is done via drift boats, starting at the access west of Colliding Rivers and running to Whistlers Park (with one steep drop). Fishing from boats is banned above Lone Rock access, 1 mile upstream of Glide. Summer steelhead run May–October, favored in the 31-mile fly-fishing-only section from Soda Springs Powerhouse down to Deadline. Spring Chinook peak in May. Below Rock Creek, where fish congregate because of the hatchery, bank angling for summer steelhead and spring Chinook is popular.

Wild steelhead must be released, and salmon fishing is closed above Deadline Falls. Rainbows are caught in spring and fall above Rock Creek.

 The North Umpqua is among Oregon's premier whitewater boating rivers—an uncommon high-gradient stream with runnable levels all summer, more rapids per mile than almost anyplace, and a lack of crowds (see *North Umpqua Wild and Scenic River Users Guide*). Even with the road, the route feels remote. Class 2–4 rapids appear from Boulder Flat (7 miles below Toketee Dam) to the mouth, with some unrunnable drops midway.

Uppermost, a Class 3 section extends 6 miles from Boulder Flat to Horseshoe Bend. The next 7-mile reach to Gravel Bin offers the river's choice big whitewater with Class 4 Pinball Rapid (0.3 miles below Apple Creek Campground Bridge but hidden from the road), plus several Class 3 drops. Next, Gravel Bin to Bogus Creek runs 5 miles with Class 2+ and one Class 3—so favored by fly fishermen that, under a cooperative agreement, floaters are asked to stay away before 10 a.m. and after 6 p.m. and to avoid boating entirely July 15–October 31. Paddlers abide by this sensible segregation of water. Then Bogus to Susan Creek is a 7-mile Class 3 run with a pair of 3+ drops and a portage when under 1,000 cfs in late summer.

Susan to Cable Crossing is a 6-mile Class 2+ run with several turbulent Class 3 rapids, including a steep plunge at Upper Baker and 6-foot Baker Falls (2 miles above takeout). Don't miss the mandatory exit at obscure Cable Crossing access; from Deadline (on 138 just east of the Hwy 78/Rock Creek intersection) drive 0.5 miles upstream to the unsigned steep paved turnoff. Just above this, Upper Cable Rapid can be avoided by exiting at a pullout 0.2 road miles east of Cable Crossing. Below Cable, a precipitous drop feeds into Deadline Falls and other Class 5 pitches called The Narrows.

Below Idleyld Park, and less visited owing to private frontage, white-water boating continues 25 splendid miles, which are excellent for advanced canoeists at lower flows (I like 1,000 cfs). Conifers transition to oak-savanna—opalescent green in spring, golden in summer/fall, with scattered riverfront houses. This is Oregon's "Thousand Islands" of rocky knobs and bedrock slabs. Lively Class 2 drops are accented with several Class 3 plunges. Launch at Lone Rock access; from Glide drive east 1 mile, before the bridge turn right, and go 1 mile to the ramp. Squirrely Class 3 Colliding Rivers Rapid marks the Little River confluence. This is normally run on the right side of the left channel, while a Class 4 sluice foams right of the island. At low flows, the left channel bottoms out and the right side eases to Class 3. The large rock island between the two channels is worth a stop and climb for the view. A ramp popular with drift boaters lies just downstream on river-left.

From there it's 8 miles to Whistlers Rapid (scout), followed by Whistlers Bend access and a large county park. Three miles below, gnarly, under-rated Dixon Falls hides beneath a plethora of guard rocks and islands that inhibit scouting. Approach cautiously, eddy out, and if in doubt, wade and drag on the left. At high water a rocky far-left-side run missing the "falls" may be possible.

Winchester Dam lies east of Hwy 99. To avoid portage, take out in the reservoir; from Roseburg at Hwy 138 take Hwy 99 north 4.6 miles, turn east on Page Road, and go 1.2 miles to a steep unmarked gravel lane.

Below Winchester Dam, under the south side of the 99 bridge, put in at Amacher Park for a summertime tuber's favorite—Class 2+ for 7 miles to the main stem's River Forks Park.

STEAMBOAT CREEK

Length: 24 miles
Average flow: 728 cfs
Watershed: 163 square miles

Renowned Steamboat enters the North Umpqua 22 miles east of Glide. Recognizing a steelhead nursery that accounted for half the spawning in the North Umpqua basin, the Oregon Fish and Wildlife Department has closed the creek to fishing since 1932. The wisdom of establishing a fish refuge has been confirmed with good runs of summer and winter steelhead, cutthroat, a few spring Chinook and coho, plus rainbow trout, Pacific lamprey, redside shiner, sculpins, and daces.

The basin underwent heavy logging in the 1960s–80s, and critical woody debris was removed from the stream, resulting in downcutting, which now requires a long restoration process. At great cost the Forest Service has helicoptered in 1,000 large logs to replace lost tributary habitat. Old-growth reserves enacted in the 1990s protect the watershed from further logging (except to enhance habitat), and an administrative mineral withdrawal to safeguard the fishery was expanded in 1976 to the basin's 15 tributaries.

Canton Creek at Steamboat Creek confluence

FR 38 follows the length of Steamboat and its East Fork—paved, with good biking and occasional stream views. At Steamboat Falls' heavily cemented 25-foot fish ladder, steelhead can be seen; from Hwy 138 drive 5.5 miles up FR 38, turn right on 3810, and go 0.7 miles. Another 5.3 miles up FR 38, Bend Pool lies on the left. This site is monitored for poaching by North Umpqua Fishwatch; in summer you can see hundreds of steelhead (best in afternoon light) holding in cold water delivered by Big Bend Creek as the fish await winter flows enabling them to reach upstream spawning grounds.

Steamboat is closed to fishing. Expert kayakers occasionally run the Class 4+ reach below the falls.

SOUTH UMPQUA RIVER

Length: 102 miles, 118 with Castle Rock Fork
Average flow: 2,755 cfs
Watershed: 1,801 square miles

Though overshadowed by its northern cousin, the South Umpqua descends vibrantly from the Rogue-Umpqua divide through forests, countryside, and a cluster of towns. Lower in elevation and lacking the robust high-Cascades aquifer, water levels drop sooner than in the North Umpqua and bottom out far lower in summer—a regime exacerbated by water withdrawals. Though affected by logging, ranching, and the I-5 corridor, the South Umpqua remains a beautiful, underrated river, and can boast Oregon's longest reach touring the crucial but stressed habitat of oaks/grassland/conifers. Dam-free, the river's length combined with tributary Castle Rock Fork headwaters plus the main stem below total 226 free-flowing miles—second-longest dam-free reach in Oregon and the state's longest completely free-flowing river.

Winter steelhead migrate upriver November–May, and some spring

Chinook survive in what was once a great fishery. These waters were highly productive with mild temperatures (but not lethally warm until massive watershed disturbance occurred). Endangered coho still survive in a few tributaries and have been the focus of Forest Service restoration. The endemic Umpqua chub and pikeminnow are found here. Opening up significant mileage that had been blocked to migrating salmon and trout for a century, a 14-foot dam on tributary Myrtle Creek was removed in 2000. Toxic blue-green algae warnings have been posted in summer for parts of the South Umpqua—avoid bright green scum.

This important stream has tremendous potential for habitat restoration and recreation use, plus community enhancement within the populated lower valley. Umpqua Watersheds and other groups work toward these goals.

Through the I-5 corridor, a number of parks and pulloffs start with Templin Beach in downtown Roseburg; go west from Hwy 99 on Mosher Avenue, south on Fulberton, and right on Templin. Moving upstream, take I-5 exit 120, turn south on 99, turn quickly west on Happy Valley Road, and continue 1 mile to a ramp. Next upstream, take exit 119, go south on 99, then quickly west on 42 for 0.6 miles to a ramp at the mouth of Lookingglass Creek. At exit 113, go right on Dole Road toward Dillard and continue 6 miles to an unmarked access at the west side of the bridge, river-right. Next, and best, from exit 102 go west and immediately left to beautiful Lawson Bar with its beach, bedrock, and rapids. Stanton County Park is off exit 101; go east on 99 a mile. For Canyonville (Picket) Park, take I-5 exit 98, go east on 227 for 1 mile, and left.

The upper river ranges from wild to pastoral. From Canyonville take Hwy 227 east 18 miles through the town of Days Creek to an unmarked state access below the Milo covered bridge. Upstream 4 miles farther, a

South Umpqua River near Milo

roadside park has a path to the water, and 2 miles farther at Tiller the stream can be reached at the Forest Service headquarters. Three C Rock Campground lies east of Tiller 5 miles, and 10 miles farther Campbell Falls plunges through old-growth forest. Another 7 miles upstream is the granite-bottomed South Umpqua Falls.

 The lower river is fished throughout and considered Oregon's most productive smallmouth bass stream. Hatchery trout are no longer stocked, and the river is closed to angling above Jackson Creek. Winter steelhead are a big draw from Three C Rock down, January–March, with drift boats popular on the lower river. Canyonville to Roseburg is favored with its hatchery run. Summer steelhead are extinct and spring Chinook imperiled owing to diversions and high temperatures. Without vulnerability to summertime flows, fall Chinook find good spawning habitat and do well.

 Owing to low summer levels, steep gradient in upper reaches, and towns and rural development from Canyonville down, the South Umpqua is not a top paddling destination. However, guidebooks report a 5-mile springtime run below Three C Rock—Class 2–3 with one Class 4 rapid about 1.5 miles above the takeout at Tiller. From there to Days Creek is a scenic 17 miles of Class 2+ with a steeper, easily portaged drop about 2 miles above takeout.

Below Days Creek, the South Umpqua runs 59 miles as Class 1–2 to the main stem, with a Class 3 drop below Canyonville (downstream from Stanton Park; portage left). See intermediate accesses listed above. Flows are likely adequate with 250 cfs at Tiller and 500 below Brockway. In early summer, the 176-mile reach from Tiller and continuing down the main stem to Reedsport is Oregon's third-longest dam-free river expedition (the Willamette trip is slightly longer and with far fewer rapids, while the John Day with its North Fork is longer and more turbulent).

COW CREEK

Better than it sounds, this largest stream draining the east side of southern Oregon's coastal mountains is also called

Length: 76 miles
Average flow: 829 cfs
Watershed: 498 square miles

the Coast Fork of the South Umpqua. Its forested course semi-circles Siskiyou Mountain terrain by angling west, then north, and finally east to Riddle. Though scarcely developed, the basin is heavily cutover, tinged by abandoned mines near the West Fork plus ongoing suction dredging for gold, and blocked at headwaters by Galesville Dam, which in 1986 was Oregon's most recently built dam to bar steelhead and now-threatened coho from spawning grounds. Today hatchery coho are stocked. Lower in the main stem, some fall Chinook continue to spawn. Though clearcut, the West Fork has potential for wild coho and steelhead recovery.

 To reach upper "Coast Fork," take the I-5 Azalea exit, then Hwy 36 east 17 miles to Devil's Flat Campground and Cow Creek Gorge Trail. Continue 2 miles farther on 36, go right

Cow Creek above West Fork

on FR 3232 for 1 mile to another trailhead into old-growth, and hike up-stream 7 miles (visit at low flows for fording).

A rural byway follows Cow Creek downstream from the sawmill town of Glendale. The quiet paved road is ideal for biking as it loops 45 miles west between I-5 exits 80 and 102 (22-mile shuttle via Interstate).

It's hard to catch the sweet spot on this flashy, low-volume stream, but *Soggy Sneakers* reports a 10-mile rainy season Class 4 run from Reuben to West Fork Cow Creek; from I-5 exit 80 go to Glendale, turn right on Reuben (becomes Cow Creek Road), and go west. After 8 miles from I-5, at the sign *Reuben,* walk on a lane to the river (poor parking). To take out, continue northwest on Cow Creek Road 10 miles to West Fork Bridge. On my springtime to-do agenda, a 10-mile Class 2 run with one Class 3 drop is listed from West Fork to a roadside gravel bar, followed by 9 miles of Class 2 with one Class 4 to Council Creek Road. Finally, 7 miles of Class 1–2 on 300 cfs reach the South Umpqua; from I-5 exit 103 go west on Riddle Bypass Road 6 miles, to Cow Creek Bridge and its north-side put-in. Take out at Lawson access on the other (east) side of the South Umpqua, west of I-5 exit 102.

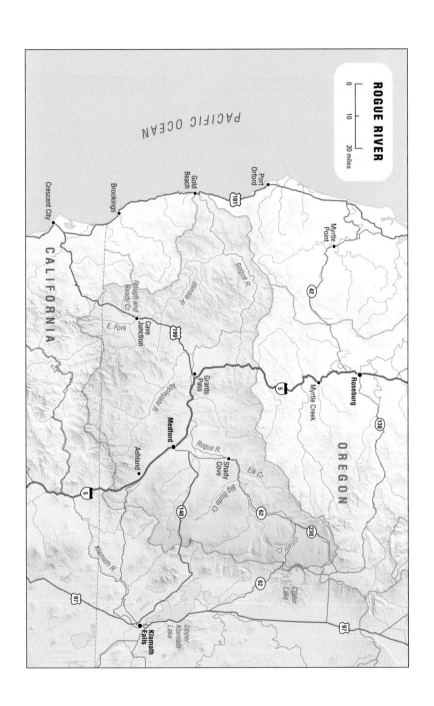

CHAPTER 6

ROGUE

Simply magnificent in southern Oregon, the Rogue has geologically fascinating headwaters, a heavily settled valley, and a lower canyon through the Siskiyou Mountains that for generations has been regarded as a quintessential wild river of the West. Like the Umpqua, it swells with winter rainfall in lower elevations but also drinks headwaters from snowy Cascade highcountry, giving the main stem ample flows for fishing and boating throughout a hot summer and lingering, endearing autumn.

ROGUE RIVER

Length: 216 miles
Average flow: 6,730 cfs (including Illinois River)
Watershed: 5,159 square miles

Extraordinary with its salmon and steelhead, diversity of plantlife, and Pacific-bound free-flowing wildness, the Rogue is especially renowned nationally for its excellent whitewater expedition. An archetype in the lore of the West, its canyon fastness inspired novels by Zane Grey and provided a powerful impetus for passing the original Wild and Scenic Rivers Act. The state's seventh-largest river, it begins in the Cascades north of Crater Lake and presses westward to Gold Beach as one of only three streams in Oregon and six on the West Coast that rise in the interior mountains and transect the entire Coast Range

Rogue River Canyon and drift boat at Tyee Rapid

(others are the Chehalis, Columbia, Umpqua, Klamath, and Pit-Sacramento). Only the Rogue, Klamath, and Umpqua cut through rugged sections of the coastal mountains, and the Rogue has by far the longest wild reach.

Not far north of Crater Lake, the Rogue's source at Boundary Springs is believed to be the principal underground outflow of this deepest lake in the United States. The river then drops 40 miles through steep rapids, enchanting pools, and spared strips of 200-foot sugar pines and Douglas-firs backed by heavily logged tracts. Shorelines dramatically reveal the ancient flow of lava, with blackened cliffs and basalt potholes deep enough to hide a grown person.

Above Prospect, a 50-foot hydroelectric dam sluices flows of the Rogue (called North Fork there) into a power plant, and the stream tumbles down its final Cascade canyon to the reservoir behind 327-foot-high Lost Creek Dam. Below, the middle river then navigates the Rogue Valley—heavily developed but with riparian enclaves through the Cascade-Siskiyou Mountain interface. Gaining force downstream of Grants Pass, the river cuts its storied wild canyon for 34 miles transecting the Siskiyous. Fishing outfitters here in the early 1900s routinely dynamited rocks to open up rapids that must have resembled those of today's Illinois River. At Foster Bar the canyon widens, and below Lobster Creek the Rogue riffles through a coastal valley before entering tidewater 6 miles from the ocean.

NATURAL HISTORY

The Rogue showcases geologic and hydrologic phenomena from its spring-fed source, to lava tubes at Union Creek, to the dramatic crossing of the Siskiyous where water carves into a resistant topographic backbone and surges along fault lines at the crux-like Mule Creek Canyon. Unique in the West, this memorable gorge of metamorphosed volcanic rocks and sheeted dike complexes stretches a mile long and barely 20 feet wide in places—remarkably narrow for a large river. Just downstream, erosion-resistant conglomerate boulders and muscovite schist create Blossom Bar—the lower river's most challenging rapid.

While headwaters accumulate heavy snows in winter, the middle river through Grants Pass receives a sparse 18 inches of precipitation, but then lower reaches enjoy three times as much rainfall. Reflecting this schizophrenic climatic journey, the watershed hosts one of the greatest cross-sections of plantlife on the Pacific coast—Douglas-fir intermingling with Port Orford cedar, ponderosa pine, sugar pine, white fir, incense cedar, red cedar, Pacific yew, Oregon white oak, California black oak, Pacific madrone, myrtle, and bigleaf maple. The basin is central to the Klamath-Siskiyou Ecoregion—biologically the richest temperate coniferous forest on earth and an Area of Global Botanical Significance designated by the World Conservation Union.

Wild fall Chinook spawn in the main stem from Shady Cove down to Mule Creek. By heading quickly out to sea, smolts escape high summer water temperatures, enabling populations to remain somewhat healthy. But the Rogue's wild spring Chinook, spawning above Shady Cove, along with summer steelhead, are in jeopardy. Threatened wild coho spawn in middle Rogue and Illinois tributaries, but most coho come from hatchery stock. Winter steelhead survive at 20 percent of historic numbers. Many of the summer steelhead come from hatcheries; wild "summers" spawn in tributaries of the Applegate and middle Rogue. The lower Rogue is one of few rivers with spawning green sturgeon.

Threatened in Oregon, Steller sea lions swim up the tidal river to eat lamprey, salmon, and invertebrates (a state-approved harassment program seeks to keep them away from anglers' lines). Seals often appear several miles up from the sea.

CONSERVATION

The Rogue's 85-mile reach from the Applegate (below Grants Pass) to Lobster Creek was among the original 12 rivers (including tributaries) protected as Wild and Scenic in 1968. Two decades later, the upper 40 miles were also designated.

With the threat of new dams past, the Rogue has become a model for the removal of dams that are now unnecessary. Elk Creek enters 5 miles below Lost Creek Dam and once accounted for 30 percent of spawning coho in the basin. But here a 186-foot concrete dam, with no fish ladder, was one-third complete before legal appeals by the Oregon Natural Resources Council halted construction in 1987. The Army Corps of Engineers eventually agreed with the state and others that the project should be abandoned, and its dismantling marked one of the largest dam breachings in the United States (much of the valley-wide concrete edifice remains).

Meanwhile on the main stem, the antiquated 8-foot-tall Gold Hill Diversion Dam was removed in 2008. The next year, 39-foot Savage Rapids Dam was torn-down after a decades-long effort. The dam and its inadequate fish ladder had hampered salmon since 1921; without it biologists predicted a 22 percent increase in fish. No longer needed for irrigation, 800 cfs were transferred from a diverted water right to an in-stream flow—perhaps the largest such transfer in the West. Then in 2010 Gold Ray Dam—a 38-foot relic of past hydropower generation north of Medford—was demolished. The Rogue's four dam removals constitute one of the most significant river restorations nationwide and increased free-flowing mileage from 107 to 157—among the West Coast's longer dam-free reaches.

Not to be removed, Lost Creek Dam discharges cold water that benefits downstream trout in summer, much to anglers' delight, but its construction in 1976 inundated one-third of the Rogue's spring Chinook spawning habitat and reversed natural runoff regimes by releasing high flows in summer and low flows in winter. Dam-induced temperature changes interfere with spawning cycles below, especially for wild spring Chinook, though the Army Corps strives to adjust its releases. Moreover, a lack of large floods has allowed alien weeds to invade the Rogue's gravel bars and caused less scouring of pools, which are critical for fish that hold in deep cool pockets while awaiting autumn rain.

Unlike most rivers, the wildest sections of the Rogue lie not upstream, but downstream from cities; between the protected upper river above Lost Creek and lower river through Siskiyou canyons lies the 59-mile Rogue Valley, including Medford and Grants Pass. Here development, sewage, and diversions have degraded water quality. Problems are evident simply by traveling with the current; the Medford sewage plant is the cause of odor at its discharge below Tou Velle State Park, and foam lingers on eddylines from there downstream. Addressing effluent temperatures that peaked far above standards in 2012, local authorities avoided costly structural options and instead embarked on a program to reforest cutover riverfronts. With the help of Freshwater Trust and federal grants, $8 million will be spent to lease land from private owners and plant trees to bring the river's temperature down. Meanwhile, suction dredge gold miners vacuum the riverbed where nobody else would be allowed to randomly dig; permits for dredging statewide have quadrupled in the past five years, with more in the Rogue than any other basin. Yet *Oregon's Living Landscape* considers the middle Rogue especially important because it harbors fall Chinook and coho, and also because the river links Cascade, Siskiyou, and Coast Range ecosystems.

Commercial jet boats here mean big business, touring 27 miles from Grants Pass down to Galice, and also 45 miles from Gold Beach up to Blossom Bar (lower terminus of the "wild" designation). Repeatedly through the day, the large powerboats throw wakes onto shorelines causing erosion and siltation that's evident simply by looking in areas where the banks are not armored in rock. According to Forest Service reports on the lower river, operators routinely perform "riffle maintenance" by scouring shallows with "prop wash," deepening the channel by 1.5–2.5 feet in selected areas for 29 miles. But in its 2005 Environmental Impact Statement on jet boat operations, the agency maintained that the current numbers and practices of jet boats do not threaten fish or water quality.

Seeking better protection of key tributaries as well as the main stem, Klamath-Siskiyou Wild, American Rivers, and others in 2014 proposed Wild and Scenic designation to thwart BLM old-growth logging along 16 tributary creeks: Anna, Big Windy, Dulog, Grave, Hewitt, Howard, Kelsey, Jenny, Little Windy, Mule, Missouri, Montgomery, Quartz, Rum, Whiskey, and Wildcat. Rogue Riverkeeper also works to reduce pollution and minimize damage from mining.

TRIBUTARIES

Union Creek flows from Thousand Springs at the western border of Crater Lake National Park and joins the upper river at the popular Union Creek resort. A trail leads upstream 4 miles through old-growth forest to small waterfalls.

The South Fork Rogue joins in Lost Creek Reservoir; see this small tributary from a trail running both up and down stream from South Fork Campground, southeast of Prospect.

Big Butte Creek—important for spawning salmon and steelhead—joins below Lost Creek Dam; from Medford take Hwy 62 north 14 miles,

Bear Creek at Phoenix

turn east at the sign for Butte Falls, go 15.3 miles and turn left to the 15-foot falls. This stream has the distinction of being the Rogue basin's most polluted stream, posted with bacterial pollution warnings and meeting the Rogue just upstream of Tou Velle State Park.

Bear Creek flows from the Cascade and Siskiyou Mountains into Emigrant Reservoir, then through Ashland and Medford, with many accesses. Fall Chinook can be seen spawning in late October; from I-5 exit 21 go just west on Valley View Road to Newbry Park. From Talent take N Pacific Highway north 2 miles and turn right into Blue Heron Park. The stream and bikeway are also reached just west of I-5 exit 24 in Phoenix, Bear Creek Park in south Medford off Highland Drive at Greenwood Street, Hawthorne Park at Hawthorne and East 8th Streets in Medford, and Railroad Park on Berrydale Avenue off Hwy 62.

Downstream from Grants Pass, Galice Creek is an important salmon/steelhead tributary. And near the ocean, Lobster Creek is the largest producer of fall Chinook in the lower basin. Though heavily logged on steep slopes slanting into the river, an undeveloped corridor remains. Because water temperatures exceed standards and put fish at risk, the Lobster Creek Partnership works to reinstate floodplain conifers. From Hwy 101 at Gold Beach turn east on Jerry's Flat Road, go 12 miles, turn north, cross the Rogue, and go left to Lobster Creek Bridge, with access possible on river-left. Also drive up gravel FR 3310 and in 5 miles turn left to Bark Shanty Bridge. Though seldom paddled, and with log hazards, Lobster Creek here is a fine Class 4 springtime kayaking run.

 The Rogue's unusual source is reached by trail at Boundary Springs along Crater Lake National Park's northwest edge; from Diamond Lake take Hwy 230 southwest 4 miles to

Crater Rim Viewpoint and look for a 2-mile path first headed west, crossing the small stream, and continuing 2 miles south above the Rogue's west bank.

From southbound Hwy 230 the growing stream is seldom seen, but the Upper Rogue River Trail follows closely for 50 miles with some trailheads. Near the Hwy 62 turnoff to Crater Lake, Rogue River Gorge is a highlight. Downstream, Union Creek Recreation Area offers access to waterfalls and lush thickets of vine maple, willows, and cottonwoods brilliant in autumn. A scenic 2-mile trail leads down to Natural Bridge; here the river disappears underground, then foams up 200 feet farther. .

For another superb section of the Rogue River Trail, go 3 more miles south on Hwy 220, turn west to Woodruff Bridge, and hike downstream 2 miles through Takelma Gorge. The trail continues past River Bridge and 9 miles onward to Prospect and North Fork Reservoir.

Below there, the 10-mile-long Lost Creek Reservoir and its dam are followed by a widening river flowing well all summer in riffles and small rapids, reached at boat ramps near the dam, then 4 road miles down at Elk Creek, 10 miles down at Shady Cove's Upper Rogue Park, and 16 miles down at Dodge Bridge—all off Hwy 62. Tou Velle State Park follows; from Medford, take 62 north 6 miles, turn west on Antelope Road, then north on Table Rock Road.

Downstream, the river riffles past the former sites of Gold Ray and Gold Hill Dams, now restored to free-flow, and over two steep rapids. From I-5 exit 35 head north on Blackwell Road, then right on Gold Ray Road for 1.6 miles to the old dam site. Continue on Gold Ray Road 4.5 miles to the former Gold Hill Dam site and just below to Powerhouse Rapid's big plunge. Continue downstream on Upper River Road to I-5 exit 40 and the town of Gold Hill.

Rogue River and mountain ash, upper gorge near Union Creek

Valley of the Rogue State Park with its campground/boat ramp lies another 5 miles downstream at I-5 exit 45B. Here you can bike the Rogue River Greenway Trail 4 miles down to Fleming Park at Rogue River City's Depot Street Bridge. The trail will be extended down to Tom Pearce Park near Grants Pass; also upstream to Gold Hill and then Central Point and Ashland via the Bear Creek Greenway.

The abutment remains of Savage Rapids Dam—a landmark of dam-removal in the West—can be seen downstream from Valley of the Rogue State Park; from there on river-left drive west on Rogue River Hwy 7 miles to a pullout.

In Grants Pass, Riverside Park offers summertime shade on the south bank—a stroll from downtown or an entangled drive to East Park Street (north of Hwy 199 and east of 238). Downstream, the popular middle river has county-road accesses for 26 river miles between Grants Pass and Galice. A local landmark, the Galice Resort is boater-central; many people begin their "wild Rogue" trips there (at least with breakfast and shuttle arrangements) or at several boat ramps in the 7-mile reach downstream.

Grave Creek marks the last major road access for one of the finest 34 wild-river miles in the Northwest. From I-5, take the Merlin exit and Merlin-Galice Road (later Almeda Road) to Merlin and west 22 more miles to Grave Creek ramp. A 2-mile trail on river-left leads to thundering Rainie Falls—Oregon's best place to see salmon jumping in October. On the north side at Grave Creek, hikers start a 40-mile riverfront trek to Foster Bar. I recommend a bear canister for food here, plus Tecnu for poison oak.

The lower Rogue can be reached from the Galice area via Bear Camp Road, but only in summer and autumn. Just upstream of Galice turn west on Galice Access Road (BLM 34-8-36), continue on Forest Service 23, go right on FS 33, and turn right at the Foster Bar sign. In winter take Hwy 199 to the coast. To reach the lower Rogue from there, take Hwy 101 to the north end of Gold Beach, turn east on Jerry's Flat Road (which becomes Agness Road and leads to FR 33 or Agness-Illahe Road), go 36 miles, then right to Foster Bar—terminus of most float trips. To find the lower end of the Rogue River Trail (Grave Creek—Foster Bar), take FR 33 another half mile east from the Foster turnoff.

Though it's short on river views and access, the Lower Rogue River Trail resumes farther downstream. For the upper (eastern) end, drive from Gold Beach up Jerry's Flat Road 33 miles, cross the Illinois and then the Rogue, turn left on Hwy 375, go 3 miles, and turn right before the Agness Post Office. This path leads downstream 13 miles (poison oak). For its lower terminus take Jerry's Flat Road 12 miles east from Gold Beach, turn north, cross the Rogue, and go right on 3533 for 6 miles.

For lower Rogue access, Quosatana recreation site is 14 miles east of Gold Beach, and Lobster Creek Campground is 3 miles downstream. The harbor at Gold Beach is dredged and jettied, but from there you can walk to the wave-swept mouth.

Historically the Rogue has been a world-renowned salmon/ steelhead fishery. Though greatly diminished, it still ranks as Oregon's second-largest salmon producer after the Columbia (with all its tributaries).

Above Lost Creek Reservoir the river is stocked with rainbow trout. For 0.5 miles below the dam the Rogue is a revered catch-and-release, fly-casting hotspot for large rainbows, open year-round, best in April and September–October. Drive north from Medford on Hwy 62 to milepost 29, then north on Takelma Drive.

From Lost Creek Dam to Tou Velle, a steelheaders' paradise includes half-pounders in from the ocean after one season, plus mature 4- to 8-pound fish headed for both hatchery and native spawning grounds, August–November. Bank fishing and drift boating both work here, popu-lar in a September–October fly-fishing-only season at the upper section. If boating, don't miss Tou Velle takeout—rapids below! Hatchery spring Chinook peak June–July; summer steelhead in July and December. Win-ter steelhead peak March–April. Resident rainbows and cutthroat are also caught. Shorelines are public for a mile below the dam/hatchery.

For 31 miles from Tou Velle to Grants Pass, 10 parks offer fishing access. Spring Chinook are caught April–June, fall Chinook July–September, sum-mer steelhead in autumn, winter steelhead January–April. Then from Grants Pass down to Grave Creek the Rogue gets heavy fishing at 17 public sites and from drift boats (rapids pick up below Hog Creek ramp). Below Grants Pass, jet boats and their big wakes—along with jet boat–related safety regulations preventing anchoring in productive spots—discourage many anglers.

The Rogue's wild section from Grave Creek to Foster Bar is legend-ary for Chinook, May–June and in autumn, and for winter and summer steelhead. Half-pounders return from sea early and are caught in autumn. Some anglers hike in; most take drift boats or rafts (permits required). Rainbow trout can be hooked in creeks: Big Windy, Kelsey, and Missouri.

Below Foster Bar, steelhead and Chinook migrate in strong runs compared to other West Coast rivers. Spring Chinook peak in May. Fall Chinook move upriver in August–October. September–December brings hatchery and wild coho. Steelhead can be caught throughout, especially December–March. The lower river from Foster Bar to Gold Beach is served by nine ramps. Estuary fishing from Gold Beach is heavy for spring Chinook, April–May, and fall Chinook and coho, August–Septem-ber. Flotillas of boats blanket the lower estuary in-season.

 The Rogue is one of the best-known American rivers for over-night whitewater trips. Outside the local area, it's less known for day trips, but those are also exceptional.

On the upper river, expert paddlers occasionally tackle 9 miles of Class 4–5 with portages below Woodruff Bridge and beyond to North Fork Res-ervoir, facing steep drops, log hazards, and difficult portages, but with adequate volume all summer—unusual for a river this high in elevation.

From Lost Creek Dam to Tou Velle State Park, 27 miles of Class 2 riffles have clear water, a green corridor, and riverfront cabins. Less developed but with some evidence of treated sewage, the 6 miles from Tou Velle to the former Gold Ray Dam is followed by Fisher's Ferry access, then in 3 miles by an irrigation weir, easily passable in the center. Immediately below, eddy left and scout Nugget Rapids' turbulent left-side Class 4 run. A mile later, opposite a river-right concrete water intake structure, eddy left for the long scout of Powerhouse Rapid. This 6-foot Class 4 plunge is run in the center of the river after avoiding confusing island channels left and right. A mile below, a right-side ramp marks Gold Hill Sportsmen's Park along Hwy 234 east of Gold Hill.

From there to Grants Pass makes a fine one-day trip featuring some big-wave Class 2 rapids, with access at Pierce Riffle Park on the right above Grants Pass, then Chinook, Baker, and Riverfront Parks on the left.

Below Grants Pass, the river riffles delightfully 20 miles to Hog Creek ramp, with interim access. A mile below, Hellgate Canyon constrains the Rogue with pushy Class 2+ whitewater, then more rapids for 16 miles to Grave Creek. Without even entering the canyon below, one could spend a weeklong river vacation on the middle Rogue.

The river's classic wild section starts at Grave Creek, where drops increase to Class 3–4. BLM's *Rogue River Float Guide* details this (and the full 103 miles, Grants Pass to Gold Beach). Permits are required for Grave Creek to Foster Bar, and numbers are rationed May 15–October 15 (120 people per day). Call 503-479-3735 or see Rogue River permits on the Internet. Passes are also given on a first-come basis at 7 a.m. at the Rand Visitor Center 2 miles west of Galice. Chances improve if your group is small; better yet in spring or autumn. Typically on a two-person trip, I've rarely failed to score a last-minute permit on weekdays in autumn. Shuttle via Bear Camp Road in summer (see above, plus Rogue River Shuttle on the Internet).

Rogue River above Plowshare Rapid

In the Rogue's wild canyon, Class 3 rapids with a few Class 4 drops keep rafters, kayakers, and drift boaters engaged. This is also the premier multiday trip for expert whitewater canoeists (raft support helps). Avoid the Class 5 Rainie Falls, 2 miles below Grave Creek, by bumping down the extreme right rocky passage—blasted out as a fish ladder long ago. Highlights of the wild section include the bubbling trough of Mule Creek Canyon and then the intricate passage through Blossom Bar. Serious problems occur here when people fail to move sharply right just below the initial left-side entry. Scout right and watch someone who knows the way! Summer/autumn levels of 1,000–3,000 cfs are favored by most.

Campsites are first-come first-served. Large ones fill early (outfitters send probes before noon); smaller sites remain available. Deter black bears with proper food storage; on the lower portion the Forest Service provides electric-fence food corrals.

Below Foster Bar, a few strong Class 2 rapids soon flatten to swift riffles for 32 miles to Gold Beach. The road recedes far from the waterfront through this underrated canyon of grand scale and immense gravel bars. Heavy jet boat traffic and afternoon wind deter most paddlers, but I relish this run as one of the coast's few overnight summertime canoe trips, and I travel during relatively calm mornings. Take out at Quosatana or Lobster Creek, or for the full Rogue experience continue on 6 miles of tidal flow to Gold Beach harbor.

APPLEGATE RIVER

Length: 56 miles including California
Average flow: 712 cfs
Watershed: 770 square miles

The Applegate flows from the Siskiyou Mountain crest in California and joins the Rogue as its second-largest tributary 7 miles downstream from Grants Pass. Applegate Dam impounds upper reaches; in 1980 this was one of the last large Army Corps of Engineers dams to be built. Opponents exposed the dubious justification for real estate speculation on the floodplain downstream (flood control "benefits" for future development), but a county referendum to halt the project failed against advertising that "160,000 jobs" depended on it—more than existed in the entire region. Dam-release flows to the lower river now meander through a fine mix of forest, ranch, and farmland.

At headwaters, the Middle Fork drains Red Buttes Wilderness; a trail ascends there for the length of Butte Fork.

The Applegate's largely private-land corridor includes only a few public access sites. From Grants Pass take Hwy 199 west 4 miles, cross the Applegate, and in 1.8 miles turn left at the sign for Murphy. Continue on Fish Hatchery Road 4 miles to Fish Hatchery Park, where salmon might be seen spawning in late October. Continue upstream, turn right on Hwy 238 at Murphy, and in 1 mile pull off at a swimming hole. In 10 more miles a pulloff lies just before Applegate. Upstream another 6 miles, bear right on Hamilton Road and go 1 mile to Cantrall-Buckley Park for swimming/camping. A mile farther, turn right

Applegate River below McKee Bridge

on Applegate Road, bear right again where the Little Applegate (very little in summer) enters, and continue upriver. In 7 miles turn left to McKee covered bridge/picnic area. Beyond, a Forest Service campground sits below Applegate Dam.

 The stream is known for stocked and wild steelhead, but the lack of public land limits access. Some wild fall Chinook spawn in lower reaches. Upper tributaries support wild rainbow, cutthroat, and alien brook trout.

 Above the reservoir a Class 3 reach with portages is run by a few kayakers in spring. Below the dam, the 9-mile reach from McKee Bridge to Cantrall-Buckley Park looked like uneventful topography to me, so I was surprised to find several steep short Class 2–3 drops in a shallow gorge entrenched within the ranching valley (300 cfs late-summer dam release). Applegate Road crosses 4 miles below McKee with an access lane to the river. Below, at a hazardously low bridge, stop and measure! Another sharp drop is hidden virtually underneath a second low bridge. I haven't yet paddled below Cantrall-Buckley, where the river winds through its ranch valley with a low dam below Hwy 238 at Murphy. Flows can be diminished here by diversions.

ILLINOIS RIVER

Largest Rogue tributary, the Illinois gathers Siskiyou Mountain runoff, winds through rolling terrain, then plunges

Length: 56 miles, 81 with EF
Average flow: 1,257 cfs
Watershed: 990 square miles

northwest through a canyon that's honored among river runners. This sizable stream has superb water quality, salmon, steelhead, challenging whitewater, and complex geology. Much of its length is roadless, a third of it in Kalmiopsis Wilderness.

Illinois River at the Green Wall

Below headwater tributaries, the main stem's rambunctious course through a bewildering topographic maze is the result of sharp cutting into an uplifted plateau. Easily eroded mudstones were worn down; harder rocks such as gabbro cap resistant ridges and rapids. Northbound faults repeatedly confine the Illinois into deep, short canyons. At lower flows, crystalline pools alternate with formidable boulder-choked rapids. Notorious flash floods in winter/spring spike from 1,000 to 20,000 cfs in a day, which means anyone caught out there has a serious problem.

With some of the Rogue basin's best salmonid habitat, the Illinois and its tributaries support a diversity of species free of hatchery supplementation, which is rare among large watersheds. Upper tributaries are important for Chinook and threatened coho spawning. Headwater streams and lower reaches of Lawson, Silver, Indigo, Briggs, and other streams provide cutthroat and winter steelhead habitat. A remarkable mix of 1,400 plant species grow in serpentine soils of the Josephine ophiolite formation, which limit vegetation growth but enable unusual species to flourish.

Tributary Sucker Creek flows through private and public land to the East Fork with the basin's most important coho habitat but suffers water quality infractions by instream miners. Fine lower Illinois tributaries include Silver, Indigo, Lawson, Collier, Briggs, and Klondike Creeks—several threatened by placer claims. National Wild and Scenic designation of 50 miles in 1984 banned Buzzard's Roost Dam, proposed 10 miles above the mouth. Like the Rogue, the Illinois is unusual in having its wild reach downstream from towns, where further development, pollution, and diversions could pose threats.

The lower West Fork, with its swimming hole just above the East Fork confluence, is reached at Illinois River Forks State Park; from Hwy 199 just south of Cave Junction turn west. Chinook can be seen here in October, especially in the East Fork just above the confluence, and also at Little Falls; from Cave Junction take 199 north 5 miles, turn west on Eight Dollar Mountain Road, in 2 miles park at the trailhead, and walk 0.5 miles. To see more river, take Hwy 199 north from Cave Junction 7 miles to Selma, turn west on Illinois River Road, and go 17 miles to Miami Bar access and Briggs Creek Trailhead. In the seldom-visited section upstream from Miami, the river mostly lies far below the road but can be reached at the Store Gulch recreation site, 8 miles west of Selma, or 2 miles farther at McCaleb Ranch.

For the lower river, take Hwy 101 to north Gold Beach, turn east on Jerry's Flat Road, go 27 miles and right on Illinois River Road, then 3 miles to Oak Flat Campground. Here the Illinois River Trail leads upstream, though it sits far back from the water. Buzzard's Roost, 2 miles up, has a bird's eye-view to the stream. At mile 4 the trail crosses Indigo Creek, then at mile 8 Silver Creek. In all, this rugged route traverses 27 miles eastward to Briggs Creek Trailhead.

Spur trails reach the Illinois at remote Pine Flat and Collier Bar via difficult routes and long roads, but fallen timber riddles the paths and brush envelops quickly in this sub-maintained area; inquire with the Forest Service before relying on maps.

 Rarely kayaked, the Illinois' upper canyon is a 10-mile Class 3–4 run with a waterfall portage; put in at Store Gulch (see above); take out at Miami Bar. Below there, the main Illinois canyon tests boaters with a 31-mile whitewater menu including the Class 5 Green Wall, which appears about halfway through the trip. This is among the West's premier challenging river outings, best at 1,000–1,500 cfs (the lower river might be double the flow at Kerby gauge—15 miles above put-in). When above 2,000 cfs (lower river), the Illinois flushes extremely hard. April–May offers the best windows for boating, but beware: flash floods leave little option but to wait on scarce high ground in the canyon. Assiduously stay away when storms approach or flows are rising. Some or all of the eight Class 4–5 rapids should be scouted. Campsites are few. Self-issue permits, portable toilets, and firepans are required. Put in at Miami Bar; take out at lower Oak Flat (see above).

For an arduous but rewarding summertime adventure on low flow, experienced boaters with inflatable craft can paddle here and drag over boulders. Far easier, sample this magnificent place by paddling and dragging upstream from lower Oak Flat, with care to avoid foot entrapment. Three easy rapids and one boulder-scramble lead to a sublime pool at Buzzard's Roost's vertical wall.

ROUGH AND READY CREEK

Length: 6 miles
Average flow: 122 cfs
Watershed: 36 square miles

Largely wild, road-free, and unknown, this stream flows from the heights of the southeastern Kalmiopsis Wilderness eastward to the West Fork Illinois, 5 miles south of Cave Junction. The Josephine ophiolite formation blankets the watershed and produces

Rough and Ready Creek at Hwy 199

serpentine soils that are calcium deficient and nutrient poor; pygmy forests are the norm here, and the watershed may have the highest concentration of rare/endemic flora in Oregon and one of the highest in North America. Cutthroat trout and winter steelhead spawn and rear in clean gravel beds. The summertime creek goes subsurface in places.

The 19-acre Rough and Ready Creek Forest Wayside State Park was created to protect unusual plantlife, and combines with a 1,164-acre BLM Area of Critical Environmental Concern and 1,560-acre Forest Service Botanical Area, all near the Hwy 199 crossing south of Cave Junction. The Forest Service has found R&R eligible for Wild and Scenic River designation and in 2004 recommended that headwaters be added to Kalmiopsis Wilderness.

The tectonic processes that delivered the unusual minerals also left nickel laterite, and miners have claimed 4,000 acres for future prospecting—18 percent of the biologically unique watershed. Friends of the Kalmiopsis opposes strip mines and nickel smelting and supports congressional withdrawal of the land from further claims.

 The braided lower creek can be seen at the Hwy 199 bridge 5 miles south of Cave Junction—park and walk on the short trail. Nearly all the basin lies in Siskiyou National Forest with nominal road or trail access.

 A few kayakers hike in for a short but beautiful Class 4 springtime adventure; portage a dangerous weir above Hwy 199.

CHAPTER 7

WILLAMETTE

The Willamette is the largest river flowing entirely within Oregon. While the Umpqua and Rogue drain the west slope of the southern Cascade Mountains, the Willamette picks up the northern two-thirds of Oregon's Cascades. Stellar tributaries here include the Middle Fork Willamette, McKenzie, Calapooia, Santiam, Molalla, and Clackamas. These tumble among steep forests and carry clear water through wildlands, reservoirs, and settled valleys, then join the Willamette's quieter windings north. Prior to upheaval of the Coast Range, rivers flowing from the west slope of the proto-Cascades likely aimed directly toward sea, but the coastal uplift blocked that route, forcing those streams north and eventually into today's Willamette. The river also gains smaller tributaries from the east flank of the Coast Range, which lacks extended runoff from high snowmelt. Then the lower river funnels past Portland to the Columbia.

The basin accounts for 10 percent of Oregon's land but 30 percent of its runoff—a ratio similar to that of the Coast Range. Some tributaries once hosted outstanding anadromous fisheries; today they support surviving runs heavily influenced by hatcheries, plus trout and warm-water game fish.

Cascade tributaries slumber under winter's snow and then remain chilled through the whims of springtime when some of the state's finest whitewater churns powerfully down from the heights, often lasting into hot days of an idyllic summer. In autumn, with lower flows and bygone mosquitoes, the high-elevation streams are superb for waterfront hiking. Another draw for many of us scrambling along riverbanks: elevations above 2,500 feet seldom have poison oak.

WILLAMETTE RIVER

Length: 187 miles, 272 with MF
Average flow: 33,054 cfs
Watershed: 11,400 square miles

If any stream rates as the "river of Oregon," the Willamette is it. Coursing more than halfway through the state, south-to-north, this is the third-largest waterway (19th in the United States) and by far the largest entirely within state. The main stem is a valley river through farmland buffered by cottonwood forests acutely reduced from past grandeur but still impressive and partly restorable. It bisects 20 of Oregon's 25 largest cities; 70 percent of state population lives in this basin. Though 15 sizable dams plug most tributaries, the main stem is blocked only once—and nominally—just above tide-line at Willamette Falls. In an unusual configuration, this dam arcs across the

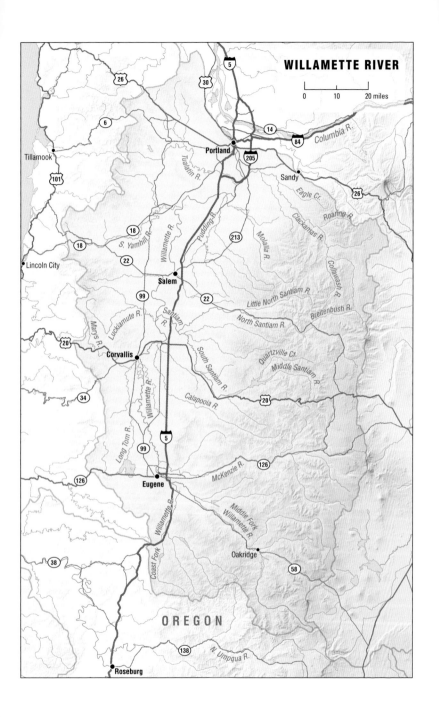

WILLAMETTE RIVER

0   10   20 miles

Columbia R.

Portland

Sandy

Tillamook

Eagle Cr.

Clackamas R.

Roaring R.

Tualatin R.

Pudding R.

Molalla R.

Collawash R.

Willamette R.

S. Yamhill R.

Lincoln City

Salem

Little North Santiam R.

Breitenbush R.

North Santiam R.

Santiam R.

Luckiamute R.

Marys R.

Corvallis

Quartzville Cr.

Middle Santiam R.

South Santiam R.

Calapooia R.

Willamette R.

Long Tom R.

Eugene

McKenzie R.

Middle Fork Willamette R.

Coast Fork

Oakridge

OREGON

N. Umpqua R.

Roseburg

river at the brink of a waterfall—America's second-largest by volume and largest in the West. Anadromous fish going up the Willamette benefit by not encountering massive Columbia River dams, which all lie upstream from the confluence. Unfortunately, however, Willamette fish face other challenges.

NATURAL HISTORY

Most of the main stem was inundated by ice-age Missoula Floods when cataclysmic high water thundered down the Columbia and backed up the Willamette like a lagoon at high-tide, nearly reaching today's Eugene and depositing silt 10 feet deep (see Chapter 8). Geologists believe that this occurred 50–100 times, delivering erratic 3-foot boulders to the Willamette Valley on icebergs that incredibly floated intact from Montana. More consistently over the eons, alluvial fans created by the Willamette's powerful Cascade Mountain tributaries piled sand and gravel into the valley to depths of 1,500 feet and pushed the main stem incrementally westward, along with the river's innumerable back channels, sloughs, and oxbows lush in riparian thickets.

Though thin and discontinuous, the Willamette's remaining bottomland forest still accounts for one of the longer cottonwood corridors in the West. The Luckiamute State Natural Area is the largest intact woodland, 918 acres opposite the Santiam River's mouth. This choice birding spot supports rare willow flycatchers and may be selected for reintroduction of yellow-billed cuckoos. Most riverfront parks have excellent bird habitat.

At Willamette Falls, spring Chinook, winter steelhead, and lamprey on spawning journeys historically ascended the cataract at high flows, and Indians fished here much as they did at the more celebrated Celilo Falls

Willamette River at sunrise downstream of Eugene

Willamette River and cottonwoods at Half Moon Bend, below Corvallis

on the Columbia. But with the damming of Willamette Falls in the late 1800s, and with decreased flows in winter owing to upstream reservoirs, the natural migration route was blocked, so fish ladders were constructed enabling Chinook and steelhead to persist. Yet all native fish populations are at a fraction of past numbers. The majority of game fish now come from hatcheries, which are prevalent enough to compromise the genetic stock of many wild fish.

The watershed hosts 34 native and 32 alien fishes, while the main stem has 24 natives and 17 exotics. The system is near a tipping point, with aliens abetted by habitat degradation stemming from dams, channelization, pollution, and warming waters. Exotics total 70 percent of all fish near the mouth. Warm-water species include the native northern pikeminnow along with alien catfish, carp, perch, and pumpkinseed, plus walleye below Willamette Falls. Introduced panfish including bluegill, crappie, and bass live in sloughs and pools.

The endangered Oregon chub—a 3-inch native with an olive back and white belly—lives in slack waters having silty vegetated bottoms. Numbers plummeted with the loss of channel complexity in the wake of revetments, riprap, and dikes; some restoration efforts are underway.

CONSERVATION

The Willamette is fundamental to a vast ecosystem and also the urban lifeline of Oregon, beloved in parklands through Eugene, Corvallis, Albany, Salem, Portland, and smaller towns. The river has suffered the full range of abuse, from clearcutting to agricultural sludge, pulp mill foam, sewage, channelization, levees, damming, and withdrawals, and the combined effects killed off nearly all the fish in the early 1900s. Major reforms were thwarted for decades, but then in 1962 television commentator Tom

McCall aired "Pollution in Paradise," building momentum to address industrial and sewage waste. The charismatic McCall took leadership as governor and established better clean water regulations, and in the 1970s authorities declared the river safe for swimming.

Today, Willamette water is mostly clear, but pesticides, toxins, and polluted runoff persist, especially in lower reaches. Portland Harbor's Superfund hazardous waste site, contaminated with mercury, PCBs, and pesticides, extends 9 miles from Fremont Bridge to Sauvie Island. Debate continues about how much of the tainted sludge should be removed. Residual toxins lie in the Newberg Pool above Portland, warranting limits on children's eating of bass and catfish. Combined sewer overflows flush raw sewage into the lower river during rainstorms, but the city's "big pipe" project is designed to treat 94 percent of this elusive effluent.

To protect open space, stop floodplain development, and support recreation, Governors Tom McCall and Bob Straub called for a Willamette River Greenway, and the legislature adopted a program to establish buffers and parks in 1974. Opposed by farmers, the effort stalled, but five regional parks were established and smaller parcels acquired. The Oregon Parks and Recreation Department administers the scaled-back program while the needs for open space inexorably increase. Between 1970 and 2010 Oregon's population doubled and, in the absence of adequate floodplain and setback regulations, riverfront house construction boomed. In one decade, 13 percent of streamside vegetation was lost to development in Benton and Linn Counties. Willamette Riverkeeper supports revival of the greenway program.

While protecting open space has been a challenge, entrenchment caused by revetments and dikes is even more difficult to fix. Once an elaborate corridor of channels, sloughs, oxbow lakes, and wetlands spanning 4–8 miles in width, the Willamette was incrementally channelized, diked, and leveed into today's confined path. Trees that had fallen into the river once provided a rich source of habitat, but for steamboat traffic the Army Corps of Engineers removed 68,500 snags from Eugene down. Between there and Albany the Willamette's meandering length was shortened by 53 percent. Revetments of rock and riprap armor two-thirds of the mileage of bends (most of the outside-bend mileage—see photo in Chapter 3). With 70 percent of the sloughs and backwaters cut off, a comparable share of bottomland forests have disappeared. Valley wetlands were reduced from 175,000 to 7,200 acres by 1990. As a result, spring Chinook, winter steelhead, Oregon chubs, western pond turtles, northern red-legged frogs, and foothill yellow-legged frogs are at risk. Yet buffers of magnificent cottonwoods and thickets of willow, Oregon ash, bigleaf maple, alder, and occasional Oregon white oak remain, and can be expanded.

After the flood of 1996 lapped levee tops in Portland, hydrologist Philip Williams and Associates found that reinstatement of 50,000 acres of riparian forest could reduce flood levels by 18 percent, and the Western Rivers Conservancy launched efforts to acquire floodplain property and reinstate its role as a sponge of high water. The group bought several parcels, but restoration at anything near the necessary scale remains elusive. Other restoration efforts have been launched at Green Island below the McKenzie confluence where degraded floodplains have been replanted, levees removed, and side-channels reconstructed. Now aware of better methods for bank maintenance, private owners below the Long Tom River confluence have avoided riprapping by sculpting a steep cutbank, anchoring logs, and planting native trees.

Dams have also taken a toll on the river's nature. Basinwide, the Army Corps of Engineers' 13 impoundments for flood control blocked 400 miles of streams—a prime cause of 300,000 Chinook from pre-dam years dwindling to 10,000 in 2011. Most salmon runs are ranked "very high" for extinction risk, and Chinook fishing, long in decline, faded another 75 percent between 1990 and 2010. Endangered Species listings in 1999 and subsequent lawsuits by Willamette Riverkeeper and other conservation groups propelled efforts to eliminate fish-passage barriers, improve flows, and depress water temperatures.

Dozens of public parks lie along this troubled but cherished river. For details, see *The Willamette River Field Guide* by Travis Williams of Willamette Riverkeeper. Shorter, the State Parks Department's *Willamette River Recreation Guide* is available online, as is information about the Willamette Water Trail. I'll highlight the most useful and revealing sites I've found for access, hiking, fishing, and boating. Most larger areas require fees; smaller ones do not.

Starting where the Middle and Coast Forks form the main stem, Eugene and Springfield share one of the great urban river park complexes in America with open space and bike/pedestrian trails. For Island Park's ramp and paths in Springfield, take I-5 exit 191, go north on Glenwood 0.5 miles, right on Franklin, cross the bridge, and right on Mill Street. City parks line most frontage from the I-5 bridge down, with popular open space on the west bank; from downtown take High Street (1 block north of Pearl) north into the park. Bike the 12-mile Ruth Bascom Riverbank Trail along both sides; just west of I-5 the paved bikeway begins at Knickerbocker Bridge and runs to Owosso Bridge south of Beltline Highway, which has access on the west bank.

For access downstream of Eugene and below the McKenzie confluence, use Marshall Landing; from I-5 in north Eugene go west on Beltline, north on River Road 7 miles, and right at the sign. For Browns Landing, go 1 mile farther north on River Road and turn right. Harrisburg appears 7 more miles downriver, with east bank access below the bridge.

Willamette Park lies 2 miles upstream of Corvallis on the west bank; from Hwy 99W just south of the Hwy 20 intersection turn east; here a hiking/bike trail tours bottomland woods and connects to other downtown parks, and summertime tubers put in for an easy drift past Downtown Waterfront Park and take out at Michael's Landing (Aquathusiast Park), river-left at the north end of town.

Willamette Falls and dam at Oregon City

Immediately upstream from Albany, Bryant Park on river-right offers access and paths through old-growth riparian forest. Bowman Park lies below the Albany bridge on the right.

Below Albany 10 miles, Luckiamute Landing and its sizable wild park on the left offer hiking in riparian woods where bald eagles can be seen; from the west side in Albany take Spring Hill Drive north, then right on Buena Vista Road.

Upstream from Salem, on the right, Minto-Brown Island Park's mature forest offers some of the best riverfront hiking. Downtown Salem has Wallace Marine Park on the left, plus another ramp at the city's north end on the right.

Downstream from Salem 12 miles, Willamette Mission State Park is one of the largest public spaces, with a ramp on river-right and a trail to the world's largest black cottonwood, a truly awesome giant 1 mile south of Wheatland Ferry.

Below Newberg 5 miles, Champoeg (Sham-POO-ee) State Park's riverfront trails and ramp appear on the right; from I-5 exit 278 go west on Ehlen Road, which becomes Yergen Road, then McKay Road, then right on River Road, and right on Champoeg Road. East of Wilsonville, Molalla River State Park on the east bank has trails through an exceptional riparian forest gracing the Willamette and lower Molalla.

Above Willamette Falls, Willamette Park on the west bank in West Linn lies at the Tualatin River mouth, with access, fishing, and urban park amenities; from I-205 at West Linn take 10th Street exit, go south on 10th to a T, turn right, go 2 blocks, and left on 12th.

The 41-foot Willamette Falls/dam is an interesting industrial site seen from a roadside overlook; just northeast of the I-205 bridge at Oregon City take 99E south. Below the dam, Pacific lamprey spawn, and in April–May sea lions migrate here to eat fish.

Willamette River in downtown Portland

Below Willamette Falls, Clackamette is a large river park with grand cottonwoods at the Clackamas mouth; take Hwy 99E north of the I-205 bridge. Meldrum Bar Park lies just below in Gladstone; from McLoughlin Boulevard go west on West Gloucester Street, right on River Road, and left on Meldrum Bar Park Road. On the west side of the Willamette, Mary S. Young State Park has access/trails; from Hwy 43 south of Lake Oswego turn east into the park, where a footbridge after April 15 serves Cedar Island. George Rogers Park has paths east of Hwy 43 and Stafford Road. On river-right, Elk Rock Island is a wild refuge reached west of Hwy 99E at Sparrow Street and SE 19th. The Jefferson Street ramp is reached via city bus on 99E south of 224.

Sellwood's access is on the east side just below the bridge. A bike and footpath extends from Sellwood downstream to the Oregon Museum of Science and Industry north of Ross Island Bridge. Below that, the East Bank Esplanade runs 1.5 miles from Hawthorne Bridge north to Steel Bridge with a path for walkers and bikers, connections to downtown streets, and a dock. In downtown Portland, Tom McCall Riverfront Park has frontage with walkways between Hawthorne and Steel Bridges; a seawall prevents access.

Portland Harbor dominates the lower 12 miles from Steel Bridge north—Oregon's most intensively developed industrial shoreline with hardened embayments, cranes for ocean freighters, levees, and riprap. The Army Corps of Engineers dredges a 40-foot-deep channel; proposals to dig deeper are resisted for their effect on habitat, water quality, and embedded toxics. Cathedral Park has a ramp on the northeast side of the St. Johns Bridge; take Hwy 30 north from downtown 6 miles, cross to the east side of the bridge, and take North Edison Street and Pittsburgh Avenue to the park. Finally, Kelley Point Park, on the Willamette's east side, has paths to the tide-washed confluence with the Columbia; from I-5 north take exit 307 and go west on Marine Drive. Do not leave valuables in cars at these lower river areas.

Anglers fish from boats and shore throughout the Willamette's course. Mouths of tributaries are often the best angling sites.

The tidal river up to Willamette Falls is one of Oregon's most popular spots for fishing from motorboats; hundreds ply the water in early spring, especially between Sellwood and Oregon City. Hatchery spring Chinook are popular April–May.

Stocked spring Chinook dominate anadromous runs, entering the river in February and moving upstream in May. A small fall Chinook run occurs August–September. Both summer and winter steelhead migrate upriver, passing Willamette Falls March–October and November–May (steelhead remain in the river most of the year). Hatchery coho, Clackamas-bound, pass through the lower Willamette September–November. A few white sturgeon venture in from the ocean and swim up to the Long Tom River, and introduced shad draw anglers to Willamette Falls, May–June. Introduced bass, bluegill, crappie, and walleye are hooked in the lower Willamette.

Farther upstream, spring Chinook are caught at Willamette Mission State Park April–May. Native cutthroat trout—a catch-and-release fishery from the source to Harrisburg—migrate to tributaries in autumn. Related to trout, whitefish are plentiful in the upper river. Bass fishing is popular throughout the main stem. Crappie, bluegill, catfish, and carp are other warm-water catches.

Fishing spots highlighted in the *Willamette River Recreation Guide* or the Department of Fish and Wildlife's *50 Places to go Fishing Within 60 Minutes of Portland* follow.

At the Willamette mouth, the Multnomah Channel flows down the west side of Sauvie Island, reached for bank fishing on the island (north) side or at ramps along Hwy 30. In Portland, the west side of Cedar Oak Island shelters bass and panfish, protected from the main current during high flows. The Clackamas confluence is one of the best spots for winter steelhead/fall Chinook.

Above Oregon City 4 miles, Rock Island is good for bass, panfish, and catfish, reached from Coalca Landing on the right bank and Rock Island Landing on the left. At the mouth of the Molalla, channel catfish are caught along with bass, crappie, and bullhead. The mouth of the Yamhill has smallmouth, bluegill, perch, and catfish.

At Luckiamute Landing Park, 10 miles below Albany, bass and blue-gills are caught. Above Albany, the mouth of the Calapooia (Bryant Park) is good for bass, panfish, catfish, steelhead, and Chinook. From Corvallis up to Peoria, 10 miles of river have good warm-water fishing, especially in sloughs behind islands and in pools.

The Willamette is the "Huck Finn river" of Oregon, where a delightful trip can be stretched to weeks if you want to camp, fish, birdwatch, resupply at riverfront towns, and read some good books. Almost the entire length is boatable in canoes, drift boats, rafts, or ocean kayaks. Motorboats are used from Corvallis down, and heavily below Newberg. Summer is hot and great for swimming. Fall is glorious, with ample water when other rivers have dropped. See *Willamette River Recreation Guide* or *Willamette River Water Trail Guide*, but beware: many facilities are not seen from the water.

The longest dam-free journey in the watershed runs from the base of Leaburg Dam on the McKenzie, down the lower 41 miles of that river and into the Willamette, then another 148 miles to West Linn (above Willamette Falls Dam, which has no locking or portage), for a total of 189 miles of Class 1–2. This is one of America's great pastoral canoe journeys. After driving around the Falls and relaunching in Clackamette Park, you can paddle another 27 wide tidal miles to the Columbia for an epic voyage of 216 miles. You can also start this Willamette adventure at Dexter Dam on the Middle Fork and enjoy 177 miles to West Linn.

Afternoon headwinds sweep the lower river, and motorboats dominate below Newberg, but above there the Willamette offers a getaway that feels amazingly remote considering its location in the ag and urban belt of Oregon. Camping is possible and often excellent on islands, secluded gravel bars, and public sites above Newberg. Always be cautious and respectful regarding private (and public) property. I keep my campsites low-key and build no fires. For long-distance travelers, drinking water is a concern. Some large parks have tap water but it can be difficult to find and require long carries. I pack my own water—a gallon a day per person—even when canoeing the entire river. No drinking water is available for 40 miles from Spongs Landing (6 miles below Salem) to Boones Ferry Park (left side in Wilsonville).

The upper Willamette, through Springfield and Eugene, flows the fastest—Class 2 in places. Beware of diversion dam remains just above the Springfield I-5 bridge, with clear passage on the far right. Through Eugene the river is full and clean, with several rapids big enough to surf a canoe. From the water you hardly know you're in a city.

For 26 miles from the main stem source to Harrisburg, this powerfully riffling reach is the most beautiful section of the Willamette, imparting a flavor of the natural waterway before widespread channelizing and rip-rapping occurred. Avoid fallen trees—plentiful to Corvallis. Sloughs are interesting to explore, but beware of dead-ends; 11 miles below Harrisburg I sought the mouth of Long Tom River, but logs eventually blocked my channel, and the mandatory return upstream was nip and tuck. Other tributaries are interesting to explore; at Corvallis you can paddle up the Marys River, and later, the Luckiamute, Yamhill, and Molalla.

I seek out riverbank walks on all my Willamette canoe trips. Just upstream of Corvallis on the left, Willamette Park has fine trails. Good paths skirt the banks at Bryant Park, half a mile above Albany's bridge. Eight miles below, Luckiamute Landing offers excellent canoe camping on the left and a wide trail through riparian forest. In another 12 miles, on the left, Independence is the finest riverfront town—an easy stroll to restaurants. Another 10 miles downstream, Minto-Brown Island Park has excellent trails, followed by Salem, high on the right bank. Below Salem 6 miles, on the left, obscure Darrow Bar Park barely has a spot to tie up but features paths through a fine cottonwood/Douglas-fir forest.

Below Wheatland Ferry, Wheatland Bar offers good canoe camping; I take the western slough to a remote site on the right side of that channel. Just above there a smaller slough on the left has been partially bulldozed shut, making evident the process that dried up countless back channels rich in habitat for fish and wildlife.

Below Newberg, the 24-mile Newberg Pool's flatwater is heavily flanked by riverfront houses, abuzz with motorboats and jet skis, and hampered by headwinds. But on the right, Champoeg State Park has riverfront trails, and in another 10 miles camping is possible at the mouth of the Molalla, with access to paths and giant cottonwoods. This forest may be the lower Willamette's least affected by alien weeds.

Below the Molalla, on a clear day, the snow-cone rise of Mount Hood can be seen from the river—one of few places in America where you can canoe at nearly sea level with a view to a snowcapped mountain, and one of few views to an Oregon stratovolcano from a sizable river. Willamette Narrows—a basalt gorge with intriguing back channels—lies 2 miles above West Linn, where the Tualatin River enters. Here, Willamette Park is a mandatory takeout; 1 mile below, Willamette Falls Dam drops 41 feet—do not approach! Paper mills and a hydro plant crowd the industrial scene (the east-side mill is closed and may be acquired for riverfront restoration). Portaging is impossible short of walking several miles on city streets, so carry by car to Clackamette Park, on the right below Oregon City.

A mile of paddling back upstream from Clackamette takes you to the base of Willamette Falls; even with its cement dam and industrial buildings, the force of this cataract is impressive and worth a close-up view. From there downstream, 26 miles are the province of the motorboat. The river is tidal, noisy, and windy, with many accesses. Below Sellwood Bridge, small channels east of Ross Island can be used to avoid powerboats. In downtown Portland, just south of the east end of Hawthorne Bridge, a dock offers access to city streets and parking.

The huge lower river presents tides, wind, ocean freighters, motorboat wakes, murky water, and industrially paved shorelines—not for everyone. Then 9 miles below Broadway Bridge, the Willamette's left half sluices behind Sauvie Island in the 22-mile windswept Multnomah Channel, which doesn't join the Columbia until 15 miles downstream from the main confluence. So hug the Willamette's opposite (right) bank above Sauvie if you want to go to the mouth at Kelley Point. The last takeout is 0.5 miles upstream from the confluence; paddle east into the Columbia Slough to the boat ramp. To drive there, take I-5 exit 307 and go west on Marine Drive/Suttle Road. Canoes or kayaks can be launched on the slough for a short paddle to the Willamette/Columbia confluence.

I've enjoyed the entire Willamette trip to West Linn and recommend it to all capable boaters. This is the longest easy-water canoe voyage in Oregon and one of the best long river journeys in the West without difficult rapids.

Middle Fork Willamette below Oakridge

MIDDLE FORK WILLAMETTE RIVER

Length: 85 miles
Average flow: 4,078 cfs
Watershed: 1,365 square miles

In everything but name, the Middle Fork is the upriver continuation of the main stem Willamette. Headwaters from Timpanogas Lake flow 28 miles to Hills Creek Reservoir, then through Oakridge and 10 more miles of current to Lookout Point and Dexter Reservoirs, and finally 17 swift miles to the much smaller Coast Fork, where the main stem officially begins.

Threatened bull trout have been reintroduced in the Middle Fork. In Bristow State Park below Dexter, the Middle Fork Watershed Council has eradicated weeds and planted trees, and at the mouth, the Oregon Nature Conservancy has launched its most extensive restoration program to reclaim gravel pits and 6 miles of frontage.

Fall Creek enters the Middle Fork from the north upstream of Jasper Park; see its pleasant pastoral mileage from a covered bridge above the Jasper-Lowell Road and from Forest Service recreation sites upstream of Fall Creek Reservoir.

 For lower Middle Fork access, take I-5 south of Springfield, exit Hwy 58 east, and in 6 miles turn north to Jasper County Park with its riparian paths. Boat access lies just downstream at the bridge. Up Hwy 58 another 4 miles, Bristow State Park's trails lead to the riverfront and connect with an anglers' path up to Dexter Dam.

Above Lookout Point Reservoir, three campgrounds lie along the river, and then Oakridge is a logging town transitioning to tourism—now a premier mountain biking destination becoming known throughout the West.

Upstream from Oakridge and Hills Creek Reservoir, at Sand Prairie Campground, the Middle Fork Trail leads upriver 27 miles. The first 10 up to Campers' Flat pass old-growth forest, pristine frontage, and occasional access to the dynamic channel with its logjams and sloughs. Another 10 miles with fewer river views offer good hiking to Indigo Campground (just east of the campground take a spur path to the river trail). The route continues up to the Middle Fork source, Timpanogas Lake, reached via FR 21 eastbound. Mosquitoes are insufferable in summer at upper elevations; if you're averse to bug repellent, as I am, save this worthy trek for autumn. The lower two-thirds of Middle Fork Trail are a popular challenge for mountain bikers, while the paved road through the valley is excellent for easy biking or hiking shuttles up to Indigo Springs. Beyond there, the road's a steep dusty climb.

 Anglers fish for hatchery spring Chinook from drift boats or from shore below Dexter Dam May–June, summer steelhead May–September, and rainbow/cutthroat trout. Entering the Middle Fork 5 miles downstream from Dexter, Fall Creek offers good trout fishing.

 The 10-mile reach from Oakridge down to Lookout Point Reservoir is a Class 2+ canoe run through a fine cottonwood corridor. Lower, the 16-mile reach from Dexter to the mouth is a good Class 2 canoe, raft, or drift-boat outing running all summer. Launch on either side at Dexter. Take out in 9 miles at the bridge below Jasper Park, or better, in 19 miles on the main stem at Springfield's Island Park north of the Hwy 126 bridge (an irresistible river-wide surfing wave lies just below the Coast Fork confluence).

SALT CREEK

Salt Creek meets the Middle Fork upstream of Oakridge, and in middle reaches its waterfall drops 286 feet in

Length: 29 miles
Average flow: 373 cfs
Watershed: 114 square miles

one jump—Oregon's third tallest behind Multnomah and Munson. Here

Salt Creek Falls

Salmon Creek upstream of Oakridge

glaciers had carved a U-shaped valley, subsequently filled with lava flowing from the High Cascades down through this gorge, which was again glaciated by ice that plucked out bedrock to make the cataract.

 Hwy 58 ascends the creek with frontage at Blue Pool Campground, 9 miles east of Oakridge. Drive 13 more miles up to Salt Creek Falls—dazzling from its trails at sunset. Another 2-mile loop trail reaches tributary Diamond Creek's waterfall.

SALMON CREEK

Salmon Creek enters the Middle Fork Willamette in Oakridge as an undeveloped stream from pristine headwaters in Waldo Lake Wilderness.

Length: 24 miles	
Average flow: 422 cfs	
Watershed: 128 square miles	

 FR 24 parallels the creek, with great biking and a riverfront campground 4 miles east of Oakridge at Salmon Creek Falls—an 8-foot drop.

 Expert kayakers occasionally tackle a short Class 4+ reach replete with log hazards and—I'll say no more—a drop called Holy Terror.

NORTH FORK OF THE MIDDLE FORK WILLAMETTE RIVER

Length: 51 miles	
Average flow: 780 cfs	
Watershed: 247 square miles	

Among the top streams in Oregon's Cascade Range, this deep-woods jewel highlights the Willamette basin. Rather than the official but tortured "North Fork of the Middle Fork

North Fork of the Middle Fork Willamette gorge below Hammet Creek

Willamette River," the "North Fork Willamette" seems adequate here, as there is no other North Fork Willamette, and the Middle Fork is clearly the upriver extension of the main stem. The source, Waldo Lake, is considered one of the world's purest lakes. The North Fork's upper 12 roadless miles cascade over 34 seldom-seen waterfalls. Below, the river cuts a 1,000-foot-deep wooded canyon. Anadromous fish never surmounted the waterfalls, and native trout in the upper river remain unaffected by alien or hatchery fish.

The paved FR 19 follows the North Fork 30 miles northeast from Westfir with pullouts, bridges, and views of crystalline depths, intense rapids, and mossy gorges. From Eugene take Hwy 58 east, and 2 miles before Oakridge (across from Forest Service headquarters) turn left at the Westfir sign, cross the Middle Fork, turn left, and continue 2 miles to Westfir's covered bridge. The North Fork Trail, eventually to reach headwaters, is a long-term work-in-progress beginning on the west side of the bridge and climbing 4 miles to the FR 1912 bridge.

From Westfir drive 28 miles up the canyon to magnificent Constitution Grove. Here a loop-trail tours riverfront old-growth Douglas-fir/red cedar/western hemlock. A 3-mile trail leads upriver to Shale Ridge Trailhead, and a grassy path ventures downriver 1 mile. If you go 2 miles farther up FR 19, Shale Ridge Trail heads south toward the headwaters, with a crossing in a few miles but only occasional river views (mosquitoes!).

The basin supports one of few rainbow/cutthroat trout fisheries west of the Cascade crest designated for fly-fishing only.

The upper river is replete with logjams. Lower, kayakers paddle Class 4–5 rapids in the Miracle Mile starting at the FR 1925 bridge 13 miles above Westfir, and onward through the turbulent gorge, 3 miles below FR 1925 and between two FR 19 bridges spaced 1 mile apart. Below them, the North Fork settles to a superb Class 2–3+ run for 8 miles to Westfir. On low water in July of a wet year (1,430 cfs on the Middle Fork below the North Fork) this was excellent technical whitewater with three easy carries around rock jams—Class 3+ at higher flows. Start at a pulloff below the first FR 19 bridge upstream of Westfir; take out at a lane 0.8 miles above Westfir. The North Fork continues with Class 2+ rapids for 3 more miles to an informal access off the Westfir Road just above the Middle Fork confluence; scout or portage a weir half-way through this reach.

COAST FORK WILLAMETTE RIVER

Length: 40 miles
Average flow: 1,593 cfs
Watershed: 624 square miles

The Coast Fork collects water from the Siskiyou-Cascade interface of low mountains and flows north to Cottage Grove Reservoir, through Cottage Grove, and then joins the Middle Fork near Springfield. Reservoir and development dominate much of the upper reach while the lower traverses an agricultural valley and the I-5 corridor. Hydropower releases from dams govern flows, and banks have been riprapped through farms. The Row River (rhymes with cow) joins from the east below Cottage Grove.

 The Coast Fork and Middle Fork form the main stem Willamette at Buford Regional Park; from the I-5 Hwy 58 exit go east, turn immediately north on Seavey Loop Road, and wind

Coast Fork Willamette River above Willamette confluence

Row River below Dorena Reservoir

2 miles to the Coast Fork bridge, with access on river-right and downstream. For a Creswell swimming hole and access, take I-5 exit 182 and follow Cloverdale Road 1 mile east.

Along tributary Row River, the Row River Trail for bikes and walkers runs 8 miles on an abandoned rail line from Cottage Grove up to Dorena Reservoir but offers only a glimpse of the river.

 The *Willamette River Field Guide* lists a 10-mile Class 2 paddle on the lower Coast Fork in springtime from Cloverdale Road to Dilley Landing (from the I-5 Hwy 58 exit go east 2 miles and left at the sign). Row River has a Class 3 run above Cottage Grove.

MCKENZIE RIVER

From high in the Cascades, this Oregon classic of cold water, foaming rapids, and excellent trout habitat drops west

Length: 88 miles
Average flow: 5,916 cfs
Watershed: 1,216 square miles

to join the Willamette 5 miles downstream of Eugene. With the Rogue and Deschutes, the McKenzie forms a triad of Oregon's most popular recreational rivers. Undeveloped above McKenzie Bridge, the upper river lies largely in Willamette National Forest; lower, private-land reaches have roads and homes, but a riparian corridor and sense of wildness remains.

Headwaters include some of the most recently formed volcanic landscape in America. Clear Lake formed when lava impounded the McKenzie. Incredibly, snags and remains of a fallen forest drowned by the lake 3,000 years ago can still be seen underwater. Below the outlet, volcanic tuff forms rapids that course through old-growth Douglas-fir and western hemlock, and the truly awesome 120-foot Sahalie Falls is followed by 90-foot Koosah Falls. Farther down, the summertime flush of 500 cfs mysteriously

McKenzie River below Sahalie Falls

disappears underground for 3 miles before emerging in the otherworldly blue depths of Tamolitch Pool—the largest spring you're ever likely to see, several hundred feet across. Downstream, small reservoirs at Carmen and Trail Bridge Dams produce hydropower, and were built as an alternative to dams and diversions upstream. With the Metolius, the McKenzie is Oregon's coldest major river, and also one of the cleanest.

Much of the stream seems enticingly wild considering that Hwy 126 tracks alongside—usually out of sight. The upper McKenzie has fallen timber, mixed pools and rapids, and deeply shaded sloughs that all illustrate

McKenzie River and Koosah Falls

the kind of channel complexity sought in restoration projects elsewhere. Old-growth shades the banks and a fine fishery features cutthroat, stocked rainbows, native redband, introduced summer steelhead below Leaburg Dam (41 miles above the mouth), and the only native bull trout remaining on the Cascades' west side (reintroduced elsewhere from this core population). Native spring Chinook dwindled from 40,000 to less than 1,000—most below Leaburg. From the source down to Scott Creek, 13 miles are a National Wild and Scenic River. This is one of few Oregon streams not over-appropriated for lower basin diversions, though in 2012 a private water developer unsuccessfully sought rights to extract 250 gallons per second.

TRIBUTARIES

Some of the McKenzie's headwater streams were cut off from the main stem by lava flows 3,500 years ago, and their waters now disappear underground. One of these, Hackleman Creek, supports an endemic cutthroat trout that evolved in isolation as a subspecies.

Lost Creek joins at Belknap Springs and is nourished all summer with cold water from the North Sister's Collier Glacier. Until recently this was Oregon's largest glacier, but it has receded rapidly (glaciers on Mounts Hood and Jefferson are higher and hold ice better). From McKenzie Bridge go 4 miles east on Hwy 126 and turn southeast on Hwy 242 along lower Lost Creek. A trail to its headwaters—Glacier and Obsidian Creeks—starts 6 miles west of the pass.

Horse Creek enters from the south at McKenzie Bridge; the paved FR 2638 leads up this otherwise wild valley 18 miles, with access at a group campground 2 miles up. Its tributary, 13-mile-long Separation Creek, rises on the South Sister, whose glaciated 10,358-foot summit guarantees snowmelt when other sources wither. Separation plunges through

French Pete Creek 2 miles upstream of South Fork McKenzie

old-growth forest in the 286,708-acre Three Sisters Wilderness—Oregon's second-largest.

The South Fork McKenzie flows north from the wilderness for 30 miles through a deeply forested corridor until blocked by Cougar Dam, 3 miles above the mouth. FR 19 has pullouts along mid-reaches.

French Pete Creek is a superb South Fork tributary, added to Three Sisters Wilderness in the early 1970s as one of the first wilderness areas to be protected where timber values were high. Its trail through old-growth climbs 5 miles; from Cougar Reservoir take FR 19 a mile south.

The Blue River is essentially the McKenzie's north fork. From Blue River community go 3 miles east on Hwy 126, turn north, and continue 4 miles to the bridge—a beautiful but trashed site needing a local steward. Dammed near its mouth, the Blue drains Andrews Experimental Forest of Oregon State University, plus heavily logged terrain.

 Hwy 126 parallels the McKenzie with campgrounds and 20 access points. Near the source, the Clear Lake interpretive site lies south of Santiam Pass. Another mile south, Waterfall Trail offers rapturous views of Sahalie and Koosah Falls. Below there, an underground interval of the McKenzie reemerges in Tamolitch Pool; take Hwy 126 east of McKenzie Bridge 14 miles, turn left at the Trail Bridge Campground sign, right on FR 655 to the trailhead, and walk upriver 2 miles to this enchanted spot.

The 26-mile McKenzie River Trail is among the best riverfront paths in the state, headwaters to Belknap Springs, with old-growth forests and crystalline water. The trail is also among the best for advanced mountain biking. My favorite sections are at Sahalie Falls, Tamolitch Pool, and above/below Deer Creek.

Below that trail, at the South Fork confluence, Delta Grove has an interpretive path through fine old-growth; from Blue River on Hwy 126 go east 4 miles, turn south on FR 19 (Aufderheide), cross the main stem, and go right on FR 400 to the end of Delta Campground. Below McKenzie Bridge, private frontage is interspersed with recreation sites every 5 miles or so.

 Rainbow and cutthroat trout anglers revere the McKenzie, especially above Leaburg Dam in springtime, but also the lower river. ODFW introduced non-native summer steelhead in 1972—a popular fishery directly below Leaburg hatchery, April–autumn. Keep only hatchery fish (clipped adipose fin); catch-and-release applies in many locations. Below Hayden Bridge in Springfield, the McKenzie is open to fly fishing year-round.

 The upper river is one of few long whitewater reaches that can be floated all summer and fall, beginning downstream from Olallie Campground, 75 miles east of Eugene. Boating goes way back on this river; drift boats are sometimes called "McKenzie" boats for their early use here and for local innovations in design.

The run from Olallie to Paradise Campground is 9 miles, Class 3+. Paradise to Finn Rock adds 18 miles of Class 2–3 with takeout on the south bank 3 miles below Blue River. Excellent Class 2 paddling continues 10 miles from Finn Rock to beautifully wooded Dorris State Park and ramp. Marten Rapid (Class 3) follows, with Leaburg Dam 5 miles beyond.

Below the dam, 30 miles of Class 2 reach to Hayden Bridge, with intermediate accesses; to put in, take Hwy 126 east from Springfield 21 miles and turn south across the dam to the boat-slide. To drive to the takeout, use the I-5 exit for I-105, take 126 east, turn north on Mohawk Road, and go 1 mile to the bridge (river-left). A Class 1–2 reach runs 8 miles from Hayden to Armitage Park north of Springfield; to reach Armitage from I-5, take Beltline Hwy west, then Coburg Road north to the river. From there, 4 miles of swift Class 1 riffles to the Willamette; take out downstream on the left at Marshall Landing, 7 miles north of Eugene.

The 41 miles of Class 2 from Leaburg Dam can be combined with the Willamette to West Linn for a rare portage-free trip of 189 miles. Private land dominates on the lower McKenzie, but islands, remote bars, and public areas can be found.

LONG TOM RIVER

Length: 57 miles
Average flow: 753 cfs
Watershed: 410 square miles

With runoff from the narrow east side of the Coast Range, the Long Tom pools into Fern Ridge Reservoir west of Eugene. Then it mirrors the Willamette's alignment, only in miniature, just 3–7 miles to the west, winding modestly north through farmland. The curiously parallel route dates to Cascade Mountain tributaries of the Willamette delivering massive amounts of glacial alluvium that accumulated in the valley, pinning the Coast Range's eastbound runoff into a barely perceptible but effective trough that became the Long Tom. It channels

Long Tom River at High Pass Road, west of Junction City

Coast Range runoff north while the Willamette channels Cascade runoff north—tandem systems until they merge south of Corvallis. The lower Long Tom has largemouth bass, crappie, and brown bullhead.

 Soggy Sneakers (1994 edition) lists a 17-mile Class 1+ run with three dams requiring portages. From Eugene take Hwy 99 north to Junction City, turn west on First Avenue, which becomes High Pass Road, and go 3 miles to the bridge (I found a thicket of blackberries and only a thin highway shoulder with private land). The *SS* takeout is above the Willamette confluence 100 yards below an Old River Road bridge (or proceed down the Willamette). Flows are often adequate (though muddy) in spring, but drop to 30 cfs in the July 1–September 30 irrigation season.

MARYS RIVER

This small river flows off the east side of the Coast Range including Marys Peak—at 4,097 feet the highest in the

| Length: 43 miles |
| Average flow: 451 cfs |
| Watershed: 301 square miles |

Oregon Coast Range north of the Siskiyou Mountains. It winds past farmland and homes and meets the Willamette in south Corvallis.

 Little public access is available along this pastoral and brushy stream. If you're a covered bridge buff, check out Harris Bridge; from Corvallis take Hwy 20 west, ramp off the east side at Wren, clover-leaf southward, and proceed upstream 3 miles.

 Soggy Sneakers has listed a Class 2 run here, however, recent reports indicate logjams below Blodgett. Also, ledges below the Harris covered bridge should be scouted but can't owing to posted land. Put-in is possible below there at the Hwy 20 bridge northwest

Marys River at Route 34 west of Corvallis

of Wren, river-left, downstream side, with a 4-foot, runnable weir along the way and takeout possible at the Hwy 20 bridge west of Philomath. Below there the river is ditched and brushy with logs. I've paddled up from the mouth in quiet shaded water half a mile—a nice contrast to the wide Willamette.

CALAPOOIA RIVER

Length: 80 miles
Average flow: 898 cfs
Watershed: 374 square miles

Wedged into lower terrain between the South Santiam and McKenzie, the Calapooia drifts northwest through the low Western Cascades to Albany. Heavily logged headwaters transition to lower reaches through farmland and villages, and riparian woodlands continue much of the way.

Salmon numbers plummeted in recent decades, spurring restoration projects and one of the more significant clusters of dam removals in Oregon. In 2007 Brownsville Dam was eliminated, leaving 11-foot Sodom Dam, 2 miles above I-5, built in 1858 for a grain mill and later converted for hydroelectric power, plus 5-foot Shearer Dam, 3 miles below I-5. Both were removed in 2011. This is the uppermost Willamette tributary with native steelhead and the fourth-largest dam-free Willamette tributary.

The Calapooia's languid mouth is seen at Bryant Park near Albany. To go upstream, take I-5 exit 216, then Hwy 228 east 4 miles to Brownsville, left into town, and left to Pioneer Park. Continue east on 228 for 6.5 miles to McKercher Park and its fine swimming hole below a turbulent rapid. Resume on Hwy 228 upriver 5 miles to Holley and bear right for Upper Calapooia Drive—gated by Weyerhaeuser 11 miles farther.

Calapooia River at Brownsville

A hatchery provides spring Chinook.

Soggy Sneakers reports an 11-mile Class 2 run (800 cfs) with log possibilities from a pullout 5 miles upstream from Holley down to McKercher Park; exit above the Class 4 rapid.

From the beach below McKercher Rapid, a 7-mile Class 1 float winds through farmland and riparian forest to Brownsville. The next reach below is heavily diverted and unrunnable with logs and brush. Then, from the Hwy 34 bridge (east of Corvallis) to Albany, 10 miles of snaking Class 1+ with brush, diversions, and logjams are said to offer a "junglelike" experience for hearty explorers in springtime. From the eastbound lanes of Hwy 34 pull off just east of the bridge for a briar-tangled path.

LUCKIAMUTE RIVER

On the east side of the Coast Range, the Luckiamute (lucky-mute) meets the Willamette north of Albany and just below the Santiam mouth. Once badly

Length: 61 miles
Average flow: 878 cfs
Watershed: 315 square miles

ditched for navigation and drainage, the lower river's shores have lushly grown over with cottonwoods, bigleaf maples, and red osier dogwoods.

 To see the upper river, take Hwy 20 west of Corvallis, turn north on 223, go 7 miles to Hoskins, and west on Luckiamute Road to pullouts. For the lower stream, go south from Monmouth on 99W for 6 miles and turn west to Sarah Helmick State Recreation Area. Luckiamute delta is the richest riparian forest along the Willamette; from Buena Vista, drive south on Buena Vista Road 2.5 miles, and turn east at the Luckiamute Park sign.

Luckiamute River near Willamette confluence

A few spawning steelhead and Chinook are off-limits to fishing. Trout are caught in the upper river (lures only); smallmouth bass below.

 The lower Luckiamute's quiet waters, draped in forest and fallen trees, are best seen by paddling up from the Willamette. Surmounting just a few small riffles you can ascend 2 miles to Buena Vista Road, with steep access on river-right above the bridge. If driving there, turn into the state park south of the bridge for parking. Flatwater paddling continues upstream.

SANTIAM RIVER

| Length: 12 miles, 105 with NF |
| Average flow: 7,726 cfs |
| Watershed: 1,804 square miles |

By far the largest Willamette tributary, the Santiam gathers water from the high Cascades via the North and South Santiam, which join as the main stem 2 miles upstream of Jefferson and only 12 miles above the mouth.

I regard the lower Santiam as a jewel of the Willamette Valley with gravel bars, cottonwood shores, and swift current. Riprap here is less evident than along most of the Willamette, and the water is much clearer. Combined with either the North or South Santiam, a long river trip, possible all summer and fall, is wonderfully intimate and feels surprisingly remote.

 Jefferson Hwy crosses in Jefferson with access 1 block north at Ferry Street. Many see the riffling Santiam at the I-5 roadside rest 8 miles north of Albany, evident on the northbound side. Unnoticed to most, a good boat ramp within the rest area lies immediately west of the freeway bridge, reached via an unsigned lane in both

Santiam River downstream of Jefferson

north- and southbound rest areas. A weedy path leads downstream 0.5 miles for fishing or a dip on a hot day of driving.

 The lower river makes for a fine 10-mile Class 1 canoe trip through cottonwoods from Jefferson to the Willamette. At the confluence an obscure path penetrates one of the best big-canopy cottonwood forests; catch the swift point bar, walk up the Willamette 200 feet, and scramble up the bank to a path leading 0.5 miles back up the Santiam.

The takeout lies another 2 miles down the Willamette at Buena Vista; from I-5 exit 242 take Talbot Road west, but there's no east-shore access—ferry your car to the west side and drive just upstream to the boat ramp. Catch the ferry daily 7 a.m.–7 p.m., flows permitting. If closed, drive to Buena Vista via Albany or Corvallis.

SOUTH SANTIAM RIVER

South Santiam headwaters gather in the Western Cascades—rising like foothills beneath the High Cascades'

Length: 66 miles, 73 with Sevenmile Creek
Average flow: 2,951 cfs
Watershed: 1,040 square miles

stratovolcanoes. Here a roaded checkerboard of National Forest and industrial timberland has been heavily cut except for the small Menagerie Wilderness. The South Santiam (not South Fork!) begins at the confluence of Latiwi and Sevenmile Creeks, 25 miles east of Sweet Home along Hwy 20. Mid-sections run 12 miles down to Cascadia State Park. Foster Dam lies below, and then downstream of Sweet Home the river flows northwest through Waterloo and Lebanon to the North Santiam confluence 2 miles upstream from Jefferson.

The proposed Cascadia Dam above Foster Reservoir would have flooded Cascadia State Park's gorge in the 1970s, but the citizens' Cascadia Task Force revealed that the Army Corps of Engineers had inflated the project's value by averaging flood control benefits of all dams in the Willamette basin and, even more dubiously, by assuming damages from a 10,000-year flood rather than the standard 100-year event. The project was halted.

 Along Hwy 20 and the upper river, Forest Service campgrounds include Fernview, with a path on an overgrown abandoned road leading upstream, then Yukwah and Trout Creek. At Cascadia State Park, a 1-mile trail leads upstream to swimming holes and old-growth conifers.

Lower reaches flow mostly through private land. For the Waterloo County Campground, access, and river path, take Hwy 20 east from Lebanon 5 miles and turn north on Waterloo Road. From the lower end of the park you can scramble downstream to extensive bedrock shores and the impressive Class 4+ cataract, Waterloo Falls. Below it, at Waterloo bridge (1st and Santiam Streets), paths lead both down river and up to the Falls—a good place for angling and fish-watching when the salmon jump. This drop is the most spectacular major rapid on lower tributaries of the

South Santiam River at Cascadia State Park

Willamette. Downstream at Lebanon, a city park with river access extends above and below the bridge.

 A popular hatchery fishery for summer steelhead and spring Chinook peaks May–June. Foster Dam stops anadromous fish, which congregate there. Bank fishing is good at Waterloo. Drift boaters row from Foster to there; take out in the park above the falls! Wild trout are found throughout.

 Soggy Sneakers calls the 19-mile, springtime paddle from Upper Soda Creek to Foster Reservoir a "magnificent" Class 3–4 kayak reach, including one or more portages and log hazards, seen from a few spots along Hwy 20.

From Foster Dam to the North Santiam is a great Class 1–2 run, with 38 miles of clear water, cottonwood shores, gravel bars, swift riffles, a few rapids, and two significant portages, flowing all summer, especially beautiful in autumn. I've found 700–1,500 cfs to be a nice low flow. Put in on the south side below Foster Dam; from Sweet Home take Hwy 20 east 3 miles, turn north at the Fish hatchery sign, bear left, right, and right to Wiley Park. Ledgy Class 2 rapids come 2 miles below Foster, followed by the Sweet Home ramp; to drive there take Hwy 20 west of Sweet Home 0.5 miles and turn north on Pleasant Valley Road. Here a restoration effort has carved stair-steps into rock at the mouth of tributary Ames Creek; prior to Foster Dam, steelhead had been able to ascend here because the creek's lower ledges were routinely flooded in spring.

Two portages lie below Sweet Home: 11 miles down, at Waterloo, the Class 4+ Waterloo Falls has a rocky left-side carry. A good takeout appears 200 yards above at Waterloo Park; to drive there take Hwy 20 east of Lebanon 5 miles and turn left at the sign. Then, about 2 miles below Waterloo, the hazardous 10-foot Lebanon Dam requires right-side portage up to the road. These onerous carries can be avoided by taking out at Waterloo Park for a 1-day trip and putting in 3 miles below there at Lebanon's town park; to drive there take Hwy 20 to central Lebanon and go east on Brewster Road to the bridge and boat ramp just above. However, I found it interesting and exciting to arrive by canoe at Waterloo Falls and have to deal with that charismatic landmark.

From Lebanon down, the South Santiam is a swift Class 1+ run. In 11 miles access is possible north of Hwy 226 (west of Crabtree); on the west side of the bridge turn north on a lane, park at the gate, and walk 100 yards. Another 8 miles downstream, eddy out on the beautiful wild point bar at the North Fork confluence. Another 2 miles on the main stem lead to Jefferson; to drive there, go to the east side of the Jefferson bridge, turn north on Mill Street and left on Ferry.

Better yet, continue down the riffling main Santiam and into the Willamette, with takeout 2 miles farther at Buena Vista. To drive to Buena Vista from Corvallis, follow Hwy 20 north 6 miles, turn left on Independence Hwy for 5.2 miles, go right on Spring Hill Drive 0.8 miles, left on Buena Vista Road 4.3 miles, and right on River View Street. With the two portages, a 52-mile voyage is possible from Foster Dam to Buena Vista—33 miles if you start below the portages—either way a splendid Class 1–2 journey. Most of the corridor is private land, but gravel bars and wooded banks are mostly remote from roads and houses and the overall feel is one of a sweet riparian path through Oregon's big valley.

MIDDLE SANTIAM RIVER

Length: 38 miles
Average flow: 1,449 cfs
Watershed: 279 square miles

This little-known branch lies off the beaten track, starting in the Western Cascades. It bisects the Middle Santiam Wilderness for 5 miles, then runs 8 miles with a gated forest industry road alongside to Green Peter Reservoir. Below the dam the river foams heavily for 2 miles to Foster Reservoir, where it meets the South Santiam.

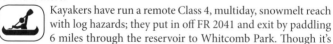 For a view that's nominal relative to the hard effort, take Hwy 20 east from Sweet Home 24 miles, turn north on Soda Fork Road, soon bear left on FR 2041, avoid logging roads and go 12.5 miles to a 3-way, take the middle road (646) to its end at Chimney Peak Trailhead, and walk 0.7 miles to the river. The lower Middle Fork between Green Peter and Foster Reservoirs hides in a thickly forested canyon south of Quartzville Road; I've given up in the poison oak trying to find it there.

Kayakers have run a remote Class 4, multiday, snowmelt reach with log hazards; they put in off FR 2041 and exit by paddling 6 miles through the reservoir to Whitcomb Park. Though it's fraught with difficulties and seldom done, *Soggy Sneakers* called this "the most pristine river run in Oregon's Cascades."

Quartzville Creek above Dogwood picnic area

QUARTZVILLE CREEK

Length: 29 miles
Average flow: 648 cfs
Watershed: 690 square miles

The Middle Santiam's major tributary, Quartzville Creek is a splendid clear river with green pools, turbulent white-water, and no development, entering Green Peter Reservoir from the north. National Wild and Scenic status safeguards 9 miles; upper reaches also deserve protection.

 From Sweet Home take Hwy 22 east 3 miles, turn north on Quartzville Road, skirt the reservoir, then drive along the stream through BLM, National Forest, and some timber in-dustry land to Dogwood picnic area, 2 miles above the backwater, and to Yellowbottom Campground, 6 miles farther. Pulloff campsites are perched on the banks; if you want to car camp at a riverfront and expend no physical effort, this is the place. But, until law enforcement gets a grip, I avoid weekends in what has become a rowdy atmosphere at this splen-did location (BLM may unfortunately have to ban roadside camping). Quieter on weekdays, the road to Yellowbottom and beyond is among Oregon's best paved riverfront biking routes, with plenty of swimming options in deep green pools.

 Class 5 kayakers paddle 16 miles above the reservoir during snowmelt, extending to early summer—"one of the best [ex-pert] runs in the state," according to *Paddling Oregon*. Difficult upper reaches are followed by 8 miles of still-challenging Class 4 rapids from Yellowbottom to Green Peter.

North Santiam River below Mehama

NORTH SANTIAM RIVER

Length: 93 miles
Average flow: 2,041 cfs
Watershed: 734 square miles

The North Santiam begins on the slopes of craggy Three Fingered Jack in the Mount Jefferson Wilderness, flows through wild headwaters to Hwy 22, then veers northbound, still within the high Cascades. Whitewater Creek adds silty glacial runoff from Mount Jefferson—at 10,497 the state's second-highest peak. A major Willamette basin reservoir, Detroit backs up 5 miles, followed downstream by Big Cliff Reservoir and 5 miles farther by Packsaddle Dam. These flood control projects block 75 percent of the river's historic salmon run. Improved fish collection facilities are being built, and further study of passage is underway. Below Detroit the river winds through private land with several parks.

The North Santiam has famously good water quality and historically had the best winter steelhead in the Willamette basin, along with one-third of the spring Chinook. Both wild fishes are threatened; hatchery stocks remain more plentiful. Cutthroat and rainbow thrive.

Hwy 22 follows the river above Detroit Reservoir with pullouts and access at Marion Forks, Riverside (user path upstream through old-growth), and Whispering Falls Campgrounds. Below the dam, Niagara County Park offers access and a trail, while Hwy 22 continues downstream. Mill City Park is followed in 2 miles by BLM's Fishermen's Bend access and paths. In 3 more miles North Santiam State Park has steelhead fishing and 1 mile of waterfront trail. John Neal Park in Mehama is followed in another 11 miles by Stayton ramp at the bridge south of town. There on river-right, a gravel trail leads upriver 0.5 miles. Roads peel away from the water for most of the lower 18 miles, which have beautiful gravel bars and occasional sloughs with the kind of riparian complexity that once made Oregon's valley rivers so rich.

 North Santiam's hatchery steelhead peak in March; summer steelhead remain into autumn. Chinook arrive May–June. Wild and hatchery trout are caught down to Stayton. Below Mill City, anglers bank fish at the parks and row drift boats.

 Kayakers paddle a 7-mile Class 4 reach above Detroit Reservoir in spring. Then, the 7-mile run from Packsaddle Park to Mill City is a popular Class 3 whitewater trip, flowing all summer. Take out on river-right at Mill City's bridge.

From there down is a good 9-mile Class 2+ run all summer and autumn with many rapids and some holes that canoeists will want to avoid. Take out at the Hwy 226 bridge south of Mehama. Below, an 11-mile Class 2 section continues to Stayton Bridge, including a low dam about 7 miles down; when a distant warning sign appears, stay left of the island (tempting to go right—don't—it's a ditch!), then stroke right of the lip of the dam, catch a tight eddy, and line the boat down the sliding-board made for drift boats.

From Stayton to the main stem is 17 miles of Class 2 paddling through farmland and riparian forest. Logs in the braided channels below the Buell Miller boat launch north of Scio are serious strainers and must be avoided. Another boat ramp lies 14 miles below Stayton at Jefferson-Scio Drive. Below the beautiful South Santiam confluence bar, 2 miles on the main stem lead to Jefferson's ramp; to drive there take I-5 exit 238, go east on Jefferson Highway 3 miles, cross the bridge, turn left on Mill Street and left on Ferry Street.

To extend this trip, continue down the main Santiam to the Willamette and another 2 miles to Buena Vista (see South Santiam)—altogether a fine 48-mile expedition on Class 2 water plus the diversion dam's boat-slide. For my excursion, 1,600 cfs in Jefferson was good. Swift, clear, beautiful, and with scarcely a house to be seen, both the lower North and lower South Santiam feel more remote than similar Class 2 reaches of the Willamette, lower McKenzie, and North Umpqua.

BREITENBUSH RIVER

Length: 10 miles, 23 with NF
Average flow: 523 cfs
Watershed: 106 square miles

This small Cascades beauty begins with its North and South Forks near the high peaks and tumbles west with lucid blue water to join the North Santiam in Detroit Reservoir. Best known for its commercial hot spring, the river flows through a narrow gorge for much of its length.

 Take Hwy 22 east to Detroit and turn northeast on FR 46—excellent biking. For a streamfront hike, continue 10 miles to Breitenbush Hot Spring (fee/reservations), go another mile, turn right on gravel, park near an old ranger station, and walk up the South Fork 3 miles to South Breitenbush Gorge.

Breitenbush River above Detroit Reservoir

Downstream on the main stem, several Forest Service campgrounds include the Cleator Bend group site—one of few places to easily reach the Breitenbush's steep-walled, brushy waterfront.

 Though challenged by difficult access, anglers catch stocked and wild rainbow and brook trout.

The lower 8-mile Class 4, springtime kayak run has steep drops requiring constant attention, with log hazards.

LITTLE NORTH SANTIAM RIVER

Length: 27 miles, 32 miles
  with Opal Creek
Average flow: 746 cfs
Watershed: 113 square miles

This exquisite, dam-free lifeline rises in Cascade Mountain wilderness, flows west through Willamette National Forest and then a BLM/private patchwork to join the North Santiam at Mehama. Deep pools at the bases of waterfalls are famous as delectable swimming holes.

In the upper basin, the Forest Service slated the magnificent Opal Creek grove for logging in the 1980s, but after a decade-long battle, the 55-square-mile basin was protected as the Opal Creek Wilderness and Scenic Recreation Area in 1996. Here the Little North begins with the confluence of Opal and Battle Ax Creeks, though the entire stream could well be called Opal River with its deep clear pools that look—of course—like opal.

To reach swimming holes and trails, go east from Salem on Hwy 22 to Mehama, and 1 mile farther turn left on North Fork Road. Several county parks border the river, along with BLM's extensive Elkhorn Valley site, 15 miles east of Hwy 22 (fee). Salmon Falls—a splendid, popular swimming hole—is 5 miles farther up. In another mile, go right on Elkhorn Drive for 0.5 miles to the Little North Santiam Trail, which tracks up the south side 4 miles to another road access. Along the way, fabulous swimming holes are segregated by small waterfalls, all elegantly wild, remote, and irresistible in off-trail enclaves. The upper section of trail is across from the famed Three Pools—more easily reached by car: continue up the North Fork Road from the Elkhorn Drive turnoff another 3 miles, turn right, and descend to the parking lot.

Three Pools is an ultimate Oregon river landmark—depthless opal pools linked by chutes and waterfalls, towering rock faces rising from the edge, shallows tiled in black-and-white rock that looks like marble. If there's a more paradisiacal river site, I'm not sure where it would be. For reverence fitting to this wonderland, avoid summer weekends, which draw teeming crowds and all the refuse one might imagine from those who don't quite get it.

To reach headwaters of the Little North Santiam, take the North Fork Road beyond Elkhorn and continue 6 miles on the gravel FR 2209 to Opal Creek Trailhead (fee). Hike or bike up the gated road 3 miles to Jawbone Flat—historic mining village turned nature center—then continue on trails into one of the Cascades' finest old-growth forests and the dead-end Opal Creek Trail.

 A 4-mile Little North Santiam reach above Three Pools is commonly called the "Opal Creek" run—Class 4–5 water that *Soggy Sneakers* says is "revered" by advanced paddlers. It features crystal clear water, old-growth forests, sharp drops, boulder sieves, and a 15-foot waterfall. For the put-in, drive up the Little North Fork Road 21 miles to Opal Creek Trailhead, hike 0.5 miles on the gated road, then cut down to the riverbank on the right. For the takeout, drive

Little North Santiam River at Three Pools

17 miles up the North Fork Road from Hwy 22, and turn right at the sign for the Three Pools parking lot.

Not immediately, but farther downstream, the Little North Santiam is known as a Class 3–4 kayak run from Salmon Falls County Park to the mouth; put in below the 25-foot drop and unrunnable gorge. In two sections, the 17-mile, rainy season paddle includes a high-water hazard called The Slot and ends at the North Santiam's Mehama Bridge.

YAMHILL RIVER

This low-gradient river winds through farmland as the Willamette's second-largest tributary lacking storage dams, ending in flatwater upstream of New-

> Length: 11 miles, 74 with SF and Pierce Creek
> Average flow: 1,998 cfs
> Watershed: 600 square miles

berg. It's also the largest river draining the east slope of Oregon's Coast Range. The North Fork merges with the larger South Fork east of McMinnville to form the main stem. In 1900 the Yamhill was dredged and scoured of logs for navigation up to McMinnville. Entrenchment damage remains, but the river has reverted to a green corridor of forest and undergrowth.

On the South Fork, a Sheridan town park lies on the south side of the Hwy 18 bridge. Downstream at the Bellevue-Amity Road Bridge, a path reaches the river on the river-right, upstream side. The best place to see this private-land river is the extensive McMinnville Marina Park; from 99W go east on 3rd Street, which becomes Three Mile Lane, and turn left into the park. Its washed-out ramp, as of this writing, requires a 200-yard carry. See the lower Yamhill in Dayton; from 3rd Street turn north on Ferry Street for a view from a footbridge or a path underneath it to the water.

Yamhill River above its confluence with the Willamette

According to *Paddling Oregon*, the South Yamhill is canoe-able at high water (700 cfs at Willamina) for 29 riffling miles, Sheridan—McMinnville. Sizable ledges are encountered above Sheridan. The next 17 miles of flatwater enter the Willamette 3 miles above the Newberg ramp. Muddy and embedded in the Willamette plain, the Yamhill still offers cottonwood-willow habitat, a surprisingly remote feel, and a long canoeable reach of slow water near Portland.

MOLALLA RIVER

Length: 51 miles
Average flow: 2,377 cfs,
1,142 above Pudding River
Watershed: 874 square miles

A low-elevation stream nested between the Clackamas to the north and Santiam to the south, the Molalla's headwaters gather in Table Rock Wilderness. After picking up its North Fork, the main stem flows from Cascade foothills across rural land to the Willamette upstream of Portland.

This is the largest Willamette tributary with no dams affecting natural flows, and has a fine cottonwood corridor. Salmon runs have plummeted, but with habitat improvements underway, spring Chinook and winter steelhead appear to be rebounding. As a rare undammed Willamette tributary, and with little development, the Molalla presents an opportunity for protection of a valuable lowland river.

 Headwaters hiking near Table Rock Wilderness is reached via Upper Molalla Road; from Molalla take the Feyrer Park Road east to Dickey Prairie Road, go right for 5.3 miles, turn right across a Molalla River bridge, and continue 12 miles to Old Bridge and a trailhead.

Molalla River downstream of Hwy 213

In Molalla, Feyrer Park offers good access and walking along the stream: from Hwy 211 at the east side of town turn south on South Mathias Road, and left on Feyrer Park Road for 1 mile. Downstream 6 miles, the Hwy 213 bridge marks Wagonwheel access; from Molalla go north on 213 for 4 miles and turn right before the bridge. On the lower river, Canby town park lies on the north side, east of Hwy 99E. Molalla River State Park occupies the mouth, where paths tour a fine riparian forest; from 99E at Canby take Ivy northwest 1 mile, go left on Territorial a block, and right on Holly Street.

 Though once stocked, the river since 1998 has been managed for wild steelhead, which peak March–April; keep only hatchery strays. Anglers catch spring Chinook April–June below Hwy 213. Catch-and-release for cutthroat in upper reaches.

 Kayakers enjoy the exceptionally beautiful 13-mile Class 3–4 rainy season run from Table Rock Fork to Glen Avon Bridge. To put in, cross the Glen Avon Bridge (see below), drive upstream 9 miles with pullout views of rapids, cross Turner Bridge, and continue 5 miles to Old Bridge.

Below Glen Avon, a Class 2 reach with one turbulent Class 3 drops 6 miles to Feyrer Park (800–2,000 cfs at Canby). To put in, go to Molalla's Feyrer Park, cross the river, go right on Dickey Prairie Road for 5 miles, cross the North Molalla, and quickly come to Glen Avon Bridge. Don't cross but park straight ahead at a pullout. A lower Class 2 reach of 7 miles runs from Feyrer to Hwy 213. These lively winter/spring runs pass through riparian habitat with clear water. Watch for bald eagles.

Another 16-mile reach continues through cottonwoods, spacious gravel bars, and occasional braided channels to the Willamette, then down it 1 mile to Molalla River State Park's boat ramp. Beware of a

Pudding River above Molalla confluence

railroad abutment 4 miles down. Unregulated by dams and only slightly encumbered by levees, this underrated but delightful reach feels more remote than it is and offers a glimpse of what back channels of the Willamette once were.

PUDDING RIVER

Entering the Molalla just 1 mile above the Willamette, the Pudding River flows from the south and carries more water

Length: 64 miles
Average flow: 1,235 cfs
Watershed: 527 square miles

than the Molalla. Small in summer, but brimming muddy with winter rain, it winds through cottonwoods and farmland and supports bass and panfish. Part of the route occupies old overflow channels of the Willamette. Much of the Pudding's water comes from Butte Creek and its showy tributary, Silver Creek, which has the most extraordinary suite of waterfalls concentrated on any one stream in Oregon.

 The Pudding can be seen from the 99E bridge in Aurora (no access). A steep approach is possible west of Canby; from 99E turn west on Barlow Road, go left on First, and continue on S Anderson Road to its end.

The big draw here is Oregon's second-largest state park—Silver Falls; from Salem take Hwy 22 east 5 miles, turn left on 214, go 16 miles, enter the park, follow signs to South Falls, and walk on the 25-mile network of trails to 10 major falls (5 others lie off-trail). The collection is an eyeful all year but spellbinding in spring runoff.

 The lower Pudding is reportedly swift-current Class 1 canoeing, with access west of Canby (see above). Beware of brush.

North Fork Silver Creek and Lower North Fork Falls

Tualatin River at Tualatin National Wildlife Refuge

TUALATIN RIVER

Length: 84 miles
Average flow: 1,463 cfs
Watershed: 705 square miles

Northernmost sizable tributary on the Willamette's west side, and second-largest stream draining the east slope of Oregon's Coast Range, the Tualatin drifts through farms and suburbs that house half a million people with associated runoff, sewer overflows, and exotic species. Sewage effluent constitutes half the summer flow. Fortunately, Tualatin Riverkeeper and Tualatin Watershed Council work for reclamation. Striving to meet temperature standards that require a reduction from 72 to 62 degrees F, local groups have planted 1.6 million trees since 2004. Some lower river floodplains lie in the Tualatin National Wildlife Refuge—under expansion for waterfowl.

Many small municipal parks offer access to the stream and tributaries; see *Exploring the Tualatin River Basin*. Mostly wetlands, the Wildlife Refuge has a trail to a river viewpoint that looks primeval considering the suburban surroundings; from 99W north of Sherwood turn west at the Refuge sign. My favorite streamfront here is above Tualatin Community Park; from 99W turn east toward Tualatin on 124th Avenue, go left on Tualatin Road, and left at the park sign. From there a wooded trail leads upstream a mile, crosses to Cook Park, and continues on the north side—perhaps the Portland area's finest urban waterfront trail.

For Brown's Ferry Park, take I-5 exit 289, go east on SW Nyberg Street, soon left on Nyberg Lane, and left into the park. Flatwater here backs up from the Lake Oswego diversion weir—hazardous to unwary paddlers 4 miles below.

Willamette Park and beautifully shaded rapids lie at the Tualatin's mouth; from I-205 take exit 6, go south on 10th Street, right on Willamette Falls Drive, and left on 12th.

Tualatin Riverkeeper reports that the lower 40 miles are generally canoeable, with adequate flows sometimes well into summer. Above the mouth 3.5 miles, a weir blocks passage; with caution, run or portage right. Below, secluded Class 2+ rapids reach the Willamette. See *Paddler's Access Guide to the Lower Tualatin River*.

CLACKAMAS RIVER

| Length: 84 miles |
| Average flow: 2,925 cfs |
| Watershed: 942 square miles |

Northernmost Cascade Mountain tributary to the Willamette, the Clackamas flows crystalline and joins the Willamette near tide-line. Elegant upper miles wind through canyons recovering from logging, and feature some of Oregon's most popular whitewater rafting plus riverfront trails. The middle reach is blocked by North Fork Dam, followed in 1 mile by Cazadero Dam, then River Mill Dam downstream of Estacada. Below, the lower Clackamas is free-flowing through private land with a series of parks—a river refuge at Portland's doorstep.

Before dams, this stream had one of Oregon's best runs of wild spring Chinook, now nearly extinct. Today's hatchery-based spring Chinook and summer steelhead rate among the top producers in the Columbia basin. Coho here may be the Willamette watershed's last viable native population, benefiting from headwater roadless areas but diminished by hatcheries, hydropower dams, logging, development, and farming. The Clackamas also supports winter steelhead and a few fall Chinook. Watershed restoration led to the successful restocking of bull trout after a 50-year absence.

Wild and Scenic River designation protects the uppermost 47 miles to Big Cliff. The river below provides water for several hundred thousand

Clackamas River above Collawash confluence

people and also hydroelectric power. With mitigation money from the dams, the Clackamas River Basin Council strove to reduce water temperatures in the lower 30 miles by planting 300,000 trees. Meanwhile, proposals to divert another 150 cfs for city supplies could endanger fish that need at least 650 cfs in the river.

Lower Clackamas tributary Eagle Creek flows as a designated Wild and Scenic River from the Salmon-Huckleberry Wilderness.

 The Clackamas has a fine network of riverfront parks that offer access, camping, and hiking. To see the mouth, go to Clackamette Park, just north of I-205 on 99E. A short walk under the bridge takes you to a gravel bar and the river's final current above tidewater. A mile upstream, Cross Park has bank-top paths on the north side; from Gladstone take East Arlington Street, right on Harvard, and left on Clackamas Boulevard.

The lower Clackamas' chain of parks is excellent; for Carver County Park, take I-205, go east on Hwy 224 for 4.3 miles, and turn right on Springwater Road (fee). Next upstream is Barton County Park; go east from I-205 on 224 for 9.6 miles and turn right. Bonnie Lure State Park is 2 miles farther on 224 and to the right. Milo McIver State Park (fee) lies west of Estacada, from I-205 go 18 miles on 224, then right on 211 and right on Springwater Road.

To reach the upper Clackamas, drive to Estacada and continue on Hwy 224. Clackamas River Trail leads to old-growth forest and the 20-foot-wide effervescing Clackamas Narrows; take 224 beyond Estacada 15 miles, turn right at Fish Creek Road to the trailhead, and walk upstream 8 miles, emerging at Indian Henry Trailhead off 224. Powerlines mar the scenery midway, but river views are good; a short spur overlooks 100-foot Pup Creek Falls.

Even better, a short streamfront trail with superb old-growth lies 4 miles upriver from Indian Henry. It wends 4 miles from Rainbow Campground (not on the Clackamas, but tributary Oak Grove Fork) upstream to Riverside Campground. The Collawash confluence comes 1 mile farther up the road, and beyond, Hwy 224 becomes FR 46 and reaches nearly to the river's source with camping, walking, and biking opportunities.

To reach lower tributary Eagle Creek, take 224 west from I-205 for 14 miles, turn left on Wildcat Mountain Road, right on Eagle Fern Road to Eagle Fern Park and continue upstream on George Road to the Salmon-Huckleberry Wilderness Trailhead.

One of Oregon's top salmon/steelhead fisheries, the Clackamas draws anglers for spring Chinook May–June. Winter steelhead run December–April; summer steelhead April–October. Most are hatchery fish; a wild winter run is hopefully recovering. Coho run September–October, mostly from an Eagle Creek hatchery; the fish congregate near the mouth of Eagle Creek in Bonnie Lure State Park. Three steelhead runs overlap for year-round fishing. Rainbow and cutthroat trout are also caught, but the river is closed to all fishing above North Fork Dam. Anglers cast from banks at public parks, especially Milo McIver. Drift boats float from Barton Park to the mouth.

Upper reaches offer Class 4 whitewater. Then from Three Lynx Power Station to North Fork Reservoir, 13 miles of rollicking Class 2–4 are runnable through summer. Varying challenges are seen from the road and selectable from different access points. Large waves appear 4 miles above North Fork Reservoir, followed by Bob's Hole—once the ultimate play-spot for kayakers. Owing to bedload movement it has shrunk but remains good at medium volume, 1,700–2,300 cfs. Below, Class 2+ at lower levels continues to North Fork Reservoir. Rafts scrape below 900 cfs, but the Clackamas is runnable to 500.

The lower river's easier rapids tour a series of parks, a cottonwood corridor, and some development—a fine float at the city's edge and good introduction to rivers for boaters, anglers, and swimmers. Below Estacada, Milo McIver State Park's ramp begins an 8-mile Class 2 reach, with a 2+ drop at the top, ending at Barton County Park. Barton down to Carver is 6 miles of Class 2; takeout is off 224 upstream from Carver Bridge (bikers beware of traffic and no shoulders; commercial shuttles are available). A final 8 miles of mostly Class 1+ ends at Clackamette Park. To drive to the takeout from Carver, cross to the south side of the bridge, turn right on Clackamas River Road, at the Washington Street/Hwy 213 intersection turn left, in 1 mile turn right, cross the tracks, and go right on McLoughlin Boulevard. Milo McIver to the Willamette makes a 22-mile Class 2 trip, often running year-round, with pushy flows possible through July.

COLLAWASH RIVER

Chief Clackamas tributary, this transparently clear stream flows north from Bull of the Woods Wilderness with sharp whitewater drops beneath craggy cliffs.

Length: 13 miles, 23 with Elk Lake Creek
Average flow: 654 cfs
Watershed: 152 square miles

Collawash River 3 miles above its confluence with the Clackamas

Hot Springs Fork Collawash River and Pegleg Falls

 From FR 46 on the Clackamas at Two Rivers picnic area take FR 63 south up the Collawash. For a striking canyon view, pull off 4.6 miles up. Near here FR 70 splits right and climbs Hot Springs Fork, with a massive logjam in 0.5 miles and Pegleg Falls in 6 miles. Just beyond, a trail ascends Hot Springs Fork 1.5 miles to the popular Bagby Hot Springs (fee), then onward 6 more wilderness miles.

FR 63 continues up the Collawash but leaves the riverfront to climb high until FR 6680 forks right and later ends at Elk Lake Creek, where an 8-mile trail ascends to the river's source.

Kayakers paddle a demanding Class 5 springtime run on the Collawash. Below, a 3-mile Class 3+ reach continues from Fan Creek Campground to the mouth at Two Rivers picnic area.

Roaring River upstream from the Clackamas confluence

ROARING RIVER

The utterly wild, 14-mile Roaring River enters the Clackamas 17 miles upstream of Estacada. Beginning in a U-shaped

Length: 14 miles
Average flow: 170 cfs
Watershed: 43 square miles

glacial valley, the small stream becomes a V-profiled, water-carved canyon replete with old-growth conifers. Wild coho, Chinook, steelhead, rainbow, and cutthroat spawn in this roadless stream; its entire length is a

 National Wild and Scenic River.

The stream can be seen from a short path above Hwy 224 at Roaring River Campground.

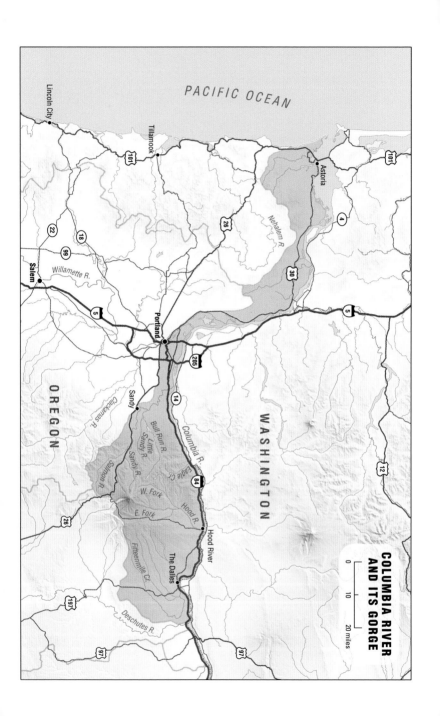

PACIFIC OCEAN

Lincoln City

Tillamook

Astoria

Salem

Willamette R.

Nehalem R.

Portland

OREGON

WASHINGTON

Clackamas R.

Sandy

Bull Run R.

Little Sandy R.

Sandy R.

Salmon R.

Eagle Cr.

W. Fork

E. Fork

Columbia R.

Hood R.

Hood River

Fifteenmile Cr.

The Dalles

Deschutes R.

COLUMBIA RIVER
AND ITS GORGE

0   10   20 miles

CHAPTER 8

THE COLUMBIA AND ITS GORGE

Principal artery of the Northwest, the Columbia already ranks as the nation's sixth-largest river when it enters the country from Canada. Then it grows larger, crossing eastern Washington and defining the border with Oregon. By the time the Columbia empties into the Pacific it carries over half of Oregon's runoff and ranks as America's fourth-largest river; only the Mississippi (593,000 cfs), St. Lawrence (348,000), and Ohio (281,000) are greater.

Now a chain of reservoirs, the Columbia has been dammed continuously through Oregon down to tide-line. In the United States, only 52 miles of the main stem remain free-flowing—all in Washington. Most of the Canadian mileage is dammed as well.

The Columbia Gorge is a pleasure year-round where tributary waterfalls—elegant in summer and autumn—become utterly spectacular, winter through spring. Rivers entering the Columbia run full and powerfully through winter while salmon migrate, and the Sandy and Hood are sustained summer-long by Mount Hood's snow and glaciers.

COLUMBIA RIVER

Length: 1,257 miles, 307 in OR
Average flow: 265,000 cfs
Watershed: 260,000 square miles

The Columbia separates Oregon and Washington for nearly three-quarters of the state's width—from north of Pendleton to the Pacific. It drains seven states and one Canadian province. After crossing eastern Oregon's drylands, the river enters America's largest gorge. The Hood River joins near the eastern end of this reach with the Sandy marking the western end. Tidal influence extends 146 miles to Bonneville Dam—farther than any other U.S. river. The massive tidal flow widens even more when it picks up the Willamette—second-largest tributary (next to the Snake, which enters in Washington). The lower river then continues 100 miles through a low, wide gap in the Coast Range, finally passing under Astoria Bridge and meeting the Pacific, where vicissitudes of this third-most perilous river-bar on earth have sunk 2,000 vessels.

NATURAL HISTORY

The Columbia predated the rising of the Cascade Range. Lava and volcanic rock from 11,239-foot Mount Hood, immediately south of the river, and 12,307-foot Mount Adams, to the north, coalesced at the river's course, but as the mountains rose the waterway continued to cut downward, maintaining its path though not without rapids at the Cascades, where Bonneville Dam is sited, and Celilo Falls, now buried in the impoundment behind The Dalles Dam. Not just water, but also basalt flowed down the gorge from sources eastward; some deposits measure hundreds of feet thick and, incredibly, 200 miles long. The river subsequently eroded through and around these basalts; some form resistant strata of today's tributary waterfalls.

For 72 miles the Gorge extends westward from the Deschutes River nearly to Portland and measures several miles across and several thousand feet deep. Here are the greatest concentration of waterfalls in America, exceeding even the numbers in California's Yosemite Valley. Older rocks on Washington's side are more easily eroded; tributaries there drop steeply but lack the vertical leaps seen at 77 waterfalls on the Oregon side, 11 plunging more than 100 feet.

The Missoula (Bretz) Floods carved the Gorge further. Ice-age glacial dams had serially formed on Montana's Clark Fork River, backing up that Columbia tributary with flatwater as big as Lake Ontario. When the dams melted enough to break, they released walls of floodwater 2,000 feet high, unimaginably carrying 400 times the average flow of the Mississippi. The onslaught scattered alluvial gravels onto mountainsides, denuded the Gorge, and undercut basalt cliffs. The cataclysmic floods occurred 50 to 100 times between 18,000 and 12,000 years ago, repeatedly burying today's Portland 400 feet deep.

With an extreme range of climate, the Columbia enters Oregon well east of the Cascade Range through basaltic plains rendered semi-arid by the rain shadow of high mountains. In contrast, the Gorge's western end gets 150 inches of rain a year nourishing tapestries of conifers, mosses, and lichens, springflows bubbling everywhere. Owing to its physical connection between the coast and the interior desert along with its topographic relief and variable climate, the Gorge is home to 800 plant species—one-fourth Oregon's total. *Freshwater Ecoregions of North America* recognized the middle and lower Columbia among the West's most important regions for conservation of aquatic biodiversity.

In addition to Chinook salmon migrations—greatest in the world a century and a half ago—the Columbia still supports important runs of sockeye salmon and steelhead. Once common through much of the river, white and green sturgeon now appear mainly in the tidal reach. Diminished by dams, other populations of this largest North American fish dwindled or went extinct.

Matching the river's scale, early-summer flooding was once a regular occurrence. Situated between the river and Columbia Slough, Vanport—second-largest Oregon city at the time—was obliterated by high water in 1948. The lowlands it occupied north of Portland have been spared ever since Canadian dams were built (with U.S. money) in the 1960s, and new urbanization now covers floodplains that are "protected" by flood control provisions of the international treaty authorizing the dams. That agreement expires in 2024 and must be renegotiated.

Columbia River from Crown Point east of Portland

Even with channelization, levees, and riprap diminishing the lower river, the flow nourishes marshes and forested swamps where brackish water extends 46 miles inland. Dramatic effects of the river don't stop at its mouth but continue along the coast and deep into sea. Far north and south, river-delivered sand creates spits and beaches. And the Columbia's freshwater plume can be detected 200 miles out.

CONSERVATION

Bonneville, The Dalles, John Day, and McNary Dams in Oregon's portion of the Columbia inundate the river that carried Lewis and Clark on their epic journey west. Fourteen main-stem dams up through British Columbia were erected for hydroelectric power, and four dams on the adjoining lower Snake River were built for barging commodities such as wheat, logs, and wood chips from Lewiston, Idaho—a "seaport" 464 miles from the ocean, courtesy of the Army Corps of Engineers. The hydropower and barging continue to be heavily subsidized, with many of the commodities bound for Asia. Meanwhile the unexpected problems of damming the river were formidable, and the sacrificed assets were great.

The finest array of salmon on earth has become a casualty in the river's transformation from wilderness to workhorse. Pre-dam runs of 16 million or more fish have been reduced to 2 million or less—most from hatcheries rather than wild stocks. Fish ladders get many salmon and steelhead past the dams, but casualties remain high, and smolts migrating downstream suffer heavy losses even after decades of remediation and a controversial Army Corps practice of trapping and loading the young fish onto barges, then motoring them through the reservoirs to tidewater where they are dumped out (see Chapter 13).

Columbia River, The Dalles Dam in center, John Day Dam in background

The dams are the major problem but not the only one affecting Columbia fish and wildlife. The estuary once provided abundant wildlife habitat and rearing areas for salmon and other fish; only 23 percent of original wetlands remain. Being the great conduit of water, the Columbia is also the accumulator of pollution, and the Hanford Nuclear Reservation in Washington puts this river into a class by itself. There, 60 percent of the nation's potent nuclear waste is stored, including great quantities in deteriorating tanks with leaks that have infiltrated groundwater across 80 square miles, according to the Department of Energy in 2005. Radioactive isotopes seep through groundwater and into the stream, which Northwest Environmental Advocates called "the most radioactive river in the world." Some cleanup has occurred but other advances have been mired for decades in studies and exorbitant costs. Additional toxins come from industry and agriculture.

On another front of environmental protection, the Columbia River Gorge National Scenic Area was established in 1986 from the Deschutes River down to the Sandy with intent to safeguard the remaining open space that gives the Gorge its unique beauty. But an original plan for National Park Service oversight of the private-public mix of properties was dropped in favor of a bi-state commission with Forest Service administration. Some key areas have been protected but compromises have allowed hundreds of new homes to be built. These and other conservation issues of the Columbia are as complex as the river itself.

Hundreds of access points appear along the river's course, and major highways parallel north and south shores. A highlight in eastern Oregon, the Umatilla National Wildlife Refuge northwest of Pendleton attracts vast flocks of waterfowl during the spring and fall migration seasons.

The four dams have visitor centers with facilities for watching the much-diminished runs of salmon, steelhead, and other fish as they negotiate the concrete stair-steps of fish ladders. Nearest Portland, Bonneville offers extensive visitor facilities/tours.

One can get a hint of the mind-boggling power that the now-harnessed river once had by seeing the turbulence released on the north sides of The Dalles and John Day Dams. Topping a eulogy of places lost to the reservoirs, Celilo Falls—a dramatic cataract where Indians of many nations came to fish and trade—can only be imagined beneath today's flatwater at Celilo Park, 11 miles east of The Dalles off I-84.

Also at the eastern end of the Gorge, tributary Fifteenmile Creek enters the Columbia just below The Dalles Dam after its 54-mile sojourn from the Cascades' northeastern limits. Here are the most-inland winter-run steelhead. Lower reaches are diverted for agriculture, but 11 miles of upper Fifteenmile are a National Wild and Scenic River. From Hood River, drive south on Hwy 35, take FR 44 east, go right on FR 4420, which turns into 2730, and continue to Fifteenmile Forest Camp. A trail runs east, and after 4 miles follows the creek for a few miles.

Farther west, the city of Hood River is terraced into slopes above the Bonneville pool, now a world-center of windsurfing owing to constant gales funneling through the Gorge. Westward to the Sandy River, dozens of trails lead to the Columbia's tributary waterfalls.

Toward the Portland end of the Gorge, at I-84 exit 40 (Bonneville), a 1-mile trail up Tanner Creek leads to elegant Wahclella Falls. Westward on Old Columbia Highway another 3 miles, McCord Creek drops over Elowah Falls. Another few miles west, Horsetail Creek sprays over its 176-foot drop. Just beyond, Oneonta Gorge is split between basalt walls 200 feet high. Visit in summer to wade up the creek. Oneonta's elegant Triple Falls can be reached by hiking 2 miles from the Horsetail parking lot to the east. Each of these stops—and more—seem more beautiful than the last.

Mobbed on weekends, the Gorge's big attraction is Multnomah Falls; two pitches drop some 611 feet (measurements vary), considered the second-tallest perennially flowing waterfall in the United States. Take I-84 exit 31, 14 miles east of Troutdale. You can climb the trail up Multnomah Creek, jog west, and descend an adjacent stream while passing 242-foot Wahkeena Falls. Closest to Portland, Latourell Falls drops 249 feet; take I-84 exit 28, go west on Old Columbia River Highway 3 miles, park, and stroll to Latourell or enjoy a 2.4-mile loop. Throughout the Gorge beware of epidemic car break-ins, and on weekends go early for parking.

West of the Gorge, the Columbia's once-spacious cottonwood floodplain past Portland is constrained by levees, though forests persist on islands. Side channels harbor houseboats and marinas. Chinook Landing Metro Park lies along Marine Drive near Troutdale (fee). The immensity of this broad waterway can be realized by walking or biking on a paved levee-top trail reached east of I-205 at the end of 138th Street. The mouth of the Willamette can be visited in Kelley Point Park; take I-5 north to exit 307 and go west 5 miles on Marine Drive.

The 18-mile Columbia Slough parallels the river and slants west through Portland's north edge; rich wetlands here were reduced to 1 percent their historic acreage, though some good bird habitat remains. Fouled by sewage in stormwater runoff, this was one of the state's most polluted waterways, but is now being upgraded with better stormwater catchment.

West of Portland the widening river's frontage of floodplain forest, wetlands, and dairy farms is mixed with industry at a multinational scale: grain silos, log-loading yards, mountains of wood chips bound for Asia, and anchored freighters as long as 4 city blocks. Northwest of Portland 26 miles, Hwy 30 leads to the Helena boat ramp. In another 19 miles, at the town of Rainier, conifer-clad hills recline to a dock harboring tugboats. In spite of the booming export of commodities—perhaps because of it—the Columbia's shipping towns reflect economic recession with closed mills, vacant shops, and deferred maintenance.

Westport Ferry, 24 miles west of Rainier, offers an easy way to get close to the lower Columbia; for $1 passengers cross to Puget Island hourly.

South of Astoria, the short Lewis and Clark River is beautifully wooded in upper reaches. Near the Columbia mouth, historic Astoria offers urban amenities, and from there you can drive across the 4-mile 101 bridge to Washington to grasp the scale of this tidal giant.

If you want a more extreme sense of the river's continental flush to sea, go for a rocky walk on the south jetty (low tide only!); from Astoria take Hwy 101 south 5 miles, turn right on Ridge Road to Fort Stevens, and walk across the Clatsop Spit to the jetty—all large rocks. On the Washington side, a tamer beach at Fort Canby State Park reaches the ends of the earth with runoff that has come from as far as Yellowstone and the Canadian Rockies.

Astoria Bridge and Columbia River

Fishing in the Columbia is mostly from motorboats. Fall Chinook peak mid-August–September near the mouth. Sturgeon run April–October. Youngs Bay, west of Astoria, offers comparatively protected waters fed by the tidal Youngs River, 27 miles long, fished for steelhead and Chinook. Through Portland and up to Bonneville Dam, spring Chinook peak in March; fall Chinook August–September; steelhead May–August. Public access to shoreline angling lies just below Bonneville Dam.

 Taking precautions for wind, tides, and deceptively powerful currents, it's possible to paddle into the monumental push of this river (sea kayaks are often preferred, though some canoeists paddle here when conditions are suitable). A Lower Columbia Water Trail has been established with access sites listed (www.columbiawatertrail.org). For big-river flavor that's relatively protected (but still exposed), go to Aldrich Point; 18 miles east of Astoria turn north on Ziak-Gnat Creek Lane, go 1 mile, turn right on Aldrich Point Road, and curve 4 miles to a weathered launch. Anglers and duck hunters here use motorboats. Low brushy islands screen passages from the main flow, though the side channels alone dwarf any other Oregon waterway. Strong currents, winds, and tides that come 1 hour later than in Astoria are all consequential. Cautiously paddle upriver and back down.

Farther west, the Nature Conservancy's Blind Slough Preserve, 15 miles east of Astoria and north of Knappa Junction, is the best-preserved Sitka spruce swamp on the West Coast. Paddle its backwater sloughs in May, June, or September (closed for bald eagle fledging February–March and July–August).

HOOD RIVER

This river and its forks gather runoff from the north and east flanks of Mount Hood and join the Columbia in

Length: 12 miles, 44 with EF
Average flow: 1,003 cfs
Watershed: 1,048 square miles

eastern reaches of the Gorge at the beautifully sited town of Hood River. Drawing from ice-scoured cirques, the quintessential glacial stream carries snowmelt extending through summer. Its roily waters are milky with rock dust from glacial-rock abrasion, and upper reaches braid and aggrade with a surplus of rounded cobbles tumbled by ice and water. Because of its northern aspect and glaciers, the river holds special importance in our age of global warming as other streams lose their ability to accommodate cold-water fish such as steelhead.

The short main stem forms at the East/West Fork confluence near Dee and runs through a shallow incised gorge among fruit orchards, forests, and pastoral fringes of Hood River. After blocking the flow for a century, Powerdale Dam, 4 miles above the mouth, was removed in 2010. This improved the channel for steelhead and opened an excellent whitewater run from Tucker Park down. The Columbia Land Trust hopes to acquire 3 miles of riverfront for protection below the former dam site.

Confluence of West Fork Hood River (left) and East Fork Hood River (right)

 Though it passes through a settled landscape, there are few opportunities to see the gorge-entrenched main stem of the Hood River. For the splendid confluence of the East and West Forks, walk the Punchbowl Falls Trail; from I-84 take Hwy 35 south 5 miles, turn west toward Lost Lake, cross the East Fork at Dee, turn right on Punchbowl Road, and park on the right before the West Fork bridge. The path leads north to overlook the falls and the lower West Fork, then continues downstream to the confluence.

The main stem can be reached at Tucker Bridge: from the south side of the town of Hood River take Tucker Road south, which turns into Dee Highway and crosses Hood River, where a path drops to the water. For better access, continue south about 1 mile to Tucker Park.

To reach the river near the Columbia, drive to the east end of Hood River, and just before the bridge to White Salmon take Hwy 30 west and immediately turn south on Dock Road. Or park in town and walk up the river's west side on railroad tracks, which cross and continue upstream.

 A good run of summer steelhead appear April–July; the winter run arrives February–May. Anglers use a county park on the east side at the mouth, or walk the tracks upstream, or go to Tucker Park. Spring Chinook were introduced here in 1990; returns are weak.

From Tucker Bridge, Class 2–3 water offers continuous steep gradient, with Class 3+ at the former Powerdale Dam site. Upstream from the bridge, Class 4 rapids are run by putting in at Tucker Park.

EAST FORK HOOD RIVER

Length: 31 miles
Average flow: 198 cfs
Watershed: 113 square miles

Coalescing from cobblestone braids on the flanks of Mount Hood, silty water of the East Fork enters the timber zone and charges north toward orchard country and the West Fork confluence.

The smaller Middle Fork Hood River carries runoff from Eliot Glacier— Oregon's largest. It flows past the stark rockiness of Mount Hood National Forest's Lava Beds Geological Area, but I've found few views of this river other than from the bridge on Red Hills Drive west of Parkdale. The Middle Fork enters the East Fork 3 miles above the East/West Fork confluence.

 To see the upper East Fork Hood, Sahale Falls makes a good start; from the Hwy 26/35 intersection south of Mount Hood take 35 east 8 miles to Mount Hood Meadows Ski satellite area, turn northwest on the old highway, and go 2 miles to the gated bridge at the 100-foot falls.

Heading north on Hwy 35, which parallels the East Fork, Nottingham Campground appears before the FR 44 turnoff. Here the daily cycle of high-and-low water—governed by mid-day melting of snow—is amply evident. A dead forest just above shows the effects of massive silt settlement in an aggrading riverbed—common among glacial streams. Fallen logs riddle the extremely active channel.

Farther downstream, Sherwood Campground lies 1 mile north of the FR 41 turnoff. A footbridge crosses the East Fork to trails leading upriver and down. Going up takes you through 4 miles of old-growth, views of rapids, and paths to the water. After the 1964 flood, the Forest Service removed fallen logs, not realizing the importance of trees to stream

East Fork Hood River at Routson County Park

morphology and ecology. Better informed in 1998, the agency placed 800 logs back into the East Fork, and increased channel complexity and habitat improvement can now be seen. The downriver trail soon leaves the East Fork and climbs to Tamanawas Falls on Cold Spring Creek.

Below Sherwood and 4 miles above Hwy 35's Parkdale turnoff, Routson County Park lies east of the road, with a trail to the boulder riverbed.

 Paddling the upper East Fork is nettlesome even for experts—continuous Class 4–5 in springtime with extreme log hazards from Polallie Creek picnic area (2 miles north of the FR 44/ Hwy 35 intersection) to the Hwy 35 bridge. To access the main stem, a few boaters manage a steep put-in at Dee below a parking lot on the west side, and paddle the river's last, Class 4 mile, then proceed down the main stem's Class 4 to Tucker Bridge.

WEST FORK HOOD RIVER

Length: 15 miles
Average flow: 549 cfs
Watershed: 102 square miles

This western Mount Hood basin has less glacier-effect than does the East Fork, and flows north, picking up the clear waters of Lake Branch Hood River. The West Fork basin has been heavily clearcut.

 The tiny source of Lake Branch can be seen at the outlet of an Oregon scenic icon, Lost Lake; from I-84 go south on Hwy 35 for 5 miles, turn west toward Odell and Lost Lake, cross the East Fork at Dee, turn left, and continue 15 miles. The road bridges the West Fork 4 miles southwest of Dee and crosses Lake Branch 1 mile farther. The slightly dammed Lake Branch outlet is near the Lost Lake lodge.

The best view of the West Fork is near its mouth; going west at Dee, cross the East Fork, turn right, and go 1 mile to my favorite bridge-view of any river in Oregon: cliffs of layered black basalt step-down to foaming water. Just south, park at a pullout and walk the trail east to the overlook of Punchbowl Falls, dominated by its concrete fish ladder. The Western Rivers Conservancy has acquired this site for protection.

 The West Fork's Class 4+ run in springtime is a local classic with two beautiful basalt gorges and a fish-ladder portage. Put in on Lost Lake Road at the Lake Branch Bridge near the Lake Branch/West Fork confluence; take out on the right above Punchbowl Falls with a steep climb.

EAGLE CREEK

Length: 26 miles
Average flow: 339 cfs
Watershed: 89 square miles

Among Oregon's many Eagle Creeks, this is the largest stream within the heart of the Columbia Gorge. Famous for seven waterfalls, it flows 10 miles through the Columbia Wilderness.

East of Bonneville take I-84 exit 41, go south to the trailhead, and hike up the narrow rainforest canyon. At 6 miles, the path was blasted through a tunnel behind a 120-foot waterfall. On

Eagle Creek below its East Fork, Columbia River Gorge

weekends people teem here to the most scenic streamfront hike in the Portland region. At the lower end watch for Chinook in autumn.

At the watershed rim, the Pacific Crest Trail links south to Mount Hood. The splendid 4-day backpack from snowfields near Timberline Lodge down to the Columbia via Eagle Creek is the ultimate highcountry-to-nearly-sea-level hike in America.

SANDY RIVER

The Sandy carries snowmelt of Oregon's highest peak—Mount Hood—to the largest freshwater conduit of the West

Length: 57 miles
Average flow: 2,278 cfs
Watershed: 501 square miles

Coast—the Columbia. With its tributaries the Sandy sweeps prodigious runoff from the entire southwestern half of the mountain—the wettest half owing to orographic effect here and rain shadow on the opposite side.

The river courses through lush forests, cuts multiple mossy gorges, and winds out east of Portland at Troutdale. The 7,300-foot drop is the greatest free-flowing vertical descent of any river in Oregon. It enters the Columbia below Bonneville Dam, providing the longest dam-free route for salmon and steelhead ascending the Oregon side of the great river. Here are some of the state's top-producing runs of winter and summer steelhead, plus spring Chinook, fall coho, cutthroat, and trout in headwaters. Separate upper and lower sections totaling 25 miles are in the National Wild and Scenic Rivers system. The mid-Sandy was blocked by 50-foot Marmot Dam, which outlived its effectiveness for hydropower and was blasted away in 2007—one of the most significant dam removals nationwide. At WaterWatch's urging, 600 cfs were reinstated as instream flow.

Major tributaries include Bull Run River, north of the Sandy, dammed twice for Portland's water supply. To see it, take Ten Eyck Road from the town of Sandy and bear right on Bull Run Road. But to protect water quality, the basin is closed to public use. Little Sandy River also drains mountains northwest of Hood and joins Bull Run River. The only dam on it was removed in 2008. Another Sandy tributary, Zigzag River drops from the south side of Mount Hood; see its glacial-cobble course north of Zigzag on Lolo Pass Road.

 To hike along the upper Sandy, take Hwy 26 from Portland east to Zigzag, turn north on Lolo Pass Road, go 4 miles, right on FR 1825, plus 3 miles to the trailhead. This is the best trail along a glacial river in Oregon. The Sandy cuts through volcanic and glacial debris into its formerly (and repeatedly) aggraded floodplain. After crossing the footbridge, an off-trail scramble upstream is worth the view to Mount Hood's ethereal rise in the background. A side trail leads to the exquisite Ramona Falls (6 miles from the road) with distinctive honeycomb pillars of rock.

For hiking and fishing on a mature middle Sandy, take Hwy 26 to Sandy, turn north on Ten Eyck Road, in 1 mile go left on Fish Hatchery Road, and from the hatchery walk 1 mile to riverfront cobble bars.

Dodge Park lies downstream; take Hwy 26 to the east side of Gresham, turn left on Palmquist Road, right on SW Orient Drive for 2 miles, left on SE Dodge Park Boulevard for 4.8 miles, right on SE Lusted Road, and cross the river (fee). Farther down, Oxbow Park's 1,200 acres offer access and bank fishing; from the I-84 Troutdale exit pass the truck stop and turn right on 257th Street, go 3 miles, left on Division Street (becomes Oxbow Parkway), and follow signs (fee). In autumn, Chinook might be seen from Bluff Trail. Next downstream, Dabney State Park is 3 miles south of I-84 exit 18; follow Crown Point Highway south.

Upper Sandy River and Mount Hood

Sandy River Gorge and Boulder Drop Rapid

Lewis and Clark State Park has the Sandy's last boat ramp before the Columbia; take I-84 exit 18 and go south. To reach the Sandy's swampy mouth, use exit 18, turn north to Sandy River Delta Park, and hike 1.5 miles to the riparian forest framing a view of the Columbia.

 In this excellent salmon/steelhead stream, spring Chinook peak late-April–May, with fall Chinook August–September, both fished from Oxbow Park down. Hatchery steelhead peak December–January; wild fish run January–February in middle reaches near Sandy. Parks provide bank fishing; drift boats are used in lower sections.

 Guidebooks report a Class 3+ paddle of 7 miles from Zigzag to Marmot Bridge (springtime), but both the put-in on Lolo Pass Road north of Zigzag and takeout off Sleepy Hollow Road at Marmot Bridge lack parking. Access 6 miles farther at the former Marmot Dam is being developed. Below there, challenging Class 4 rapids of the Sandy River Gorge, with portage and log hazards, follow for 7 miles to Revenue Bridge on Ten Eyck Road north of Sandy. But the steep takeout path on river-left lacks parking or even drop-off space.

Easing up, 5 miles of Class 2–3 extend from Revenue Bridge to Dodge Park. A good takeout there makes possible a challenging 12-mile run from the Marmot Dam site. More popular, 8 miles of scenic Class 2 with one Class 3 continue from Dodge to Oxbow. Flowing year-round, Oxbow to Lewis and Clark Park is Class 1+ for 8 miles.

SALMON RIVER

Salmon River headwaters gather on the slopes of Mount Hood between the upper Zigzag and White Rivers. Then this gem of Oregon's Cascades plunges 8 miles through Salmon-Huckleberry

Length: 35 miles
Average flow: 527 cfs
Watershed: 115 square miles

Salmon River above the Salmon River Road trailhead

Wilderness to a bridge near the dead-end of Salmon River Road. Below, another 10 miles continue to the Sandy confluence, 4 miles west of Zigzag. Chinook, coho, and steelhead spawn in excellent habitat below six mid-river waterfalls; resident cutthroat thrive above.

The South Fork Salmon is a road- and trail-free tributary joining the main stem just past the dead-end of Salmon River Road.

 See the lower end of this superb river at BLM's Wildwood recreation site (fee); from Zigzag take Hwy 26 west 2 miles and walk the 1-mile interpretive trail.

For one of the finest riverfront trails anywhere, take 26 to Zigzag, turn south on Salmon River Road, drive 4 miles to Green Canyon Campground, then 1 mile farther to trailheads at the bridge. The path downstream passes through old-growth for 3 miles to a lower trailhead on the road 2.7 miles south of Zigzag. From the bridge, the trail also leads upstream through 2 miles of excellent ancient forest before climbing high on canyon slopes that lack river views. Enticing waterfalls shown on maps are inaccessible except by extreme scrambles.

Salmon River headwaters can be seen just southeast of Timberline Lodge.

 A challenging Class 2–3+ paddle for 10 miles on the lower Salmon offers continuous rapids, often runnable into early summer past old-growth forest and some cabins. Among steep rocky drops, logs are a hazard; expect one or more portages. Put in at the Salmon River Bridge 5 miles south of Hwy 26. Or, to miss some (not all) Class 3 rapids, tackle the 300-yard carry down from the lower trailhead (2.7 miles south of Zigzag). A weir below Wildwood pedestrian bridge is easily portaged. Take out at the Hwy 26 bridge 4 miles west of Zigzag; drive just west of the bridge, turn south, then immediately left, and park at the bike trail. I found low but mostly runnable flow when the Sandy at Marmot ran 1,500 cfs.

CHAPTER 9

DESCHUTES

Runoff from the eastern slope of the Cascades drops to tributaries of the Deschutes River—world-renowned among trout anglers, hotspot for whitewater rafting, and lifeline of desert canyons linking glaciated mountains to the Columbia. In the rain shadow of high peaks, streams are less robust than those west of the Cascades, but owing to the volcanic landscape, snowmelt sinks underground and seeps back as steady spring-flows. Thus, the Metolius has one of the steadiest natural hydrographs known, and the lower Deschutes flows evenly as well. Good levels persist through the scorching summer and fall, providing cool relief for boaters and swimmers and excellent fishing year-round.

DESCHUTES RIVER

Length: 255 miles
Average flow: 5,827 cfs
Watershed: 9,934 square miles

The Deschutes is the state's ninth-largest river in volume, but discounting the Columbia and Snake, which originate elsewhere, it's by far the largest Oregon stream in the vast region east of the Cascades. Next to Hells Canyon of the Snake, it offers Oregon's premier big-water river trip with an exquisite 98 miles of constant current and many powerful rapids—some of the most popular

Deschutes River upstream of Bend at Dillon Falls

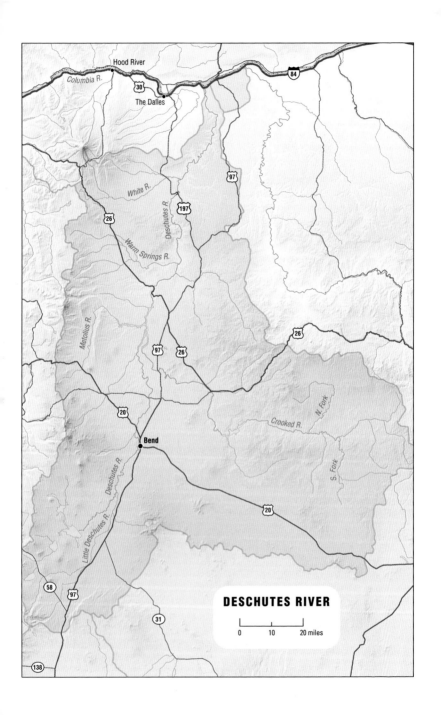

Hood River

Columbia R.

The Dalles

84

30

White R.

97

197

Deschutes R.

26

Warm Springs R.

Metolius R.

97

26

26

20

Crooked R.

N. Fork

Bend

Deschutes R.

S. Fork

20

Little Deschutes R.

58

97

31

DESCHUTES RIVER

0   10   20 miles

138

whitewater in the West. The river is also one of the better known trout fisheries in America.

Drawing most of its water from mountain springs, and regulated by upstream dams, the Deschutes crests in mid-summer—one of few major U.S. rivers outside Alaska's glacial arteries with such a delayed peak. It also claims one of the steadiest flows; the lower river tops out at only 1.7 times the low flow.

The 80-mile-long upper Deschutes begins in conifer forests, encounters two dams, and meanders lazily past ponderosa pine groves, wet meadows, and recreational subdivisions. Then, when you least expect it, the river plunges over jagged lava cataracts. It passes through the resort development of Sunriver and into Bend, where it's among the most used community rivers in the West with trails and bikeways, intense whitewater, placid interludes, and low dams above and below the city.

For the next 40 miles, the middle Deschutes pushes through dry canyons stepped with rapids and waterfalls. Round Butte Dam forms a large reservoir, followed by Pelton Reregulation Dam. Then the lower Deschutes runs 100 miles through basalt canyons a half-mile deep. Flatwater of The Dalles Dam on the Columbia backs into the Deschutes' lowest mile.

The river shares the distinctive geography of central Oregon with its sister stream, the John Day, but in marked contrasts. The Deschutes carries more water, is dammed, has ample summer flows, plunges through big rapids, and faces urbanizing pressures.

NATURAL HISTORY

The Deschutes is the archetypal river of volcanic landscapes, and dramatic bedrock of its canyon is more easily seen than on the Cascades forested west slope. In higher reaches, mixed conifers blanket the basin, followed by pines that once formed a magnificent savanna of large trees and bunchgrasses. Systematic harvest of the girthy ponderosas and suppression of ground fires resulted in thickets of small new trees that typify upper reaches today. Some road frontage has been thinned to simulate fire conditions of the past and support the native ecosystem—dependent on frequent lightning-fires at low intensities, which historically pruned brush but left the bare-trunked big pines standing.

Farther down, lava flows only 6,100 years ago filled the channel and, above Bend, created steep drops including Benham, Dillon, and Lava Island Falls. Lower reaches cut through linked canyons—some with basalt cliffs hundreds of feet high in colossal hexagonal pillars.

Cold steady flows in upper reaches support rainbow trout and kokanee; also introduced brown and brook trout. Bull trout survive in some tributaries. Rainbows on the lower river are a special strain, Deschutes redsides. Summer steelhead migrate up from the Columbia to Pelton Dam. Spring Chinook—threatened throughout the lower Columbia basin—still spawn in the lower Deschutes. Mountain whitefish, shorthead sculpin, longnose dace, largescale sucker, chiselmouth, and northern pikeminnow complete this well-rounded native fishes roster. *Freshwater*

Ecoregions of North America lists the Deschutes as important for biodiversity and as a center of mollusk endemism.

CONSERVATION

In an important but unfortunate chapter of river conservation history, the state of Oregon argued in the 1960s that the Deschutes' anadromous fish should be protected by halting the construction of Round Butte Dam, but Portland General Electric prevailed when the Supreme Court ruled that states lack authority to override the Federal Power Commission (now Federal Energy Regulatory Commission). The dam subsequently blocked hundreds of miles of salmon and steelhead habitat upstream. Turning the conservation corner, further threats from 16 new hydroelectric proposals were thwarted in 1988 when 173 miles in three sections were designated the Deschutes National Wild and Scenic River (unlike state action, this blocks FERC approvals). Today, some of the damage from Round Butte is being addressed; improved facilities for fish passage by trapping and trucking around the dam are being developed by PGE and the Warm Springs Tribes. Salmon and steelhead will reach higher spawning grounds in the Deschutes, Metolius, and Crooked Rivers, plus Whychus Creek.

Issues of flow are also important. Above Bend, the hydrograph has been turned upside down; Wickiup Dam releases more water in summer than would be natural and far less in winter. This enables irrigators below Bend to divert 98 percent of summertime runoff, cutting it to 30 cfs (below, Pelton Dam releases a steadily higher outflow to the lower river). Urban development is likewise a reason for mid-river withdrawals. The city of Bend has undertaken water conservation measures, and the Deschutes River Conservancy has leased water from farmers and reserved it for instream flows, somewhat improving the middle river in summer.

About 90 percent of the stream above Bend and half below it flow through Deschutes National Forest or BLM acreage, escaping land development that has boomed on private land in recent decades. But reflecting riparian forest removal, overgrazing, and diversions, 48 of 58 tributaries fail temperature standards.

TRIBUTARIES

In the upper basin, Fall River is a popular spring creek and fly-fishing destination; from Bend take Hwy 97 south 15 miles, go west on FR 42 for 6 miles, then south on FR 4060. A short walk downstream leads to Fall River Falls. A hatchery lies 4 miles upstream. Stocked rainbows dominate, with wild rainbows, brown, and brook trout below the falls.

West of Bend, Tumalo Creek foams from snowy crags of Broken Top and over an 85-foot waterfall; from Drake Park in central Bend go west on Galveston Avenue (becomes Skyliners Road), continue 13 miles including FR 4603 to the end, and walk the short path upstream.

Whychus (formerly Squaw) Creek carries meltwater from Broken Top and the South, Middle, and North Sister's glacial peaks through meadows and forests southwest of Sisters. Headwaters illustrate a whole textbook of glacial features seen from paths and wanderings on flanks of the Sisters. Lower, irrigation canals divert water, and the creek finally joins the Deschutes in Round Butte Reservoir.

To reach Deschutes headwaters, take Century Highway southwest from Bend (becomes Cascade Lakes Highway), pass Mount Bachelor, and continue to Little Lava Lake outlet—the Deschutes' source. Drive another mile south to a pulloff where Blue Lagoon Trail leads 1 mile to the aquamarine upper river. My favorite view of Deschutes headwaters hides between Crane Prairie and Wickiup Reservoirs; on Cascade Lakes Highway go 2 miles south of Crane Prairie, turn east on FR 42 for 3 miles, park at the bridge, and walk up the east side, exploring off-trail for views of log-riddled rapids framed by aged Douglas-firs and ponderosa pines. Brilliant red kokanee swim upriver in September.

The Deschutes winds through La Pine State Recreation Area, where Oregon's fattest ponderosa, 9 feet across, stands a stone's throw from the river. From La Pine take Hwy 97 north 6 miles and turn west at the sign.

The resort community of Sunriver offers an example of riverfront setbacks incorporated into development plans; take Hwy 97 south of Bend 15 miles and turn west into the new town ("residents only" at river ramps).

Between Sunriver and Bend, the Deschutes passes an astonishing series of lava cataracts separated by placid flows and powerful rapids. For outstanding hiking, mountain biking, and views, take Cascade Lakes Highway 7 miles southwest from Bend, turn left on FR 41, then left at the Dillon Falls sign. Trails lead upstream to Lava Island and Dillon Falls, and in 5 miles to Benham Falls. To start at Benham, drive south of Bend 8 miles on Hwy 97, west on FR 9702, and go 4 miles beyond the visitor center.

Just upstream from Bend, and running into the city, excellent bike/foot trails follow the Deschutes on both sides with views of the remarkable Meadow Camp reach—Class 5 rapids, old rebar and all, run by a few intrepid expert paddlers. Trails lead upstream from the Old Mill Mall on the east side and from Riverbend and Farewell Parks off Columbia and Colorado Streets. This is one of the finest urban riverfront recreation corridors with opportunities for flatwater paddling, biking, and walking. A nasty dam, hazardously negotiated by summertime tubers but not without casualties, lies downstream and should, by any measure, be removed. Downtown, thousands stroll Drake Park as Bend's charming centerpiece with forest and lawn along an impounded reach. See the *Bend Urban Trail Map*.

North (downstream) from Bend, Tumalo State Park offers a swimming beach; from town take Hwy 20 north 4 miles and turn west. What remains of the Deschutes after summertime diversions drops into obscure canyons. For Cline Falls, drive to Redmond, then west on Hwy 126 for 4 miles. Lower Bridge Road penetrates the canyon farther down; from Redmond go 7 miles north on 97, then west on Lower Bridge Road for 7 miles.

To reach the remote canyon above Billy Chinook Reservoir, take Hwy 97 to Terrebonne, go west on Lower Bridge Way for 2 miles, right on 43rd

Deschutes River at Sherar's Falls

Street for 1.7 miles, left on Chinook Drive for 2.3 miles, left on Mustang for 1.1 miles, right on Shad Road for 1.4 miles, right on Peninsula Drive for 3.2 miles, left on Meadow Road for 0.5 miles, then right on Scout Camp Trail to the end and a 2-mile canyon loop trail.

The 440-foot Round Butte Dam rises west of Madras. Immediately below, Pelton Dam evens out the flow, and then at the Hwy 26 crossing (Warm Springs) a boat ramp serves the lower river. Downstream, on the east side, an 8-mile trail from Mecca to Trout Creek uses an abandoned railroad grade, good for hiking, biking, and fishing; from Madras take 26 north 12 miles, before the bridge turn right on a dirt road, and go 2 miles to the Mecca Flat Trail. To reach the Deschutes at remote Trout Creek, drive to Madras, continue north on Hwy 97 for 3 miles, go left on Clark Drive for 7 miles, right on Buckley, through Gateway, cross the tracks, turn right, and follow signs.

Hwy 197 crosses at Maupin. Downstream, the paved east-side De-schutes River Access Road continues 9 miles to impressive 15-foot Sherar's Falls, where Indians dip-net for salmon spring and fall, much as they once did at Celilo Falls on the Columbia (Sherar's is also reached by driving northwest from Maupin on 197, then east on 216).

To see the lower canyon, take 216 north from Sherar's on Deschutes River Access Road—open to cars for 12 miles. This is followed by a trail, with hiking only in the upper 7 miles because of nettlesome scrambles at ravines. The lower 16 miles to the Columbia are a gated gravel road reached from the bottom at Deschutes River State Recreation Area on a fine bikeway, though it's high above the water and searing hot in summer. To reach the river's mouth, take I-84 east from The Dalles to Celilo Falls exit and follow Celilo-Wasco Highway east to the Deschutes with its west-side ramp and east-side trail and campground.

Fly-fisherman's paradise, the Deschutes is famous for trout and steelhead. In the upper river, brown trout, brook trout, and native redband are caught year-round but especially April–July from Wickiup Dam to Bend. From Tenino ramp below Wickiup down to Wyeth Campground makes a good angler's float. In the middle river, with its diversions and warmer flows, brown trout excel; early spring and late fall are best. Lower Bridge west of Terrebonne offers good fishing.

In the lower river, the canyon from Hwy 26 to Maupin is notoriously productive with phenomenally abundant insect life. The one-day float, Warm Springs to Trout Creek, is relatively calm with glassy fly-fishing water.

Below Maupin the lower Deschutes is regarded by some as the greatest rainbow trout fishery in the West, especially April–July. In June the salmonfly hatch of 2- to 4-inch insects is a prized time for fly fishing. The river is open for trout and steelhead angling all year below Warm Springs Reservation; artificial lures only except 3 miles below Sherar's Falls.

Summer steelhead arrive in July, caught near the mouth and up to Maupin until mid-September, then to Warm Springs September–December. After that they are protected for spawning. Occasional 20-pounders stray from Idaho-bound migrations up the Columbia.

Anglers boat overnight on several reaches, and many sites are served by road. Fishing and landing on the Warm Springs Indian Reservation's west bank is banned without a permit. Fishing from boats is not permitted below Hwy 26; anglers must stop and get out.

 With naturally steady runoff plus summer dam releases, the river upstream from Bend has ample paddling flows April–October. Because of diversions, the river below Bend is depleted in those months, but high (and cold) in winter. Below Pelton Dam, the lower river has good flows all year.

The Class 1 upper river—crystal blue among ponderosa pines—has easy access from Wickiup Dam to Wyeth Campground's mandatory takeout above Pringle Falls. From Bend, take 97 south 24 miles, go west on Hwy 43 for 9 miles, before the Deschutes bridge turn left on FR 44, go 6 miles, and turn right to Tenino ramp (below Wickiup). For Wyeth, take Hwy 97, go west on 43, cross the Deschutes, and turn left.

From Big River Campground to Benham Falls is an 18-mile reach of Class 1 with shoreline houses. To put in, take Hwy 97 south of Sunriver, turn west on FR 42, and go 4 miles. After Sunriver the Deschutes drops into blackened lava with forbidding waterfalls. Mandatory takeout is on the right upstream from a footbridge over an impassable logjam, followed directly by Benham Falls. To drive there, take 97 south of Lava Lands Visitor Center, turn west on FR 9702, and go 5 miles to Benham picnic area. For more Bend-area boating see *Deschutes Paddle Trail River Guide* and *Soggy Sneakers*.

Far downstream from Bend, the 15 miles from Lower Bridge to Billy Chinook Reservoir is Class 4 with portages but lacks adequate water except in winter.

Lower Deschutes River upstream of Mack's Canyon

When people talk about boating the Deschutes, they usually mean the 98-mile reach from Hwy 26 to the mouth—one of Oregon's longest raft trips with big-volume Class 2–3+ rapids. Trains rumble through but the canyon still feels remote. Toilets are found at many campsites; boaters are required to use portable equipment elsewhere. A pass is needed below Warm Springs; call 541-416-6700 or see www.boaterpass.com. This lower river offers the ultimate geological tour of volcanic landscapes—towering cliffs of somber dark basalt in hexagonal columns and massive contortions.

Glassy water and strong riffles entice boaters for the first 20 miles below Hwy 26. Then gradient increases. Hot in summer, afternoon winds are likely. Avoid stopping on the Indian Reservation—the left side down to mile 69 (17 miles above Maupin). My favorite section bisects the Mutton Mountains, river miles 75–65, where the Deschutes and its riparian ribbon of green wind beneath ridges and peaks. Scout the Class 3 Whitehorse Rapid (mile 77). An enchanting interlude follows at Davidson Flat where the tunneled railroad briefly disappears.

Easy access comes 4 miles upstream from Maupin with the paved road at Harpham Flat; also at Maupin City Park below the bridge (fee). The 10 miles from Harpham to Sandy Beach above Sherar's Falls may be Oregon's most popular whitewater. Powerful Class 3 rapids attract summer weekend mobs. On my first trip I scouted Wapinitia (mile 55), Boxcar (mile 54), and Oak Springs Rapids, 4 miles below Maupin.

With the Deschutes' steady spring-fed, dam-controlled flows, there's little evidence of flooding or sandbar development, but the White River, entering below Oak Springs, peaks with floods and carries perpetually milky runoff from glacial rather than groundwater sources. Sand and cobbles gather at its mouth on an alluvial plain unlike anyplace else in the basin.

Mandatory takeout comes on the right 2 miles below White River at Sandy Beach, upstream from unrunnable Sherar's Falls. From Warm Springs to here makes an exceptional 52-mile trip, but there's no need to go home; commercial shuttles can be arranged around the Falls, with the second-half of the lower river to go.

The lower 44 miles include four Class 3+ rapids. Start at Buckhollow via the paved road 1 mile below Sherar's. Trestle Island, 2 miles down, makes a nice stop where intimate back channels are carved in bedrock.

For a shorter trip without roads (but often with motorboats), rafters and drift boaters launch 19 miles below Buckhollow at Mack's Canyon. Perfect basalt columns rise from the river 4 miles down. Beautiful Gordon Ridge Rapids comes 6 miles above the confluence with the Columbia. The final takeout lies on the left at Deschutes Recreation Area, off I-84 east of The Dalles.

LITTLE DESCHUTES RIVER

Length: 105 miles
Average flow: 201 cfs
Watershed: 927 square miles

This low-gradient stream drains the southern end of the Deschutes basin and winds north in countless wetland meanders. The upper 12 miles, in a 1,500-foot-deep canyon reaching to Hwy 58, are designated Wild and Scenic.

Crescent Creek, a 30-mile tributary, is also Wild and Scenic for 10 miles from Crescent Dam to Hwy 61 and the confluence of Big Marsh Creek, whose 15-mile length is likewise Wild and Scenic. Riverfront there was bought by the Forest Service, diversions for pasture retired, and wetlands restored. Beavers returned, and potential for fine trout fishing is good. A highlight of the Little Deschutes basin, and entering from the

Little Deschutes River downstream of La Pine State Park Road

east, Paulina Creek plunges from Newberry National Volcanic Monument over twin waterfalls.

 The diminutive upper Little Deschutes can be reached by remote Forest Service roads and paths northwest of Crescent. Once it accumulates sizable flows, frontage is mostly private; for access take Hwy 97 south from Sunriver 6 miles, turn west on La Pine State Recreation Area Road, and go 1 mile.

Crescent Creek can be seen at a National Forest campground; from 97 at Crescent go west on Hwy 61 for 8 miles to the bridge. For Big Marsh Creek, take 97 south from Crescent, go west on Hwy 58 for 9 miles, then left on FR 5825 for 5 miles to a 2-mile trail skirting the reclaimed marsh. To see Paulina Creek, take Hwy 97 south from Bend 22 miles, turn east on Hwy 21, and go 9 miles to the falls and 8 miles of trails.

 The Little Deschutes has brown and brook trout; walk below the La Pine State Recreation Area Road bridge or canoe downstream.

 The circuitous lower Little Deschutes makes an uneventful 10-mile Class 1 paddle from the La Pine Recreation Area Road bridge to Hwy 42. Forests and meadows become scattered with housing. Takeout is west of the 42 bridge at a nominal shoulder with poor parking.

METOLIUS RIVER

Length: 29 miles
Average flow: 1,497
Watershed: 447 square miles

This exceptional stream literally surges out of the ground with springwater that has percolated through volcanic conduits from Cascade snowmelt, discharging a whopping 100 cfs and growing to 1,500 with adjacent springflows within half a mile—one of Oregon's largest spring-source rivers. Anglers fish heavily in the upper reaches' glassy riffles. The lower Metolius flumes through a swift-water canyon accessible only by trail, and terminates in Billy Chinook Reservoir (Round Butte Dam).

The upper river does not deviate from 45–54 degrees F—probably the coldest major river in Oregon—and flows at a nearly constant rate year-round. As a result, unscoured banks are lushly vegetated down to waterline. Water quality is outstanding with aquamarine pools and white rapids, and the upper reach sports some of Oregon's most picturesque glades of riverfront ponderosa pine.

Listed as an aquatic species diversity area by the American Fisheries Society, the Metolius supports native redband, kokanee that migrate from the downstream reservoir as landlocked sockeye salmon, and whitefish. Here is one of Oregon's strongest populations of threatened bull trout—affluvial migrants through the main stem between the reservoir and spawning beds in tributaries. Their survival owes largely to water that's too cold for brown and most brook trout.

The state set aside one section exclusively for fly fishing in 1939. Current improvements in fish passage at downstream dams are expected to

Metolius River below Camp Sherman

bring steelhead and some Chinook back, though waters are excessively cold for most Chinook. A hatchery at Wizard Falls (the falls is gone—drained to the hatchery diversion) raises rainbow trout, kokanee, and alien brook trout, plus Atlantic salmon, which are released to Hosmer Lake, where they cannot escape. The state last planted hatchery rainbows in the Metolius in 1996; current management favors natives, and lower reaches are designated a Wild Trout fishery.

Like elsewhere, exotic plants plague this stream. Floodplains are overwhelmed by ribbon grass, which Friends of the Metolius and the Forest Service try to eradicate. Other restoration included placement of 800 whole fallen trees along 10 miles to reestablish woody debris, essential to the stream's ecological functions.

The lower reach of this National Wild and Scenic River flows through Deschutes National Forest on the south side and Warm Springs Indian Reservation on the north—off-limits to public use. The Reservation's Whitewater River plummets from Mount Jefferson as one of few sizable Oregon streams perpetually milky with glacial silt and joins the Metolius 5 miles above Billy Chinook Reservoir.

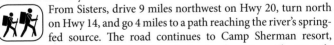 From Sisters, drive 9 miles northwest on Hwy 20, turn north on Hwy 14, and go 4 miles to a path reaching the river's spring-fed source. The road continues to Camp Sherman resort, where fish-watching from the bridge is the local pastime. The 15-mile paved upper Metolius road—great for biking—serves 12 campgrounds, rustic resorts, and cabins.

Trails on both sides offer fishing access and some of Oregon's nicest riverfront strolling. I like the west-side path for 1 mile above Lower Bridge Campground; also the 3-mile trail from Wizard Falls hatchery up to Canyon Campground through deep forest and past whitewater and bubbling springs.

Downstream from Lower Bridge, a rough gated road continues 8 miles, suitable for hiking and mountain biking with occasional windows to the river, but thick waterline vegetation hampers access. Then the route becomes a single-track footpath for 3 miles, overgrown and needing volunteer maintenance. This emerges on another rocky road that continues downstream to Billy Chinook Reservoir. Biking the spine-rattling 18-mile route—upper river to reservoir—is not a particularly pleasant ride, but it's the best way to see this unusual stream from conifer forest to desert edge. The shuttle is a 23-mile creep on washboard gravel: from the upper river near Lower Bridge take FR 1490 east to 1180, then 1170, and west on Hwy 64. To enter from the bottom, take Hwy 97 south from Madras, turn west on Culver Highway, then west to the reservoir, and follow Hwy 64 to Monty Campground, where the trail leads upriver.

 Though the river is too cold to produce large trout, it's nonetheless legendary for rainbow and bull trout, year-round, lures/flies only, fished heavily, Camp Sherman to Lower Campground.

 The upper 6 miles can be paddled on swift water with no significant rapids but possible log hazards and low bridges through private land. Put in along the road, at Camp Sherman, or campgrounds. Downstream from Gorge Campground—3 miles below Camp Sherman—turbulent Class 3 rapids hide in a remote reach. Then from Wizard Falls Bridge to Lower Bridge Campground, fast Class 2 resumes. Visit non-descript takeouts first so you recognize them from the water. Avoid anglers by staying off this stream early and late in the day.

Below Lower Bridge the Metolius is a difficult 18-mile Class 3+ roadless paddle to Monty Campground. While rapids are typically not intricate, they are continuous, and any upset in the extremely cold water would be hazardous and complicated by relentless deep current sweeping shorelines of repelling brush and logs. Swimming to shore—and even eddying out—is difficult. Especially dangerous to rafts, log blockages are common and not removed. Adventure boating here is for teams of experts only.

CROOKED RIVER

Among Oregon's major dryland streams, and surprisingly about as long as the Rogue, the Crooked starts

| Length: 127 miles, 203 with SF |
| Average flow: 1,553 cfs |
| Watershed: 4,338 square miles |

56 miles southeast from Prineville at the confluence of Beaver Creek and the South Fork, 5 miles west of Paulina. Flowing from Ochoco Mountain headwaters, the North Fork joins 12 miles down, and in 23 more miles the main stem enters 18-mile-long Prineville Reservoir behind Bowman Dam. Famous trout water awaits just below, and then downstream from Prineville the river forms the lifeline of Smith Rock State Park before cutting a forbidding canyon to Billy Chinook Reservoir on the Deschutes.

Part of a collapsed 25-mile-long caldera, the remarkable cliffs at Smith Rock resulted from lava encroaching on the ancestral river, which then eroded a new channel through a volcanic vent, exposing rhyolite ash and welded tuff that had earlier erupted under extreme heat and pressure.

In upper reaches, the Crooked's drought-stressed ponderosa pines have been clearcut and its grasslands grazed heavily, while at the bottom of the basin Round Butte Dam blocked salmon and steelhead. Some of this fishery will be restored with transport improvements allowing migration up to Bowman and Ochoco Creek Dams. Downstream from Stearns Dam (11 miles below Bowman and being considered for removal) diversions have for decades reduced summer flows to a trickle through Smith Rock State Park. Negotiations led to a 2012 agreement reserving 80,000 acre-feet for downstream fisheries (redband trout and reintroduced steelhead) while providing water for Prineville and irrigators (congressional reauthorization of the dam is needed). National Wild and Scenic River sections total 15 miles—one below Bowman and another below Hwy 97.

The 76-mile-long South Fork is the upriver extension of the main stem, with grazed headwater marshes, then flowing through an 18-mile BLM canyon where roads principally serve private property.

The Crooked's popular recreational canyon lies below Bowman Dam; from Prineville, take Main Street (Hwy 27) southeast. In 1 mile a town park fronts the diverted river. Another 7 miles upstream lead to Stearns Dam site and access just above. In another 3 miles up, the Wild and Scenic reach begins with BLM's Castle Rock Campground, the first of 11 recreation sites along the 7-mile reach up to Bowman. Midway, a trail ascends Chimney Rock with canyon views.

The spectacular Smith Rock State Park lies downstream; take Hwy 97 north from Redmond 6 miles to Terrebonne and turn east. Trails lead to overlooks of the Crooked's Grand Canyon, where cliffs above gentle windings offer some of Oregon's best rock climbing. For a 4-mile river-trail

Crooked River below Bowman Dam

loop and demanding climb, drive to the main parking area, walk down a dirt road to a footbridge, cross the river, angle right, and ascend to an 800-foot ridge with river views. Descend the west side and follow the trail back to the footbridge. Or just follow the trail along the river.

To see the Crooked's lower canyon, go north of Redmond 10 miles on Hwy 97 to its crossing of the chasm and stop at the west-side overlook. Public access to the lower canyon is possible at a rugged BLM trailhead: from Hwy 97 in Terrebonne turn west on Lower Bridge Road, go 2 miles, go right on 43rd Street for 1.7 miles, left on Chinook Drive for 5 miles, then straight on Horny Hollow Road 1.7 miles to Lone Pine Trailhead.

 Below Bowman Dam, 8 miles of tailwater is a huge draw, reached from pullouts and campgrounds. Year-round cool releases keep trout and insect life active. While other streams are too cold or have closed seasons, fall/winter remain open here; artificial lures for redbands and whitefish.

 The reach below Bowman is a fine 8-mile Class 1–2 canoe run from Big Bend to Castle Rock Campground. Avoid early and late hours to minimize conflict with anglers. Below Prineville, expert kayakers run 18 miles of Class 4–5 from Lone Pine Bridge to Crooked River Ranch, limited to April before irrigation begins (see American Whitewater's website). Then, from the Ranch to Billy Chinook Reservoir is 9 miles of Class 4 with portage at Opal Springs Dam/diversion. This remote section runs year-round with springflows from canyon walls (see *Soggy Sneakers*).

NORTH FORK CROOKED RIVER

Length: 46 miles
Average flow: 368 cfs
Watershed: 323 square miles

Little known, dam-free, this Wild and Scenic River lacks roads or trails through Ochoco National Forest and BLM land. It begins in high prairies, winds 13 miles in a wilderness study area, and penetrates a 900-foot-deep basalt canyon. Ponderosa/Douglas-fir forests transition to juniper/sage. Native redband thrive; bald eagles roost in winter.

 From Prineville take Hwy 26 east 15 miles, go right on Hwy 123, continue 8 miles up pastured Ochoco Creek, turn right on FR 42, go 23 miles up Canyon Creek and down the upper North Fork to Deep Creek Campground. Then walk south on an abandoned road, ford Deep Creek above its North Fork confluence, and wander trail-free downstream through splendid ponderosa glades along the singing stream. It eventually enters a rugged gorge with dual waterfalls, a 28-mile reach in all, with private property along the lower 5 miles before Hwy 380 crosses. This is one of Oregon's westernmost canyons where plantlife is similar to Rocky Mountain vegetation.

 A few paddlers have run the 28-mile Deep Creek to Hwy 380 reach, reportedly Class 3, plus two arduous waterfall portages and log hazards on springtime runoff.

North Fork Crooked River below Forest Road 42

WHITE RIVER

With milky water gushing from Mount Hood glaciers, headwaters collect in an active fumarole field, Devil's Kitchen.

Length: 49 miles
Average flow: 423 cfs
Watershed: 409 square miles

Also at the hydrologically significant upper river, a mudflow from 300 years ago is being downcut by the stream, exposing parts of a forest buried centuries ago. The White then tumbles over cobbles and glacial outwash in braided channels with spectacular views to Oregon's most

White River at Tygh Valley State Park

legendary mountain. The river enters forest where its pathway tightens from a U-shaped glacial trough to a V-shape eroded by water, finally ending in a vertical-wall dryland canyon. The White transitions through diverse biomes more abruptly than any other Oregon stream, dropping from Alpine to timberline, then through Douglas-fir, pines, cottonwoods, and desert sage. Headwater precipitation of 130 inches wanes to 10 at the mouth, all in 49 winding river miles.

A scenic attraction near the bottom, 90-foot White River Falls is followed by twin cataracts of 20 and 40 feet. This state park remains riddled with derelict hydropower pipes and debris abandoned in 1960; the spectacular waterfall is otherwise beautiful enough to become a showpiece of Oregon's state parks system.

The upper river supports resident redband, while salmon and steelhead spawn near the Deschutes. The White is an unusual National Wild and Scenic River where hydrology (glacial silt/bedload) is one of the officially listed values warranting protection.

 The river has few roads, trails, or bridges. To see spectacular glacial headwaters, take Hwy 26 east from Portland, pass Mount Hood, bear left on Hwy 35, and in 3 miles stop at the bridge and walk up toward Mount Hood or down on gravel bars to a trail on river-right.

To drive downstream, cross the 35 bridge, turn right on FR 48, go 9 miles, turn right on FR 43, and cross the White. There FR 3530 heads downriver 1 mile to White River Campground. Another 6 miles downstream, Keeps Mill Campground is reached via Hwy 26; take it east from Mount Hood, go left on 216 toward Maupin, then left on the jagged surface of Keeps Mill Road.

For the lower White, take Hwy 197 north from Maupin, turn east on 216, and drive 4 miles to Tygh Valley State Park's ornate waterfall. A 2-mile trail leads to the Deschutes (poison ivy!).

Kayakers run 12 miles, Class 4, from Keeps Mill to White River Bridge during snowmelt, plus 11 miles onward to Tygh Valley. For the expert paddler competent with log hazards, *Soggy Sneakers* calls this "one of the most delightful canyons in Oregon."

CHAPTER 10

KLAMATH

Vital to the West Coast, the Klamath is the third-largest river flowing into the Pacific south of Canada, and has its beginnings in southcentral Oregon where streams gather from pine and sagebrush mountains. A delightful mix, its headwaters are topographically linked to the Cascades but botanically akin to the Rocky Mountains with lodgepole/Douglas-fir forest and meadows of sage and grass, yet geologically part of the drier Basin and Range Province that continues south and eastward through Nevada. Downstream of Klamath Lake and a chain of troubling reservoirs, the river thunders through a forested gorge and transects the Cascade Mountain range with a boldness unseen in any other river. Then in California it wends its way through seven distinct geological terranes that successively collided with North America and collectively became today's Klamath Mountains. In all, it's an extraordinary tour of the Northwest and California, semi-arid steppes to sea.

Klamath tributaries swell high in springtime after the deep chill of Oregon's interior begins to warm. Trout season opens then, with waters at boatable levels in some reaches, though mosquitoes are thick along many wetland-fringed waters until late summer.

KLAMATH RIVER

Length: 257 miles, 46 in OR, 364 total with the Williamson
Average flow: 17,397 cfs, 1,767 in OR
Watershed: 14,831 square miles, 5,702 in OR

Beginning at the outlet of Upper Klamath Lake, the upper 46-mile reach of this river journeys to California. Three dams in Oregon are followed by three more across the state line, but then the Klamath flows unimpounded through 193 California miles to the Pacific—one of the longest dam-free reaches on the West Coast and by far the longest in rugged semi-wildness.

The Williamson is the main stem's upriver extension, feeding 23-mile-long Upper Klamath Lake. This and other nearby lakes and wetlands comprise the Klamath Basin National Wildlife Refuges, celebrated as the "Everglades of the West"—essential waterfowl habitat and stopover for 80 percent of Pacific Flyway birds.

Locally called the Link River where it emerges from the dammed outlet of Upper Klamath Lake in the city of Klamath Falls, the waterway soon flattens behind Keno Dam, then spills as the "Klamath," but is impounded again 6 miles farther at J.C. Boyle Dam's 4-mile pool. Below Boyle's powerhouse, the Klamath careens through 17 miles of the highest

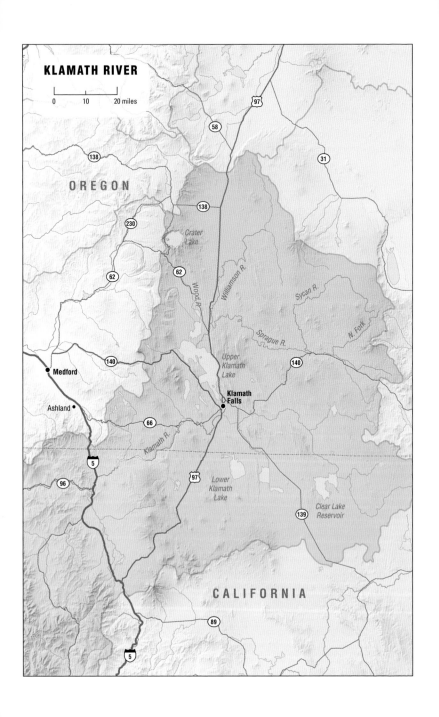

KLAMATH RIVER

0   10   20 miles

97

58

31

138

OREGON

230

Crater Lake

62

Wood R.

138

Williamson R.

Sycan R.

Sprague R.

N. Fork

140

Upper Klamath Lake

140

● **Medford**

Klamath Falls

Ashland ●

66

Klamath R.

5

97

Lower Klamath Lake

96

139

Clear Lake Reservoir

CALIFORNIA

89

5

Klamath River below Boyle Powerhouse, with black algae along shorelines

volume Class 5 whitewater in the Northwest and the Pacific slope's wildest big-water canyon. Steep rapids and sharp rocks are artifacts of recent lava flows from the Mount Shasta area. Unfortunately the river here is polluted with a soup of blue-green algae that incubate in warm water of the lake and reservoirs.

The lower-most major tributary in Oregon, Jenny Creek runs 22 miles from Howard Prairie Reservoir to the Klamath in Iron Gate Reservoir. Because of biodiversity fitting the basin's Cascade-Siskiyou Mountain pivot-point, this stream has been recommended for Wild and Scenic protection by the Soda Mountain Wilderness Council.

NATURAL HISTORY

The Klamath is among only three rivers that begin east of the Cascade Mountains and pass through both them and the Coast Range (others are the Columbia and Pit/Sacramento). Though emphatically a Pacific Coast stream, its headwaters' volcanic landscape is biologically linked to the Great Basin with fishes native to ice-age Lake Lahontan, which sprawled across northern Nevada. And connections extend even farther east: though the Snake River of southern Idaho now veers north to Hells Canyon and the Columbia, its ancestral route likely reached the ocean via the upper Klamath—a remarkable journey for waters as far away as Yellowstone.

Reflecting this heritage of geographic complexity, the upper basin endures as a hotspot of biodiversity with eight endemic fishes including 2-foot-long Lost River suckers and similar shortnose suckers, once serving Indians and then a commercial fishery but now endangered. Few suckers survive to become adults in this system where wetland habitat for the fish has been drained, water levels lowered, cold-water springs isolated, and parasite numbers elevated in the algae-infested, overwarmed lake and reservoirs. Other endemics of the watershed are the Klamath Lake sculpin, slender sculpin, and Miller Lake lamprey. America's southernmost bull trout hide in upper basins, which the American Fisheries Society lists as an aquatic diversity area (California's McCloud River once had the southernmost bull trout—sadly a victim of habitat loss and brown trout introduction by the late 1970s).

West of the Cascade Mountains in California, the lower Klamath supports 21 native fishes dominated by anadromous species, and ranks as the third-most productive steelhead and salmon stream on the West Coast. Chinook once migrated up the Klamath and into Oregon; now none can overcome the dams.

CONSERVATION

Effects of the dams and withdrawals for irrigation were known for years but became starkly apparent in 2002 when an estimated 35,000–70,000 adult salmon downstream were killed by diseases stemming from low flows—one of the worst fish kills in the history of the West. The U.S. Fish and Wildlife Service and National Marine Fisheries Service had taken steps in 2001 to nominally protect endangered species, including prescribed flows for salmon downstream and diversion restrictions for Lost River and shortnose suckers upstream. However, after crop losses and rowdy opposition from upper basin farmers, Bush Administration appointees blocked the releases in 2002 in order to return full amounts to irrigation, and the fish kill followed.

Downstream tribes, anglers, conservationists, and commercial fishermen next organized to restore the flagging fish runs by removing several Klamath hydropower dams owned by PacifiCorp. These block more than 300 miles of Oregon spawning streams and create warm reservoirs incubating toxic blue-green algae, *Microcystis aeruginosa*. In the reservoirs, the algae accumulate to 4,000 times the amount deemed risky to humans; effects can be seen 100 miles downstream (see page 53). Owing to this and problems stemming from agriculture, dams, logging, and mining, Klamath salmon runs have faded to 3 percent of historic levels, decimating not only the commercial fishing industry offshore in Oregon and California, but also the subsistence catch of tribes and one of the West Coast's finest sport fisheries.

After negotiations that had never seemed possible during the near-violent conflicts of 2002, restoration agreements were reached between farmers, tribes, agencies, PacifiCorp, and some environmental groups in 2010. The settlement called for removal of four dams—Boyle in Oregon plus the 210-foot Copco, a smaller secondary Copco, and 173-foot Iron Gate in California by 2020—plus a small allocation of water to Lower Klamath Refuge, and a cap on irrigation diversions. This will open the way for salmon and steelhead to reach the upper river (Keno Dam has fish passage that can be improved; Link Dam will remain but hydropower operations will end). Peaking flows now turned on-and-off like a spigot

Klamath River and Boyle Powerhouse, which is scheduled for removal

will become steadier. However, congressional authorization is required, and critics including Oregon Wild and WaterWatch argued that loopholes can enable PacifiCorp to keep the dams, that minimum flows for fish are not established, that irrigation still trumps endangered species, and that the dams can be removed through other means. Supporters maintained that the agreements improve the status quo, that they represent the only compromise possible, and that the effort will constitute the largest dam removal and river restoration in history.

While dam removal is essential to recovery, lower Klamath River water will remain too warm in summer; additional efforts appear to be needed to address water quality and diversions associated with agriculture in both states.

In the upper river, the endangered Lost River and shortnose suckers got a reprieve when Oregon Wild won a settlement with PacifiCorp to alter operations at Link River Dam by adjusting spill schedules to protect the endangered fish.

Parallel efforts to restore upper basin Klamath River wetlands have also attracted interest. At this essential flyway stopover, waterfowl concentrations are the largest on the continent. In winter, 700 bald eagles congregate—more than anywhere outside Alaska. Yet farmers have drained or converted 80 percent of the basin's wetlands. Even within the national wildlife refuges, 22,000 acres have been inexpensively leased to farmers. In the dry year of 2012, no water was released to wetlands of the Lower Klamath Refuge May—August, desiccating them while farmed acreage on the refuge received ample supplies. Oregon Wild, Klamath Basin Audubon Society, WaterWatch, and others work for restoration of crucial habitat.

In the thundering whitewater gorge between Boyle Dam and the state border, 11 miles of the Klamath were designated a National Wild and

Scenic River in 1994 by Interior Secretary Bruce Babbitt at the request of Governor Barbara Roberts to prevent the city of Klamath Falls from diverting 80 percent of the flow for hydropower. In 1980 188 miles of the Klamath in California had been designated—the fourth-longest Wild and Scenic River nationwide.

 Upper Klamath Lake's outlet can be seen in north Klamath Falls; from Hwy 97 Lakeshore exit go 0.5 miles west and walk or bike on PacifiCorp's trail down the Link (Klamath) River. In 0.5 miles an impressive rapid (all that's left of the real Klamath Falls) can be seen via a side path. The gravel trail runs 2 miles into the city and to "Lake Ewauna"—now the backwater of Keno Dam.

Finally called "Klamath" below Keno, the algae-filled waterway tumbles 6 miles. The upper end of this section can nominally be reached on the north side; from Hwy 66 at Keno take Clover Creek Road west, go south on Old Stage Road, and scramble down. For the lower end of the Keno section, take 66 west from Keno 6 miles, turn north into Sportsman's Park (fee), and walk to the river while avoiding the rifle range, motocross, etc. Below, the river enters Boyle Dam's pool.

To see the astonishing canyon and whitewater below Boyle Dam, take Hwy 97 south from Klamath Falls, go west on Hwy 66 for 17 miles, and turn south (gravel) at the power plant sign. Striking views of the gorge-bound river can be spotted below Boyle, followed in 4 miles by the powerhouse, where water is returned to form Oregon's most awesome pileup of big rocky whitewater. Boaters put in at BLM's Spring Island ramp 1 mile below the powerhouse. Another 3 miles of canyonside road serve a campground and continue for 7 increasingly rough miles to private land. Among Oregon's greatest river ironies, the spectacular canyon is compromised by sharply fluctuating peaking-power flows and by gross mats of black algae when the water is down—all but late-afternoon hours daily until the hydro project is retired.

 Anglers fish below Keno Dam for large native redband before June and after October (summer is closed because the fish are stressed by warm water, plus they taste bad when algae peak). Hydropower flows fluctuate radically. Below Boyle Dam is open for redband, best May–June.

 A few kayakers paddle the obscure 6-mile Class 3 run below Keno Dam, April–May before the algal epidemic begins.

The 17-mile, big-whitewater challenge from Spring Creek ramp (see above) to Copco Reservoir includes 350-yard Class 5 Hell's Corner Rapid. The dam releases 1,500 cfs during afternoon peaking hours, or a tremendously pushy double-dose when two generators operate. To take out, drive Hwy 66 west from the Boyle turnoff 17 miles, go south on West Copco Road 10 miles, turn east on Copco Road for 6 miles, cross the bridge, and continue upriver to accesses in 1 and 5 miles.

Boyle to Copco is an extraordinary whitewater run with regular commercial rafting use, however, the daily flow fluctuation of several vertical feet and poor water quality pose serious problems. Algae, especially from mid-summer to autumn, renders the water pea-soup green or brown. Thick suds mound in eddies and, most shocking, a foul slime of dead algae blankets shoreline rocks, as black and messy as an oil spill when water is drawn down. Health advisories, however, have not been issued here, as they have for the Klamath below Iron Gate Dam.

Removal of the four dams will end the daily flush-and-drain cycle and yield steadier flows; 1,000 cfs may become typical in early summer, but big runnable water will be less common later. Above the current rafting run, the sensational 4-mile whitewater torrent from Boyle Dam to the powerhouse—now a meager 300 cfs—could carry full runnable flows in early summer. If the algae problem could be controlled, this one-of-a-kind canyon would become one of the grandest whitewater attractions of the West and comparable to American classics such as California's Tuolumne River and West Virginia's Gauley.

WILLIAMSON RIVER

Length: 107 miles
Average flow: 1,038 cfs
Watershed: 2,831 square miles

Primary source of Upper Klamath Lake and a top trophy trout fishery of the West, the Williamson bubbles as a river-sized springflow from lava fissures at Head of the River, then meanders through marsh, ranch, and forest. It seeps across one of the West's largest wetlands: 34-mile-long Klamath Marsh, where a 10-mile meandering channel is planned to be re-excavated in the ancestral lakebed by the Fish and Wildlife Service for increased wildlife habitat.

In the manner of other Great Basin rivers—but unusual elsewhere—the Williamson arcs in long detours to circumvent topography thrown up in

Williamson River source at Head of River Spring

its way; after aiming north for a third of its length and then angling west, it veers due south through a lava-walled canyon at the base of Soloman Butte, finally easing into the delta separating Agency and Upper Klamath Lakes.

The hydrology within this labyrinthine geography also defies expectations. After birth as a voluminous springflow and drifting many miles, the Williamson in summer disappears into volcanic fissures south of Klamath Marsh. The lower river's powerful year-round force and notoriously steady cold discharge owes entirely to Spring Creek—incredibly only 2 miles long where it meets the lengthy but languid Williamson in Collier State Park.

Famous among anglers, the stream historically produced Oregon's largest trout, plus record redband. Introduced brown trout—competing with natives—also get hooked here. Seventeen fishes include eight endemics, with the endangered Lost River sucker, shortnose sucker, Klamath largescale sucker, speckled dace, tui chub, and a genetically distinct rainbow trout, plus 15 endemic mollusks—all imperiled. Chinook salmon once prolifically arrived here on their 300-mile migration but have been blocked by downstream dams since 1917. They're expected to return to ancestral habitat after four of the Klamath dams are removed. The Williamson delta/Klamath Lake area also boasts America's greatest concentration of migratory waterfowl—an impressive 3 million birds, though this is only half the historic number.

Grazing throughout and farming in the lower basin have extracted a toll on the Williamson and related wetlands. Only 10 percent of marshes once surrounding Upper Klamath Lake remain, though some restoration efforts are underway. The Nature Conservancy and others are reclaiming 12 square miles at the Williamson delta after acquisitions opened the way for breaching dikes and reinstating meanders.

 To see the river's delta and its restoration take Hwy 97 north from Klamath Falls 16 miles and bear left on Modoc Point Road. To reach the lower river from 97, go 2 miles north from the Hwy 62/97 intersection, turn right at the southern entrance to Chiloquin, then quickly right into a county park. Upstream, Collier State Park has beautiful frontage on the river and refreshing Spring Creek; drive 6 miles north of Chiloquin on 97. A short walk to the confluence shows that the creek provides virtually all the Williamson flow in late summer; Williamson water there is eddied backwaters of Spring Creek's flow. If you want to see what a bone-dry riverbed looks like, go 8 miles farther on 97, turn east on FR 43, and continue 0.5 miles to the Williamson bridge.

To reach Klamath Marsh, take Hwy 97 another 10 miles north and turn east on Silver Lake Road. For the Williamson's unusual spring-fed source, follow a different route: from Chiloquin go east on Sprague River Road for 7 miles, go left on Williamson River Road for 24 miles, and left to Head of the River Campground (mosquitoes). Below the source springs, ranchers divert water in its sinuous path north to Klamath Marsh.

 Large redband in a nationally acclaimed trophy fishery migrate from Upper Klamath Lake, late summer and fall. Collier and Chiloquin Parks have bank access, but most frontage is private, so anglers use drift boats July–September. A 4-mile float extends from the county park in south Chiloquin (see above) to Waterwheel RV Park (fee) where Hwy 97 crosses. Guides are available. For a longer trip, go to Sportsman's River Retreat off Modoc Point Road (fee). From the Chiloquin put-in, a 200-yard row upstream takes you to legendary Blue Hole at the Sprague confluence and the base of the Williamson's steep Chiloquin Rapid. Fishing from boats is not allowed on the Williamson above Chiloquin.

 Canoes can be launched at Collier State Park picnic area—park and walk east of Hwy 97 to the Spring Creek confluence. In summer paddle across the spritely Spring Creek and up the languid summertime Williamson for several miles, or drift downstream for 6 miles of Class 1–2 to Chiloquin Bridge, with takeout on river-right (sharp drop ahead!) Below the rapid in Chiloquin, anglers put in at the county park and drift 4 miles to the Hwy 97 RV park.

SPRING CREEK

Length: 2.5 miles
Average flow: 300 cfs
Watershed: 26 square miles

In summer this remarkable creek provides virtually all the Williamson's water above the Sprague River (and also far exceeds that lengthy tributary in volume). It begins in a robust spring and is immediately augmented by discharges erupting like miniature volcanoes through sand in the bed of the creek. The frigid, utterly clear stream soon measures 100 yards wide.

In upper reaches the creek bed is covered with rare algal water balls—*Nostoc pruniforme*. These grow in strange colonial spheres as big as grapefruits, full of air and water, clustered by the thousands like stones on the

Spring Creek with *nostoc* algal balls

bottom where the cyanobacteria requires a constant 39–43 degrees F. The unusual algae also grows in Mare's Egg Spring on the west side of Wood River basin (south of the Sevenmile and West Side Roads intersection).

 See this unique stream at Collier State Park, 6 miles north of Chiloquin on Hwy 97, with an easy stroll to glassy water above the logging museum, to whitewater rapids near the 97 bridge, and to the Williamson confluence downstream in the park. For the source, take 97 north from Collier 2.7 miles, then left on FR 9732 for 4 miles to a picnic area.

 For a distinctive, quiet paddling experience, turn west from Hwy 97 at the Collier Park logging museum, go straight for 0.5 miles to the park's upper picnic area, and launch in Spring Creek above its rapids. Paddle upstream 1.5 miles through transparent water to the source. Take out in the same upper picnic area, or probe downstream to three turbulent Class 2+ rapids with log hazards and a likely portage or two. Take out below at the Williamson confluence or continue downstream to Chiloquin, with care to exit above the Chiloquin Rapid (see Williamson River).

WOOD RIVER

The Wood River rises in springflows and supplies Agency Lake—a northern arm of Upper Klamath Lake separated

Length: 20 miles
Average flow: 319 cfs
Watershed: 220 square miles

only by delta wetlands. From its lucid groundwater source in Jackson Kimball State Park, this trophy trout fishery winds acutely as the quintessential spring creek, glassy through forest, then with forest on the east bank and pasture on the west, then with pastures all around. Water that's

Wood River below its spring-fed source

left after diversions take their toll feeds Agency Lake, where wetlands are being restored.

Tributary Annie Creek, bursting from the snowy southern end of Crater Lake National Park, is geographically linked but fails to flow directly into the Wood owing to groundwater infiltration and diversions. Bull trout survive in Sun Creek, a wild tributary.

 From Hwy 97 south of Chiloquin take Hwy 62 north 13 miles, bear right on Dixon Road toward Jackson Kimball State Park, and in 1 mile turn west to the Forest Service's Wood River access. Dixon Road continues 2 miles to Kimball, its campground, and a path to the robust headwater spring (mosquitoes).

To see Annie Creek, continue on Hwy 62 past Kimball 4 miles to Crater Lake National Park's Ponderosa picnic area and a steep user path. Drive farther to canyon-rim pullouts and Annie Falls picnic area, where the creek has sliced through hundreds of feet of soft ash and pumice.

 After July big rainbow and brown trout draw anglers who fish from boats or float tubes, mostly below the Forest Service's access. Private shorelines are vigorously posted. Guides are available.

All summer the upper Wood makes a charming canoe/fishing trip of 6 circuitous miles with swift Class 1 current and the easiest bike shuttle imaginable. Transparent water drifts through ponderosa glades from Kimball to Wood River access. In the enchanting style of spring creeks, the Wood is glassy yet swift. You can paddle up to the headwall of the spring, return downstream, lift over a log, and continue with one minor diversion-weir-drag. Below the Forest Service's Wood River access the farmland route may include low dams and fences.

SPRAGUE RIVER

Length: 86 miles
Average flow: 581 cfs
Watershed: 304 square miles

From headwaters in Fremont National Forest northwest of Goose Lake, the Sprague's countless tight bends meander marshes and forests as the secondary source of the Klamath. A watery maze at the Sycan River confluence illustrates cutoff channels and oxbow ponds where the river once flowed. Most mileage is private. Heavily logged, grazed, diverted, the Sprague is a good candidate for rehabilitation and fishery restoration with its long mileage, lack of development, and cool springflows.

The choice attraction here is 34-mile-long North Fork—a National Wild and Scenic river arcing around Gearhart Mountain Wilderness.

The main Sprague is seen from side roads off Hwy 140 between Lakeview and Klamath Falls. In upper reaches, 3 miles west of Bly, a Forest Service site offers access to the diminutive South Fork. For the lower river, take Sprague River Road east of Chiloquin 5 miles to a lane on the right. Until late summer mosquitoes are thick through this basin.

North Fork Sprague River at Lee Thomas Meadow

To reach the North Fork's meadows, lodgepole forest, and beaver dams, take Hwy 140 east from Klamath Falls to Bly, turn northeast on FR 34, then left on FR 3372 for 11 miles to Lee Thomas Meadow. Also, from 3372 turn west on FR 3411 and go 2 miles to Sandhill Crossing and stroll through glades downstream.

Redband/brown trout fishing can be good after June. Bull trout in upper reaches must be released. To catch invasive brown bullhead, visit the Sprague from Godowa Spring Road (north of Beatty) downstream to Saddle Mountain Pit Road (at Lone Pine where FR 44 turns northeast). The North Fork can be excellent for rainbow and introduced brook/brown trout.

Even with diversions and low flows, Class 1–2 canoeing is good through mid-summer when most other rivers drop. With an easy bike shuttle, put in at the first Sprague River Road bridge, 7 road miles east of Chiloquin, or at the dirt lane 1 mile west of that. At an abandoned mill 2 miles below the bridge, be ready to drag across a strange water-level pipeline, potentially hazardous at medium-high flows. A mile of intricate Class 2 rock gardens follow. The lower half of this 10-mile trip is a beautiful roadless loop. One mile above the Williamson confluence, and just above heavy riprap on river-left, Chiloquin Dam was removed in 2008.

The Sprague mouth is dramatically sited at the base of the Williamson River's Chiloquin Rapid. Take out just below; from Hwy 97 northbound continue past the Hwy 62 turnoff for 2 miles, bear right at the southern Chiloquin exit, and turn right to the ramp.

Sycan River below Sycan Marsh

SYCAN RIVER

Length: 76 miles
Average flow: 149 cfs
Watershed: 557 square miles

Sycan is the Sprague's principal tributary but, without the high terrain and snow of Gearhart Wilderness, flows are weaker. An upper reach winds through Sycan Marsh, being restored as a Nature Conservancy preserve. Below, the marshy river narrows into shallow canyons and through meadows with old-growth ponderosa pine, cutover woodland, and ranches. The lower, private 12 miles tumble over small waterfalls and past springflows. Along with the Sprague, this is a rare example of a river in the mostly arid Great Basin geographic province flowing perennially many miles and supporting a native rainbow fishery.

 To reach the stream below Sycan Marsh, take Hwy 140 east from Klamath Falls 35 miles to Beatty, continue 9 miles, go north on Camp Six (Ivory Pine) Road 13 miles, and turn left on FR 27 for 13 miles to a channel that's distinctively choked with water hemlock in summer. Angler/cow paths track downstream, river-left. Other Forest Service roads reach points below.

 Large brown trout and small redband are caught in Winema National Forest's Coyote Bucket area; take Forest Service roads northwest from Hwy 140 at Beatty.

 From Sycan Marsh to Teddy Powers Meadow the stream can be canoed through small rapids and possibly a portage or so before levels drop in June when irrigation diversions begin. Access is along FR 27 below the marsh; also at Teddy Powers Meadow (private, with access but no hiking). Follow National Forest roads north of Beatty.

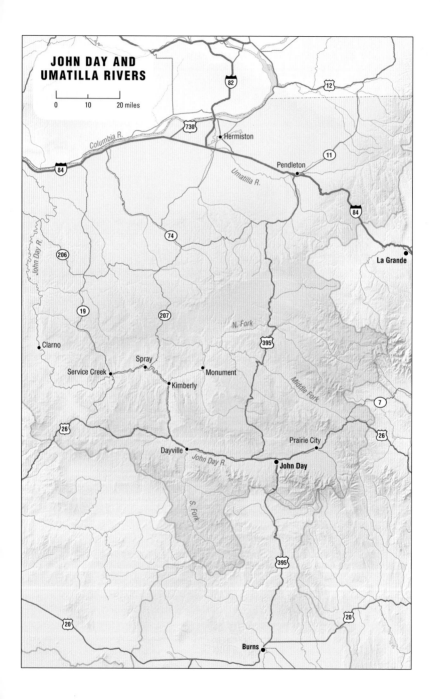

JOHN DAY AND UMATILLA RIVERS

0   10   20 miles

CHAPTER 11

JOHN DAY AND UMATILLA

Though known for big trees, rain, and snowcaps, Oregon has far more dryland than wet: two-thirds of the state's acreage lies in the eastern rain shadow of the Cascade Mountains. Rivers there are fewer and smaller; most flows emanate from snowfall on the region's peaks—principally the Blue Mountains, including the Strawberry and other sub-ranges.

Here the John Day's North, Middle, and South Forks are splendid mountain streams, while the lower main stem carves exquisite canyons through wildlands and ranches. The Umatilla likewise aims toward the Columbia. These rivers are most welcoming in late spring when snowmelt stokes the flow. Mid-summer levels drop sharply, leaving small streams in broad riverbeds through hot dry country.

JOHN DAY RIVER

The John Day is Oregon's fifth-longest river when the North Fork is included, but it's the longest flowing entirely within the state. The main stem with

Length: 180 miles, 293 with NF
Average flow: 2,060 cfs
Watershed: 7,880 square miles

its North Fork also has the longest dam-free reach in the entire Northwest—284 miles (a main stem Columbia dam impounds the John Day's lowest 9 miles, so the river is not entirely free-flowing, though it's often listed as such). This stream supports Oregon's best remaining salmon runs above Bonneville Dam. With scarcely a handful of small communities, the basin has potential for restoration from a history when logging, grazing, and mining dominated while the river's exemplary fishery was all but lost.

Covering much of northcentral Oregon, all three John Day forks drain the Blue or Strawberry Mountains. Lighter snowmelt from the Ochoco Mountains to the south and west also contributes. Lying below the highest mountains, most of the basin is semi-arid; the John Day carries less water than the Chetco but drains 23 times the landmass.

The main stem begins in Dixie Pass, receives the South Fork, and then the North Fork, which is longer and registers twice the volume of the main stem at their confluence. Below, the John Day's route through desert canyons and ranchland offers one of the longest canoe trips in the West, or a relatively carefree rafting expedition until flows plummet in June.

NATURAL HISTORY

Columbia River Basalt eruptions 16 million years ago covered much of the basin with dark volcanic rock—some exposed in signature hexagonal columns or striated cliffs soaring up hundreds of feet. Where the basalt veneer has weathered away, the older underlying 1,000-foot-thick Clarno/John Day Formation of volcanic ash appears—quite colorfully below Dayville. Welded by steam and heat that accompanied the eruptions, the ash blends from red in lower layers to greenish and then yellow-brown on top. It covered 1,000 square miles, now evident in canyonsides exposed by the river. The strata hold a wealth of leaf and bone fossils depicting one of the world's longest known continuous sequences of life—40 million years. On this colorful crust, erosive rainfall produces a badlands topography through the basin's middle reaches. There below the South Fork confluence, the river traverses the Sheep Rock Unit of John Day Fossil Beds National Monument; others units downstream are Painted Hills (at tributaries Bridge and Bear Creeks) and Clarno.

The John Day remains among the longest wild anadromous streams in the Columbia system; fall and spring runs produce northeast Oregon's largest wild Chinook. This is also the state's only major Columbia watershed virtually unaffected by hatchery fish. West slope cutthroat and summer steelhead survive in cool tributaries. Bull trout persist in the diminutive Call Creek at the main stem's headwaters and in a few other streams. Introduced bass have multiplied profusely in the main stem and draw anglers who can easily and almost invariably catch a lot of sizable fish. Bighorn sheep, once driven to local extinction, are the basin's showy mega-fauna, reintroduced near Dayville in 1978 and at the lower canyon's Thirtymile Creek in 1989.

CONSERVATION

The main stem is a National Wild and Scenic River for 148 miles from Service Creek to the backwaters of John Day Dam—the ninth-longest reach in the National Wild and Scenic system. Adding to the public estate here, the Western Rivers Conservancy in 2008 purchased 8,114 acres of ranchland on the lower river. Linked with BLM grazing allotments of 8,000 acres, the purchase will safeguard 16 miles of riverfront vital for salmon and steelhead. This Cottonwood Canyon tract has become Oregon's largest state park, managed for wildland and riparian restoration.

However, the river overall has been diminished by cattle that graze to the waterline, by clearcutting at the headwaters, and by a rapacious era of gold mining. Little monitoring is done of many diversions that weaken the flow. Temperature standards are exceeded in 9 of 16 tributaries.

Salmon downstream encounter two Columbia River dams, which take a toll, but in comparison, Chinook of the Grande Ronde in northeast Oregon or of Idaho's Salmon River encounter eight large dams on the Columbia and Snake. John Day fish, 75 percent less encumbered by dams, are doing better.

 To reach main stem headwaters, take Hwy 26 south from Prairie City 21 miles to Crescent Campground. Downstream (west) of John Day, Hwy 26 follows the main stem to the South Fork confluence at Dayville.

John Day River at Amine Canyon above Clarno

Below Dayville and east of the Hwy 26/19 intersection, the river threads narrow Picture Gorge—black basalt with red soils weathered from a volcanic eruption and later incised by the river. To hike in John Day Fossil Beds National Monument, go to Blue Basin Trailhead 5 miles north of the 26/19 intersection, where a 3-mile badlands loop offers distant river views. May is good for wildflowers. Hwy 19 continues north through the valley to Kimberly and the North Fork confluence.

For 29 miles below Kimberly Hwy 19 follows the main stem westbound to Service Creek, then bends away from the stream. Only a few remote roads touch down until Clarno, where Hwy 218 crosses at Fossil Beds National Monument with its boat ramp and nature trail. Many miles of isolated sections continue downstream to the Hwy 206 crossing at Cottonwood Canyon and its ramp; from Wasco take Hwy 206 southeast 15 miles.

In another 20 miles downstream, the lowest public access is McDonald Crossing (no bridge); from Wasco take gravel Klondike Road east 16 miles. Another 10 miles downstream is the river's largest drop, Tumwater Falls. Directly below, the river's final 9 miles are impounded by John Day Dam.

Hiking is largely restricted to BLM land, reached mainly by boat. But in the steppe-like grasslands, cross-country hiking is easy, and open ridgelines offer spectacular views. Below the 206 bridge, Cottonwood Canyon State Park has limited parking and trail access.

 The John Day supports the Columbia basin's largest remaining runs of wild spring Chinook and summer steelhead. These must be released (a few hatchery strays appear). Steelhead wait at the mouth for winter rains, which raise levels at Tumwater, enabling fish to ascend through April. Smallmouth bass are hooked in great numbers below Service Creek, May–August; they extend above the North Fork confluence and account for most John Day fishing. Typically in rafts or drift boats, anglers also have bank access at Service Creek and the Fossil Beds' Sheep Rock Unit. Cutthroat thrive in upper reaches.

 The John Day offers excellent Class 2 boating April–June (800–6,000 cfs at Service Creek), with one steeper drop. May is best; expect Memorial Day crowds below Service Creek. Canoes and small inflatables can cope at 300 cfs, often through July.

From the North Fork confluence at Kimberly to Service Creek, 23 miles of Class 1–2 boating are largely avoided because the road runs somewhat alongside. Yet the river there is beautiful—especially the mountainous south shore—and the float is pleasant. Public land/campsites are scarce but scattered. The village of Spray (14 miles below Kimberly) has access with a fine park and the only public water on the entire North Fork/main stem. From there it's 13 miles to Service Creek.

Most boaters prefer the reach from Service Creek to Cottonwood with its ranch-and-canyon mix, and many subdivide for the 48 miles to Clarno (Class 2) or the 69-mile Clarno to Cottonwood section, with one significant rapid. Private land prevents camping near Twickenham (12 miles below Service Creek), and for 8 miles above Clarno.

Wilder, swifter, the Clarno to Cottonwood section has a Class 3 rapid (Class 4 at 6,000 cfs) 4 miles below Clarno, portaged left by canoeists. Basalt Rapid, 12 miles farther, escalates from Class 2 to 3 with volume. In this beautiful reach, basalt canyonsides soar up as much as 2,000 feet.

For Service Creek to Cottonwood, BLM requires permits May 20–July 10; numbers are limited. Portable toilets are required. Headwinds can be strong. Turbidity hampers the filtering of drinking water; springwater is reportedly available at upper Devil's Canyon (22 miles below Clarno), but I carry water. For shuttles, call Service Creek Trading Post.

Another 20-mile Class 1–2 reach of fine desert canyons extends from Cottonwood to McDonald, reached via Klondike-John Day River Road (no bridge!). Downstream 10 more miles, private landowners bar access around unrunnable Tumwater Falls where a portage trail once clung to the right canyonside.

The run from the North Fork confluence to McDonald is 165 miles, and above that you can add 60 adjoining miles of the stellar North Fork for an expedition of 225 miles—the longest dam-free boatable route in Oregon and one of the longest in the West. See BLM's *John Day River Recreation Guide*.

NORTH FORK
JOHN DAY RIVER

Length: 113 miles
Average flow: 1,293 cfs
Watershed: 1,800 square miles

This stunningly beautiful stream highlights Oregon's Blue Mountains and offers the best of the John Day's salmon and steelhead habitat. It rises in the North Fork Wilderness and drops through Douglas-fir/ponderosa pine with basalt canyons, then juniper/sage drylands. It picks up the charming Middle Fork, and in another 30 miles carries twice the main stem's volume, and often more, at their confluence in Kimberly.

The Blue Mountains consist of granite and sedimentary rocks once the core of ancient volcanoes but now exposed after seismic uplifts and subsequent erosion of lava that had covered them. Quartz veins in the granite led to extensive gold mining; dredge tailings and old cabins can be seen along the upper, recovering river. The lower North Fork below Grave Creek tours a striking landscape of ponderosa pine savanna that one might expect from a natural fire regime in this fire-dependent ecosystem.

The North Fork supports 90 percent of the John Day basin's spring Chinook and 70 percent of summer steelhead—Oregon's best Columbia basin habitat above Bonneville. The river has the most intact headwaters and the largest relatively continuous riparian cottonwood groves. Yet 20 of 27 tributaries exceed temperature standards. A National Wild and Scenic reach of 54 miles is separated from the main stem's Wild and Scenic reach by a long interval of private land.

An exceptional riverfront trail follows the upper North Fork 25 miles. It starts at North Fork Campground; from La Grande take I-84 west, turn south on Hwy 244 for 14 miles, take FR 51 south to FR 73, and continue south to the campground. The trail offers frequent views of rapids framed by pines and magnificent old-growth larches. For mid-trail access, continue south on FR 73 to Granite, turn east on FR 1035 to Granite Creek Trailhead, then hike down the creek 3 miles to the river. For the western (downstream) end of the trail, from Ukiah take Hwy 531 and FR 52 southeast to FR 55 and then 5506 to Big Creek Campground.

From the Hwy 395 bridge 16 miles south of Ukiah, the dusty Texas Bar Road turns upstream (east) for 6 miles of riverfront in national forest.

Upper North Fork John Day River below North Fork campground

North Fork John Day River above Middle Fork confluence

Below or west of the 395 bridge, the highway follows the North Fork for 3 of Oregon's prettiest roaded riverfront miles before veering north. There, north of the Camas Creek bridge, a dirt road angles west (downstream) with nominal traffic, excellent biking, and remote car camping on scattered BLM riverfronts for 18 miles until encountering posted private land.

Avid steelheaders fish the North Fork January 1–April 15 and September–December 31. Some seasoned anglers regard this catch-and-release fishery as their favorite wild steelhead stream. Summer bass fishing is excellent, especially from Monument to Kimberly.

Some kayakers have run the wild section from North Fork Campground to Hwy 395, with log portages. Though I saw it only at low flow, this looked like Class 3–4 to me—no doubt an epic wild river adventure.

Boaters paddle or row on snowmelt (May–early June) from Hwy 395 for 44 miles of lively Class 2–3 water to Monument (800–2,500 cfs at Monument), with the option of continuing another 17 miles to the main stem at Kimberly. If you want an early-summer, overnight, wildland river trip with whitewater substantially easier than the Rogue, this is the place. The lyrically beautiful ponderosa forest and grassland is partly roadless with little development, good campsites, and easy walking in glades and up ridgelines with grand views. Put in at Tollgate Campground; from the 395 bridge south of Ukiah go east on FR 55 half a mile and turn right. Or, for more water, drive 3 miles northwest of the 395 bridge, cross the Camas Creek bridge, turn left, and follow the gravel road 1 mile to BLM's access and camping spot.

At the Middle Fork confluence, reachable only by boat, a trail winds up that scenic tributary. Downstream, between Cabin Creek and Neal Butte, a dirt lane through BLM land provides 4 miles of good walking on the west side (posted above and below).

Beyond Monument's ramp and town park (0.5 miles below the bridge) the canyon opens up in ranchland alternating with canyons and a scenic southern shore for 17 miles (Class 2) to Kimberly. At 2 miles below Monument a low dam can be run on the left. Several miles farther, just above a blue bridge, stay left at a concrete weir. Two BLM campgrounds with road access lie just above Kimberly—the area's best access. The North Fork can be combined with the main stem for one of the finest relatively easy long float trips in the West. Service Creek Trading Post offers shuttles.

MIDDLE FORK JOHN DAY RIVER

Length: 75 miles
Average flow: 256 cfs
Watershed: 774 square miles

This tributary to the North Fork begins in the Blue Mountains east of Austin and flows with fast current northwest amid forests, ranches, and a wonderfully scenic ponderosa pine savanna.

At low flow, summer temperatures reach 80 degrees F—lethal to spawning salmon that linger too long—yet the stream remains important for the John Day's spring Chinook, ascending 480 miles from the ocean, and summer steelhead, spawning in Granite Creek (Hwy 395 bridge) and Boulder Creek (14 miles west of Austin). These cold streams also support redband and westslope cutthroat. Bull trout once thrived in many tributaries and survive in Big, Boulder, and Clear Creeks. The Nature Conservancy is restoring riparian habitat along 4 miles and reinstating meander channels, log debris, and spawning gravels 13 miles west of Austin.

A paved but quiet road parallels the stream excepting the lower 9 miles, which have no road access. Near the top, from Hwy 7 at Austin, take Upper Middle Fork Road west (downriver) through Malheur National Forest's lush riparian belt to two

Middle Fork John Day River above Hwy 395

campgrounds. At 7 miles below Hwy 7 the Warm Springs Tribes have launched significant riparian restoration. At 22 miles, below Galena, mine tailings dominate for 2 miles. Though the effects are aging, the disturbance still offers a glimpse of the abuse that this river and others once endured in the gold-mining belt of northeast Oregon.

For the next 20 miles downriver the paved Middle Fork Road is one of the finest of all riverfront bikeways as it passes by pines, junipers, grassland, rolling hills, and rocky peaks. The final 10 miles of pine savanna above Hwy 395 are exceptional in springtime. Below 395, Heise Road continues for 10 private-land miles to Ritter, then angles away, leaving a splendid wild canyon extending to the mouth.

 Though most frontage is private, fishing opportunities include catch-and-release steelhead January 1–April 15 and September 1–December 31. Trout are stocked.

 At this seldom paddled stream, I've found 8 blissful miles of Class 2 canoeing above Hwy 395 on the waning flows of spring when the hills were still vivid green. The road is perfect for bike shuttles. Springtime paddling may extend farther up, with fence hazards, and possibly downstream with reportedly larger rapids—an alluring route at the top of my list of rivers to explore.

SOUTH FORK JOHN DAY RIVER

> Length: 61 miles
> Average flow: 225 cfs
> Watershed: 606 square miles

Flowing through drier country than other John Day branches, and clearer than the main stem, the South Fork in its deep canyon separates the Ochoco Mountains to the west from the Aldrich Mountains to the east. A

South Fork John Day River above Black Canyon Creek

diminutive upper reach tumbles over 55-foot Izee Falls. The South Fork has 47 miles designated Wild and Scenic, and the American Fisheries Society noted the stream for biological diversity.

 From the mouth at Dayville, the South Fork Road follows the stream to its upper reaches; after a paved mile, expect gravel washboard. Ranchland yields to wilder country and a lush riparian corridor. Bear left in 8 miles and enter a striking basalt canyon that runs 5 miles before terrain opens up again. Black Canyon Creek enters 12 miles from Dayville; its 12-mile trail is reached at the bottom by a South Fork ford that's deep and swift until summer.

 The entire river is closed to salmon and steelhead fishing but open for redband and mountain whitefish May 27–October 31. With restoration efforts, habitat and fishing has improved, and 15-inch trout are common.

UMATILLA RIVER

Gathering snowmelt at the northwestern face of the Blue Mountains, the Umatilla flows from second-growth conifers down to Columbia plateau

Length: 89 miles
Average flow: 501 cfs
Watershed: 2,328 square miles

drylands, through Pendleton, then in riffling cottonwood-lined currents to Columbia backwaters of John Day Dam at Umatilla.

The river supports hatchery summer steelhead, spring and fall Chinook, coho, and rainbow trout, plus redband and bull trout in upper reaches including the North Fork. Margined sculpins occur only here and in the Walla Walla basin. The American Fisheries Society listed the Umatilla for species diversity, and *Oregon's Living Landscape* notes this as the only river on the Columbia Plain retaining a strong network of riparian habitat (the lower Deschutes and John Day riverfront forests were reduced to isolated remnants).

However, the basin has been affected by clearcut logging and fire suppression in headwaters, grazing, and farm diversions. In 1988 the Confederated Tribes of the Umatilla Indian Reservation led the Umatilla Basin Project to restore some flows, which for 70 years had been desiccated by summertime diversions. To do this without cutting farmers' supplies, the Bureau of Reclamation pumps Columbia River water to Cold Springs Reservoir near the Columbia in Hermiston, which replaces Umatilla water that had been withdrawn from the river. Anadromous fish, including lamprey, responded with new runs in long-abandoned reaches. A salmon season has opened in most years since re-watering began.

Another stream of note in this region, the Walla Walla flows mainly in Washington but its South Fork comes from Oregon's Blue Mountains; at Milton-Freewater take Hwy 600 east to Harris Park Trailhead for 20 miles of streamfront hiking. Avoid motorbikes by driving Hwy 11 to Athena, east on Hwy 204 to Tollgate, left on 64 past Jubilee Lake, and left to the upper South Fork Trail.

Umatilla River in Pendleton

 Umatilla headwaters lie 33 miles east of Pendleton; drive Hwy 30 east but instead of getting on I-84 take Mission-Cayuse Road, which becomes Thorn Hollow and then River Road and leads to the North/South Forks confluence in Umatilla National Forest. Here the North Fork Trail enters a wilderness canyon, ascending the stream 5 miles before climbing sharply. FR 32 continues up the South Fork 2 miles. The middle river is off-limits to public use through the Indian reservation—from 7 miles below the North/South Fork confluence down to Pendleton's Hwy 11 bridge.

In central Pendleton an urban river parkway, built on a levee dating to 1877, offers 3 miles of trail; to reach the downstream terminus, take I-84 exit 207 and Westgate (Hwy 30) east for 2 miles, then turn left at Westgate Place to Trailhead Park. In mid-town, Roy Raley Park, next to Pendleton's Round-Up Grounds, has parking for trail access. Upstream (eastern) access to the trail is west of the Hwy 11 bridge at Little League Park.

Below Pendleton, I-84 exit 207 leads to Reith Road on the north bank. Downstream 1.6 miles, a left on Birch Creek Road drops to a bridge and informal access on river-right. Reith winds onward through farms with occasional river views and re-joins I-84 at Echo.

Downstream in Hermiston, Riverfront Park's paths offer nominal access; from Hwy 395 take Orchard Avenue west. Roads, tracks, city streets, and diversion dams all encroach on the lower river.

Following the tribes' restoration work, hatchery steelhead and salmon including coho are again being caught, especially below Three Mile Dam (3 miles above the Columbia), where shorelines are public. Fall Chinook and coho peak October–November, spring Chinook mid-April–June, and steelhead October–December. Smallmouth bass, perch, and crappie are always there. Most frontage is private, so anglers cast from bridge and park sites below Pendleton. The upper river has good catch-and-release rainbow angling.

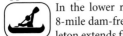 In the lower river, diversion dams are problematic, but an 8-mile dam-free reach with a sharp drop in downtown Pendleton extends from a ramp at the ODFW office east of town to Reith Road. Anglers float this in spring (too low by May/June). Take I-84 exit 210, go north to the first light, right on Court Avenue/Hwy 30, exit at Mission Road, turn left at the light on Mission (frontage road), left on Mytinger, and right at the ODFW chain-link fence. For the Reith takeout, use Old Pendleton River Road west of Pendleton. Below MacKay Creek, which joins the Umatilla above Reith, summer flows along the farmland river are stronger.

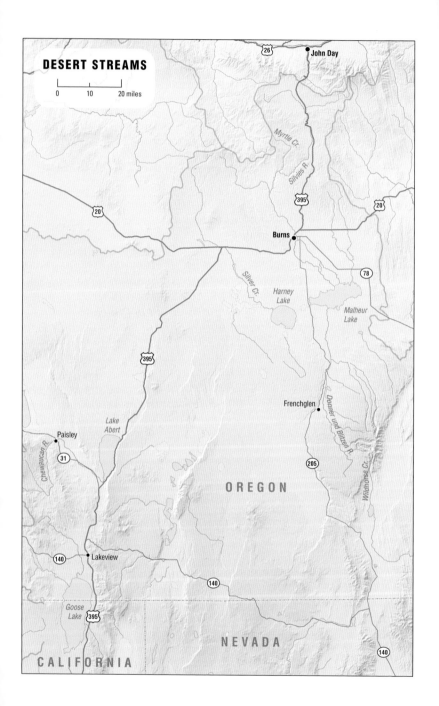

DESERT STREAMS

0   10   20 miles

John Day

Myrtle Cr.

Silvies R.

Burns

Silver Cr.

Harney
Lake

Malheur
Lake

Frenchglen

Donner und Blitzen R.

Wildhorse Cr.

Lake
Abert

Paisley

Chewaucan R.

OREGON

Lakeview

Goose
Lake

NEVADA

CALIFORNIA

CHAPTER 12

DESERT STREAMS

The southcentral part of Oregon's desert lies within the Basin and Range province of geography where surrounding mountains trap meager runoff that's destined to evaporate in lakes, marshes, and parched playas rather than flow to the ocean. Once linked in a sprawling complex of wetlands fed by meltwater from mountain glaciers, remnants of rivers remain and support 18 endemic and imperiled fishes dating from the Pleistocene.

Frigid in winter, desert streams burst with early spring snowmelt, then recede to trickles or dusty riverbeds in the scorching summer. Compared to Oregon's robust waters elsewhere, it's difficult to consider these tenuous waterways "rivers" at all, but across a landscape the size of Vermont and New Hampshire, these streams are all the more precious to the community of life that depends on them.

CHEWAUCAN RIVER

Length: 53 miles, 71 with Elder Creek
Average flow: 223 cfs above diversions, 54 cfs below
Watershed: 564 square miles

This stream may win the least-known-but-most-beautiful river award in Oregon. With year-round flows, it offers the region's best native redband habitat. From rolling ponderosa pine highlands in the Dairy Creek headwaters of

Chewaucan River upstream of Paisley

Gearhart Mountain Wilderness, the Chewaucan (chew-WAH-can) flows north 25 miles to Paisley, hooks sharply around uplifted mountains in the way of Great Basin rivers, crosses a broad irrigated valley, and empties into Lake Abert—the only landlocked southcentral Oregon lake that has never gone dry in historic times. Vestige of a climatological past, the Chewaucan still feeds the 15-mile-long Abert just as other rivers spanning from the Columbia Plateau to Death Valley once nourished dozens of Great Basin lakes during the Ice Age melt-off. Irrigation, however, consumes much of the river's flow before it gets to its historic destination.

Redband 3 feet long used to migrate between the upper river and 42,000-acre Chewaucan Marsh south of Paisley. Weirs subsequently blocked migration, drainage ditches destroyed habitat, hatchery fish displaced natives, and alien species multiplied. But starting in the 1990s the Department of Fish and Wildlife and ranchers began to collaborate. Stocking was stopped in 1999, troublesome culverts replaced, and fish ladders attached to weirs, all allowing native trout to prosper. A sport season has grown in what could become a trophy fishery. Downstream diversions continue to affect Lake Abert.

 From Lakeview take Hwy 395 north, turn left on Hwy 31, go 22 miles to Paisley, and turn west on Mills Street (FR 33) to the canyon, with pulloffs and campgrounds. BLM land transitions to National Forest where the road winds 8 delightful miles through park-like ponderosa/juniper—excellent biking.

 Fishing above Paisley is good for native redband, brook, and brown trout, artificial lures only. The lower river has largemouth bass and brown bullhead.

 Paddling Oregon notes the Chewaucan as "exploratory." Some sections appear to be Class 2–3, though I've not seen them in the requisite flows of late spring, and some sections are hidden from the road.

SILVIES RIVER

Length: 119 miles
Average flow: 185 cfs (above diversions)
Watershed: 1,350 square miles

Carrying precious runoff from the Aldrich Mountains, the Silvies drains into the basins of Harney and Malheur Lakes with their 180,000 acres of wetlands—the West's largest freshwater marsh. The upper river draws from a larger mountain complex than other streams of the closed-basin desert region, and so carries more water through meadows, forests, and a 16-mile untracked canyon, followed by ranchland. Lower reaches are diverted to hayfields. Other than in coastal estuaries, rivers rarely have distributaries—branches that take water away from the main stem but, much like an estuary, the Silvies splits into East and West Forks as it enters landlocked Malheur Lake basin.

Upper reaches support native redband and hatchery rainbows. Other native fishes include speckled dace and mottled sculpins; aliens are bass, carp, bluegill, and yellow perch.

Silvies River below Forest Road 31

 At Seneca, the upper river nourishes a robust riparian corridor of willows. Downstream, and south on Hwy 395, the middle river is diverted in the ranchlands of Silvies Valley.

For the Silvies finest reach, continue south on 395 to FR 31 (17 miles north of Burns), turn west, and go 7 miles to Silvies Bridge. Below, an 8-mile roadless canyon deepens through Malheur National Forest, its upper end easily toured via cow paths and open terrain with pine savanna, rocky bluffs, sagebrush, and riparian willows. In summer expect only an algal trickle.

For trail hiking, take FR 31 another 7 miles north to the bridge over tributary Myrtle Creek. Here a path leads 8 miles down Myrtle through ponderosa glades, almost reaching the Silvies confluence before encountering private land.

Below Myrtle Creek confluence, the Silvies meanders through a 16-mile canyon of mixed ranch-and-public frontage, but BLM does not recommend access here. The lower river's remnants can be seen from Hwy 205 south of Burns.

 Fishing for native redband and hatchery rainbows is considered fair in the upper Silvies. Anglers catch smallmouth bass and other warm water fish in middle/lower reaches after May. Myrtle Creek has redband.

DONNER UND BLITZEN RIVER

Length: 78 miles
Average flow: 78 cfs
Watershed: 618 square miles

Steens Mountain rises to 9,773 feet, towering over southeastern Oregon's Basin and Range geographic province and accumulating heavy snowfall as an orographic monolith in the middle of the desert—one of the state's notable

Donner und Blitzen River above Frenchglen

landmarks. The region's only glaciers once carved spacious U-shaped canyons here. Ice age evidence remains starkly apparent because coniferous forests don't block the view in the Steen's semi-arid landscape. Glaciated tributaries include Little Blitzen River plus Kiger, McCoy, Bridge, Mud, Fish, and Indian Creeks. All flow into Donner und Blitzen, which feeds wetlands and landlocked Malheur Lake.

Like glaciated highlands of the Rockies, these streams flow past aspen groves brilliant in autumn orange while bighorn sheep roam high meadows. In shaded alcoves heavy snow persists into summer. Endemic redband evolved with desert conditions; before wetlands were drained they likely migrated to Malheur Lake.

 This unusual river can be sampled upstream from diversions, channels, and Malheur National Wildlife Refuge; from Burns take Hwy 78 east 1.7 miles, go south on Hwy 205 for 60 miles to Frenchglen, east on Steens Mountain Loop Road 3 miles to Page Springs Campground, and walk upstream until cliffed out.

The glacially sculpted canyons are practically inaccessible owing to brush, but spectacular views into them can be seen from Oregon's highest-elevation road. This gravel byway ramps 20 miles up the seismically tilted Steens from Frenchglen. At Kiger Gorge viewpoint catch a stunning vista of the 4-mile-long National Wild and Scenic Kiger Creek deep in its canyon. The road continues to Steens Summit Trail—exhilarating at the head of Little Blitzen Creek. The Loop Road down the south side of the mountain is passable after snowmelt and dry-off.

For streamfront hiking go to Big Indian Creek. Take 205 south from Frenchglen 10 miles to the south entrance of the Loop Road, ascend it 19 miles to South Steens Campground and walk up an old lane past choice backcountry campsites and spectacular scenery for 8 miles to the headwall. Fords and mosquitoes make this trip challenging until July or so. Hiking is also possible along Little Blitzen River; from the Loop Road's south entrance drive 20 miles up to the trailhead.

 The intimate Donner und Blitzen is a favorite of fly fishermen who start at Page Springs Campground and work upstream. Renowned for native redband, this Wild Trout fishery is not stocked. High runoff clouds the water until July, followed by heat and bugs. This process of elimination leaves autumn delightful with golden willows, cottonwoods, and aspens.

 Soggy Sneakers calls a 17-mile reach of the South Fork along with the main stem "one of the finest whitewater runs in Oregon." But the Class 3+ snowmelt (500–800 cfs at Frenchglen) is for experts with its relentless flush, brushy shores, icy water, and inaccessibility. A few competent boaters put in by driving 16 miles up from the south entrance of Steens Loop to the South Fork's Blitzen Crossing. Take out at Page Springs Campground, but remember, anglers value undisturbed waters here.

WILDHORSE CREEK

While Donner und Blitzen drains the snowclad west slope of Steens Mountain, the drier eastern escarpment yields a much smaller Wildhorse

Length: 19 miles
Average flow: 5 cfs
Watershed: 27 square miles

Creek. Snowmelt from a glacial cirque beneath the summit plunges gorge-bound to Alvord Lake—a graben sunken by earthquakes into the shadow of the great mountain and seasonally reduced to a dry playa— one of the continent's harshest deserts enjoying only 5 inches of rain. Also feeding Alvord, Trout Creek carries lean flows north from the scenic Trout Creek Mountains bordering Nevada. With its imperiled Alvord chub and the endangered Borax Lake chub nearby, this lake is recognized in *Freshwater Ecoregions of North America* as a center of aquatic biodiversity.

 From the Steens Mountain Loop northern entrance, drive 25 miles up to a 3-way, take the middle fork, and go 2 miles to the trailhead, where a steep path drops southward 2.6 miles to Wildhorse Lake. The 9000-foot altitude may challenge the unacclimated. Lahontan cutthroat reproduce in the lake. The creek's 10-mile, trail-less descent begins at the outlet.

WHITEHORSE CREEK

Whitehorse and its tributary Little Whitehorse rank among the longer isolated streams of Oregon's southern

Length: 36 miles
Average flow: 21 cfs
Watershed: 140 square miles

desert. Gathering snowmelt from the Trout Creek and Oregon Canyon Mountains near Nevada, they flow north to drylands east of Alvord

Desert. Along with the Owyhee canyons, this is one of the more remote geographies in Oregon and, for that matter, America.

The stream is primary habitat for endemic Whitehorse cutthroat—a variety of Lahontan trout. When the huge Pleistocene Lake Lahontan dried up after the glaciers' retreat, this fish was isolated in Whitehorse and neighboring Willow Creek. Likewise, five of six remnant populations of Oregon's Lahontan trout live in these two basins. But heavy grazing along Whitehorse led to compaction of soil, loss of native plantlife, and downcutting of channels, all reducing habitat and increasing water temperatures for the threatened fish. Increasing rancor was reversed when the Trout Creek Mountains Working Group formed in 1988 with a commitment to restoring the stream without bankrupting local ranchers. Declines bottomed out in 1989 with 8,000 fish. By removing cattle from sensitive BLM land, fencing waterfronts, and pasture rotations, the streams have begun to recover; numbers climbed to 40,000 one year. WaterWatch took further action to prevent new dams and diversions that threatened the fish. The creek survives as an example of a relatively intact desert stream in a deep canyon with riparian vegetation and beaver dams.

Drive south from Burns Junction (not Burns!) on Hwy 95 for 20 miles, turn west on Whitehorse Road, go 21 miles to the creek/wash, then walk or drive on an unimproved road south 4 miles to the Whitehorse/Little Whitehorse confluence.

CHAPTER 13

THE SNAKE RIVER AND ITS TRIBUTARIES

In its epic route from wilderness heights of the Rockies to agricultural lowlands and arid canyons, the Snake River scribes the Oregon-Idaho border. The Owyhee River joins from wild desert terrain in Oregon, Idaho, and Nevada, and the Malheur flows in from its ponderosa-pine headwaters and drylands. Then below its agricultural zone, the Snake plunges through Hells Canyon. Feeding this artery from Oregon's northeast corner, the Wallowa Mountains—still seismically rising—rake-off 100 inches of precipitation and spawn one of the finest clusters of high-elevation natural rivers in the West, rich in imperiled aquatic species including bull trout and once-prolific runs of Chinook and steelhead.

The Snake pushes powerfully toward the Columbia all year. Springtime on the main stem brings massive flows and enticingly green canyonsides, summer broils but the water refreshes, autumn grows tinderbox-dry but sharply beautiful. Tributaries pump strong in spring when hiking along lower-elevation streams is excellent and boating is good. This region's mountain streams appeal in summer when the highcountry sings with fresh water; in autumn the bugs have gone and the days shine warm, bright, perfect.

SNAKE RIVER

Length: 1,056 miles, 235 in OR
Average flow: 56,255 cfs at mouth,
19,970 in OR at Hells Canyon Dam
Watershed: 109,000 square miles,
16,900 in OR

Flowing from headwaters in Wyoming and then across Idaho to Oregon, the Snake is the Columbia's largest tributary and twelfth-largest river in the United States. Only a small percentage of its flow comes from Oregon, and half enters via Idaho's Salmon and Clearwater Rivers in the lower Snake basin. In length, the Snake exceeds the Columbia by 126 miles at the confluence, but coming from a profoundly drier region, it carries only 30 percent of the flow there.

Soon after entering Oregon from Idaho the Snake becomes the states' boundary, easing north through dusty farmlands, agricultural processing towns, and the I-84 corridor. Then it cuts the misnamed Hells Canyon (this spectacular landscape was formerly called "Snake River Canyon")— once a continuous wilderness chasm of 200 miles. This lacked the sheer-wall, red-rock sublimity of the Colorado River's Grand Canyon but was otherwise comparable in length, whitewater, and wilderness. Deeper, its slopes drop 5,620 feet from Oregon's Wallowa Mountains and 7,900 feet from Idaho's Seven Devils. The full gulf of topographic extravaganza is

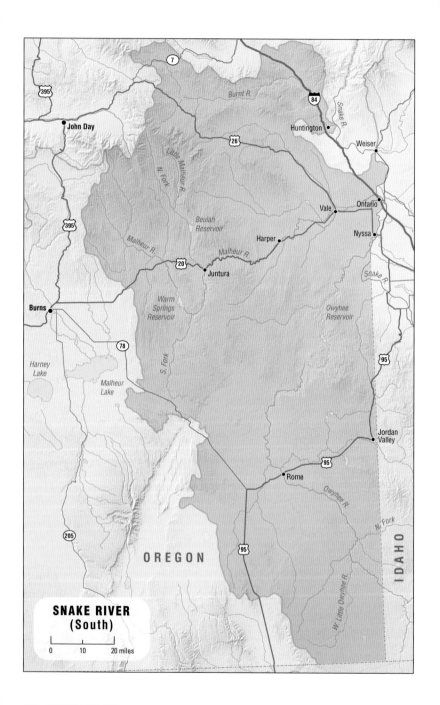

SNAKE RIVER
(South)

0   10   20 miles

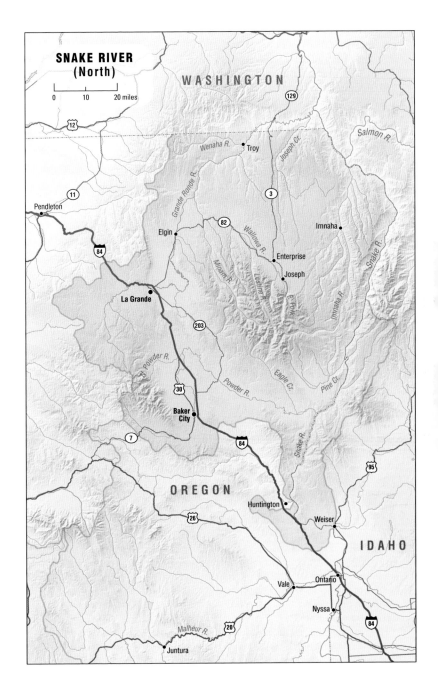

SNAKE RIVER
(North)

0   10   20 miles

WASHINGTON

129

12

Salmon R.

Wenaha R.   Troy

Joseph Cr.

11

3

Grande Ronde R.

Pendleton

Elgin

82

Imnaha

Wallowa R.

84

Enterprise

Minam R.

Lostine R.

Joseph

Snake R.

La Grande

E. Fork

Imnaha R.

203

Powder R.

Eagle Cr.

Pine Cr.

30

Powder R.

Baker
City

7

84

Snake R.

95

OREGON

Huntington

Weiser

26

IDAHO

Vale

Ontario

Nyssa

Malheur R.

20

84

Juntura

virtually unseen because canyon walls and sub-peaks block the view even to a river of such enormity.

By 1964 Idaho Power Company had built three reservoirs that flooded the upper half of Hell's Canyon's length and five of seven great rapids. But below the dams the river still surges, 18,500 cfs on average released after silt from the Snake's troubled agricultural journey across southern Idaho accumulates in the upstream reservoirs—like big septic tanks—leaving the water downstream brilliant green.

The Snake exits Oregon just below the end of Hells Canyon and proceeds north as the Washington-Idaho boundary to Lewiston, where it encounters flatwater from the first of four lower-river dams in Washington. Below them it enters the Columbia's back-to-back, four-dam complex, which continues nonstop to tide-line.

Rafters, drift boaters, and kayakers nationwide come to Hells Canyon, which is also popular among jet boaters, whose unrestricted numbers soared for decades while quotas sharply limited the numbers of non-motorized boaters. This became the West's most infamous conflict between motorized and non-motorized river enthusiasts shouldering conflicts regarding noise, wakes, crowding, camping, and inequities of management, but most river runners assiduously maintained a personal sense of courtesy and friendliness. After years of debate, some restrictions were placed on jet boat use, with prescribed days free of motorized activity above Pittsburg Landing, and some limits on total numbers in the Hells Canyon National Recreation Area, ending above Heller Bar. Powerboat use is heaviest below Pittsburg Landing and on weekends.

NATURAL HISTORY

Half Oregon, half Idaho, Hells Canyon is all landmark of the West with thunderous rapids and wild shorelines beneath basalt walls and steep arid slopes tiered up to forests, meadows, and peaks—altogether a museum of biological diversity spanning a mile-and-a-half vertical rise above continental cleavage separating the Seven Devils and Wallowa Ranges. The remaining free-flowing river scours America's second-deepest canyon; only the Middle Fork Kings in California's Sierra Nevada churns deeper beneath summits (8,000 feet up on both sides there). But the Snake has more of a canyon feel—big river beneath steep walls—while the Kings describes a mountain stream tumbling among sky-high peaks.

Lava flows once blocked the water's passage north and formed the ancient 300-mile-long Lake Idaho, extending upstream to today's town of Hagerman. From this virtual sea, the ancestral river amazingly spilled west across Oregon to the Klamath basin and out to the Pacific on the shores of today's California. Faulting eventually fractured the north side of the impeding lava flows, and a Columbia-bound stream along those seismic cracks eroded into its headwalls below the mouth of today's Pine Creek, incising the lava-dam enough to tap the enormous southern Idaho lake and release it northward. This surgically downcut the route of today's Snake River by eroding through a patchwork of volcanoes, Columbia

Snake River in Hells Canyon at Wild Sheep Rapid

basin basalts, and underlying sedimentary/igneous rocks from old accreted terranes that now variegate the inner gorge of Hells Canyon in gray and brown. This is Oregon's best example of river currents cutting the entire way through the massive Columbia River Basalt, which overlays much of the state's landscape. Then another cataclysm descended only 15,000 years ago when ice-age Lake Bonneville—big as Lake Michigan—broke free from bedrock barriers upstream in Utah and ripped through the Snake's corridor as an unimaginable 400-foot tidal wave and earthmover.

Today, harsh volcanic slopes above the shores blend to ponderosa pine, Douglas-fir, and grasslands; lower sections remain rocky, arid, notoriously hot in summer but starkly lovely with the spotty shade of hackberry trees.

A large mix of 24 native and alien fishes includes bass, trout, catfish, sturgeon, black crappie, suckers, and pikeminnows. The lower end of Hells Canyon is critical to imperiled steelhead and Chinook returning to the Grande Ronde and Imnaha Rivers and also to Idaho's Salmon River—once the world's most robust migration of Chinook. All the spawners must now overcome eight dams downstream before reaching their natal tributaries. Critically threatened, fall Chinook spawn directly in the Snake below Hells Canyon Dam. This is also one of the best river reaches supporting rare white sturgeon, which grow as long as some of the boats on the river.

CONSERVATION

Agricultural wastewater badly pollutes upper mileage of Oregon's Snake above Hells Canyon, and the state has issued advisories regarding fish consumption. Further handicapping that section of river, riparian vegetation has been systematically cleared, but the 86-island Deer Flat National Wildlife Refuge remains a reprieve. Water quality can be improved with wider riparian buffers, reduction of pesticides, and irrigation efficiency.

For all its problems, the 116-mile reach from Idaho's Swan Falls Dam to Brownlee Reservoir is the longest free-flowing section remaining on the entire four-state Snake, and dedicated people are working to reduce farm runoff.

Below the three-dam, 95-mile chain of hydropower reservoirs, 104 miles of river still flow through Hells Canyon to Asotin, all protected in one of the great sagas of river conservation history. In the 1960s the 700-foot Nez Perce Dam was proposed by the Bureau of Reclamation below the mouth of the Salmon River and would have flooded that legendary stream as well as the Snake's Hells Canyon. Conservationists and private power interests, which wanted to build their own dams nearby, halted the plan, but then the threat shifted to build a 670-foot High Mountain Sheep Dam, 1 mile above the Salmon in the heart of Hells Canyon. Utter ruin of the river was averted when Brock Evans of the Sierra Club and others succeeded with National Wild and Scenic River legislation in 1975—a conservation victory that signaled the beginning-of-the-end of the big-dam building era in America (see *Endangered Rivers and the Conservation Movement* about this heroic campaign). A 1980s proposal to build another dam downstream at Asotin—death knell to surviving salmon—was likewise halted.

Hydropower produced at the dams is inexpensive if the external costs are not counted. But before Idaho Power Company and earlier dam builders arrived, millions of salmon and steelhead migrated up the Snake to the Boise, Payette, Malheur, Owyhee, and other tributaries; some swam the whole way to Nevada. That enormous food supply of fish is now barred from 368 miles of the Snake to Shoshone Falls (near Twin Falls) and from 3,000 miles of spawning streams in all. For perspective on this loss, consider that today great efforts are made and millions of dollars spent to eliminate a single culvert barrier or obsolete dam that might block only a few miles of spawning habitat elsewhere.

The river suffers not only above the dams, but below too. Because suspended silt settles to the bottom of reservoirs, "hungry" water below erodes the banks but fails to deposit silt in the way that free-flowing rivers typically do when balancing erosion with deposition. Furthermore, Idaho Power manages the Snake for hydropower peaking, dumping a lot of erosive water in the afternoon and storing it at night. The combined effect of imbalanced input of silt and decades of extreme peaking-power flushes resulted in the disappearance of a once-rich riparian belt of willows, plus 80 percent of the spacious sandy beaches that had hallmarked an extraordinary place. Below the mouth of the Salmon River—still dam-free—larger beaches prevail where one can see a marked difference between the manipulated and free-flowing river regimes.

Yet wildness remains in the awe-inspiring canyon, the main stem still supports spawning Chinook, and the Snake continues as a conduit for fish en route to the Salmon River's free-flowing wildness. Federal law now requires updated licenses for the Hells Canyon dams, and with them, an opportunity for management improvements. Renewals have been withheld pending—among other things—resolution of water quality infractions; reservoir releases are too warm.

The hotter current debate, however, is about the four lower Snake River dams that hinder or bar salmon and steelhead on their journeys up and down river. These and the Columbia dams reduced the greatest runs of salmon in history—16 million or more fish basinwide—to endangered species. Current numbers even in rare good years are far below thresholds considered essential to the species' long-term survival. In the exceptionally good year of 2006, only 1 million salmon and steelhead returned to Bonneville Dam on the Columbia, according to the Fish Passage Center, and the great majority of those were from hatcheries, which may not be sustainable in the long-term. The Army Corps of Engineers' fish passage facilities and down-river transport—ironically done by trapping the young fish and motoring them as captive passengers in barges to sea-level—have failed to stem the salmon's long-term decline. Spilling more water over the dams during migration appears to have helped fish in several recent years, as have the ever-cycling conditions in the ocean.

Turbines at the four Snake River dams generate less than 4 percent of the Northwest's electricity—easily replaced through efficiency measures according to the Northwest Power and Conservation Council. To motor barges full of grain and wood products from Lewiston, 450 miles from the ocean, was the impetus for building the dams, but the barging system, with its commodities bound for Asia, is almost completely subsidized, and only a small fraction of the Columbia River's traffic goes the whole way up to Lewiston. If the four dams from Pasco to Lewiston were breached, railroads could easily fill the gap, as they used to do. Even in Lewiston, where people vociferously backed the damming of their river, support for removal now grows because the uppermost reservoir pool, lapping at the town's edge, constantly aggrades with silt deposits, which inexorably raise the riverbed and promise to eventually flood parts of the community.

Touting economic as well as fishery benefits, groups including Idaho Rivers United and Save our Wild Salmon Coalition argue for removal of the four dams. In 2011 Judge James Redden agreed with them that the federal government's position regarding endangered species was flawed, and for the fourth time in 20 years the court ordered the agency to prepare a better plan. This time, consideration of dam removal was required, but the initial response in 2014 showed little change in the federal plan. The outcome of this drama will become either one of the greatest river conservation stories in our history or one of the greatest ongoing tragedies.

The agricultural Snake can be seen from boat ramps in Adrian, Nyssa, Ontario, and Farewell Bend (upper Brownlee Reservoir). Hells Canyon Dam—and the boaters' put-in for Hells Canyon just below—is reached from Halfway, Oregon, or more often via the Idaho side; from I-84 at Ontario take Hwy 95 north to Cambridge, turn west on Hwy 71, and go 29 miles past Oxbow Dam to Hells Canyon Dam.

Hells Canyon remains largely inaccessible by car, except for a steep gravel road to Pittsburg Landing; from Hwy 95 at White Bird (Idaho) cross to the west side of the Salmon River and take gravel Deer Creek Road (493) west 16 miles. From Pittsburg you can walk upstream along the east side trail 35 miles to Brush Creek (3 miles below Hells Canyon Dam)—great hiking, spring or fall.

More remote, Dug Bar Road (4-wheel recommended) rattles to the canyon's bottom on Oregon's side; from Joseph drive east 30 miles to Imnaha and continue north on Lower Imnaha Road, which becomes rough in 7 miles but continues another 25 miles; cross the Imnaha, then bear left to Dug Bar and the west-side Snake River Trail, which clings to canyonsides for 56 miles up to Battle Creek (4 miles below Hells Canyon Dam).

Or, for fit hikers, drive to the crossroads at Imnaha, turn south on Upper Imnaha River Road, go 13 miles to just before the Imnaha bridge, angle left on FR 4230 at signs to Saddle Creek Trail, and continue 3 miles to Freezeout/Saddle Creek Trailhead. Hike uphill 1,700 feet to Freezeout Saddle, then down Saddle Creek to the Snake. From there the River Trail reaches upstream to Battle Creek, while the longer hike aims downstream—25 miles of canyon to Pleasant Valley Creek or beyond. Summertime in Hells Canyon is insufferably hot; May is ideal; autumn is pleasant. Beware of rattlesnakes.

My favorite hike to the canyon is easy via the Imnaha River; from its lowest bridge walk down the west-side Imnaha Trail 4 miles to the Snake (poison ivy). Several other trails reach the bottom of Hells Canyon—long, strenuous, hot, remote routes with interminable approaches.

A canyon overview can be seen from the Hells Canyon Overlook via paved road between Imnaha and Halfway, but even there the Snake remains hidden within its inner gorge. Hat Point has the only road-accessible view of the distant river from the rim, though the arduous approach doesn't make much sense unless you're planning an extended tour of the region; go to Imnaha, take the more easterly of two gravel roads headed south (FR 4240), wind 22 miles and turn right to Hat Point. For serious hikers, Somers Point has a great view if you backpack 27 miles round-trip; go to Hat Point's turnoff and continue on the main road 4 miles to the Warnock Creek Trail (see *100 Classic Hikes in Oregon*).

Just downstream from Hells Canyon and north of the Oregon-Washington line, Heller Bar offers access to the Snake and takeout for Hells Canyon trips. From Clarkston go south on Hwy 129 to Asotin, bear left at the light, and follow Heller Bar Road.

 Much of the Snake has great bass fishing. See accessible locations listed above and below. When steelhead and salmon runs are adequate, a sport season opens as a major regional economic event. Heller Bar is a favorite spot that's easily reached. In this large river many anglers prefer fishing by boat, either in the canyon or from Heller Bar to Asotin.

Through its agricultural valley upstream from Brownlee Reservoir the Snake is rarely visited by recreational boaters, but from Swan Falls Dam to Weiser, this broad flow is worth doing once for real river aficionados. The eye-opening tour of industrial farmland in an ignored corner of Oregon includes remnants of riparian corridors and unvisited islands of the Deer Flat National Wildlife Refuge. Put in on the north side at Swan Falls Dam, or below at Homedale's park just north of Hwy 19 (6 miles east of the state line), or at Nyssa—best known for colossal white piles of sugar beet processing waste rising from the banks. With flows diverted and banks overgrown in weeds, the mouths of the Owyhee and Malheur Rivers are scarcely noticeable. Then the comparatively refreshing flows of the Boise and Payette Rivers enter. Take out at a ramp on the right just upstream of Weiser, or continue to Brownlee Reservoir backwaters for a trip of 116 miles from Swan Falls.

The big prize here is Hells Canyon, second only to the Colorado's Grand Canyon for enormous rapids in a high-volume western river. Summer flows up to 13,000 cfs are manageable by experienced rafters or kayakers. The most challenging big water occurs at 20,000 cfs, though springtime peaks of 60,000 create an other-worldly sense of scale. Boats of any kind in the wrong place (monstrous holes) can be flipped at any level, and long swims are especially hazardous early in the season. Flows in the lower-gradient reach below the Salmon River can double with that tributary's inflow.

Spring boating in Hells Canyon thrills with its soaring sweep of green grasslands, but includes high-water challenges. Summer sizzles with little shade but delightful conditions on the water. Fall is exquisite with good weather lingering to early October. Permits are required and numbers are limited; call Hells Canyon National Recreation Area (208-743-2297).

To put in, drive to Hells Canyon Dam (see above). Most boaters run 79 miles to Heller Bar. Some exit after only 31 miles at Pittsburg Landing to avoid a longer shuttle, heavy jet boat traffic, and gentler rapids. I, on the other hand, recommend continuing on enjoyable water with nice campsites the whole way to Asotin for a truly significant 104-mile journey—longer than almost any other big-water expedition in the West (headwinds and motorboats increase below Heller).

The uppermost 17 miles present the biggest whitewater: Class 4 at Wild Sheep (scout left 6 miles down from Hells Canyon Dam), Granite Creek (2 miles later, scout left or right), and then Lower Bernard Creek, Waterspout, and Rush Creek, plus scores of smaller but powerful drops. At 20,000 cfs early in the season, Granite Creek Rapid's "Green Room" has the largest glassy green wave anywhere.

Though most of the sand has disappeared with hydroelectric peaking, good campsites remain. Beware of the hydropower release, which can rise and fall 1 foot per hour and 5 vertical feet total, ramping from 5,000 cfs to 20,000 in seemingly no-time. Alone once, I had to swim in heavy current to retrieve my raft, which I had pulled far onto the beach but foolishly forgotten to tie.

In the heart of Hells Canyon boaters can access good hiking on the west and east side trails, plus paths up tributaries that are difficult to reach from land: Battle, Granite, Saddle, Sluice, and Temperance Creeks.

The shuttle for Hells Canyon is long, and the jet boats annoy non-motorized boaters, yet this trip remains an exquisite adventure, an American classic, and the premier big-water wilderness voyage of Oregon.

OWYHEE RIVER

Length: 347 miles, 198 in OR
Average flow: 1,213 cfs
Watershed: 10,569 square miles

The upper Owyhee basin endures as one of the wildest, most rugged regions in the state and one of the least accessible desert-canyon complexes in the West. Fourth-longest river running wholly or partly in Oregon, it drains canyonlands extending to southern Idaho and northern Nevada, but owing to the desert climate, runoff is light (comparable to the Wilson River, which is only 36 miles long). With irrigation diversions in the lower basin, there's scarcely any summertime flow at the mouth. The main stem is joined by the North and Middle Forks at Three Forks, 21 miles downstream from the Idaho line. From Three Forks to Owyhee Reservoir, the river flows through 96 miles of roadless and nearly trail-less canyons; one highway crosses.

Lava flows of dark basalt and tan, orange-tinted rhyolite have eroded to ledges, pinnacles, and intriguing sculptures decorating a canyon half a mile deep in places. Fantasy-land cliffs veer 1,000 feet from the river. The resistant basalt and rhyolite create steep rapids with rock that's dangerously sharp for raft fabric and swimmers.

On the lower river, 417-foot-high Owyhee Dam was the world's tallest in 1932 and prototype for Hoover Dam, backing up a 55-mile reservoir. It extinguished a unique run of Chinook that had migrated to this unexpectedly rich desert spawning grounds. Except during rare, high spring runoff, the Bureau of Reclamation releases 40 cfs or less from the dam in winter and 200 during summer's irrigation season, but most of this is extracted not far below the dam and never makes it to the river's lower 30 miles.

Along Oregon's upper Owyhee, remarkable cliff faces, warm springs, and geologic curiosities abound, as do bighorn sheep, rattlesnakes, and raptors. Most of the canyon is publicly owned except 10 miles through Rome. In a region overrun with alien cheatgrass and tumbleweed, Owyhee canyons remain relatively unaffected. But a legacy of upstream mining has left heavy metals including mercury in sediments; the state issues fish consumption advisories for the reservoir.

The Owyhee is a National Wild and Scenic river for 86 miles from Three Forks to Owyhee Reservoir, excepting 10 miles above and below Rome. Additional headwater mileage, including other Wild and Scenic reaches with intriguing boatable waters, lie in Idaho.

 To reach remote Three Forks, take Hwy 95 east from Rome 16 miles, turn south on the dirt Three Forks Road for 35 miles, right on Fenwick Ranch Road (impassably greasy

Owyhee River downstream of Owyhee Dam

when wet, even on the flats), and drop steeply to the river (4-wheel-drive recommended).

For an Owyhee hike, best in springtime, take Three Forks Road to the Fenwick Ranch (Soldier Creek) Road intersection (3 miles short of Three Forks), continue 0.8 miles west toward the rim, park, and look for the unsigned, nominal Wes Hawkins Trail to the right, or to a jeep track angling right. Another 2.5 miles westward lead to views at the rim. To reach the river from there, walk to a cairn at the rim and down the brushy trail. Better—once the water drops (by June)—drive or walk the steep pitch to Three Forks, ford the main stem, scramble downstream to the military grade switchbacks, and climb to the western rim for river views.

To see the lower end of the Three Forks to Rome reach, take Hwy 95 just west of Rome, turn south on Skull Creek Road, and bear left on a lane to the river, good for a cool dip.

The lower canyon can be reached via a 4-wheel-drive road to Birch Creek; from Jordan Valley take Hwy 95 north 8 miles to the Jordan Craters sign, turn west on Cow Creek Road, and follow Owyhee signs 28 miles to BLM's Birch Creek Historic Ranch (avoid when wet).

The easiest way to see the Owyhee is by paved road below the dam. Though the river there is shorn of natural flows and wildness, its beauty and vitality came as a complete surprise to me. Clear water from the reservoir winds through a spectacular canyon above the major diversion point, and the road's great for biking. Take Hwy 20 south from Ontario to Nyssa, then Hwy 201 southwest 8 miles, follow signs, and enter the 13-mile canyon of public land, with Snively Hot Springs 3 miles up, plus campsites.

 The upper river has smallmouth bass and channel catfish, while native redband survive in some tributaries. Below the dam, cold tailwater attracts many fly fishermen to the popular hatchery rainbow/brown trout fishery.

The main stem offers challenging short-season whitewater for experienced boaters. Oregon's upper run, Three Forks to Rome, descends a deep wild canyon with no access for 36 miles, runnable (1,200–4,000 cfs at Rome) while snow melts April–May on good years (sometimes lasting to June, sometimes not at all). The put-in road closes on short notice with mud. Class 4 rapids intensify to Class 5. Below the put-in 20 miles, a 200-yard narrow stretch of Class 3 feeds the gnarly Class 5+ Widowmaker—an arduous portage complete with rattlesnake hazards. This is usually lined on the right; medium-sized rafts up to 15 feet recommended. If you're motivated to see this remarkable canyon but you miss the springtime flush, or you sensibly don't want to deal with the big drops, you can paddle and drag a canoe or kayak up from the Rome access—determined paddlers have gone the whole 16 miles to Widowmaker.

More popular, a wider canyon below Rome is a Class 2–3 run with some Class 4 for 67 miles, April–June (1,000–4,000 cfs) on a good year. Small inflatables can be paddled and dragged on flows as low as 300 or maybe less. Midway, Lambert Rocks rise on the right, with Chalk Basin on the left. Trails lead to colorful cliffs, arches, and hoodoos. Watch for bighorn sheep. Class 3 Whistling Bird Rapid lies 30 miles below Rome, followed in 2 miles by Class 4 Montgomery, and 5 miles later by Nuisance Rapid with its nasty wrap-rock. Birch Creek takeout (see above) involves rough roads but avoids the day-long 11-mile row on Owyhee Reservoir, ending at Leslie Gulch. For this takeout, follow Hwy 95 north from Jordan Valley 19 miles, turn west on Succor Creek Road, left on Leslie Gulch Road, and continue 14 miles. An attraction in its own right, the trail at Leslie tours a colorful canyon maze of rhyolite.

Variable weather—intense heat to freezing in the Owyhee's short springtime boating season—makes the alternative appealing: low-flow, early-summer trips with inflatable kayaks. Floater numbers are not restricted but self-issue permits are mandatory at the launch; portable toilet/firepan required.

Below the dam, the lower canyon offers excellent Class 1–2 summer canoeing for about 8 miles—rare in the desert. Do your best to avoid anglers.

WEST LITTLE OWYHEE

Among Oregon's wildest rivers, the West Little Owyhee has no dams, diversions, development, roads alongside, or trails,

Length: 63 miles
Average flow: 18 cfs
Watershed: 310 square miles

and it just so happens, almost no water. Though nearly dry much of the time, this is one of the longer streams designated Wild and Scenic from source to mouth. Cattle have grazed heavily in places; bighorn sheep can be seen in others. BLM manages the watershed as a wilderness study area.

 For the few who are up for such remote geography, take Hwy 95 south from Burns Junction (nowhere near Burns), go 40 miles, turn east on a gravel road, go 1.2 miles, bear right, go 14 miles, turn right (southeast), follow the main road across Antelope

Creek, go 19 miles to Anderson Crossing, and walk upstream or down. Canyoneers have tackled the rigorous 40-mile trek/scramble down to Three Forks.

MALHEUR RIVER

Length: 190 miles
Average flow: 201 cfs
Watershed: 4,703 square miles

Precipitation is scant through the Malheur basin, with most water in the main stem coming from the Strawberry Mountains while the Blue Mountains feed the North Fork. The river is best known along Hwy 20 where it wanders arid ranchland and where diversions leave only weedy trickles. But above there, a rare section of desert river maintains strong summer-long flows, and higher yet, headwaters tumble through magnificent ponderosa pine canyons.

On the upper river, through Malheur National Forest, 12 miles are designated Wild and Scenic in a 1,000-foot-deep basalt canyon. Native redband and bull trout led the American Fisheries Society to identify the upper main stem, North Fork, and Little Malheur as aquatic diversity areas. Before Warm Springs Dam was built downstream in 1919, Chinook and steelhead spawned far up in highly productive habitat.

Below Warm Springs Dam, sizable flows are released through the irrigation season and reduced afterward, though the stream is still fished in autumn. Given good productivity here, some anglers believe that, with more attention to releases from the dam, the middle Malheur could become a trophy trout fishery rivaling the Deschutes.

Below Harper the river is shunted into 370 miles of canals and ditches; return flows cause phosphorus, bacteria, pesticide, and high-temperature

Upper Malheur River below Middle Ford

Malheur River below Warm Springs Dam

pollution in the lower 67 miles. Riparian habitat here is some of the West's most degraded according to *Oregon's Living Landscape*. Confronted with pollution problems, the Malheur County Soil and Water Conservation District and landowners in 2004 created a 13-acre wetland to filter farm waste, and their success spurred additional plans. Meanwhile the Malheur Watershed Council helped farmers convert to water-saving sprinklers.

The small South Fork Malheur starts in drylands east of Malheur Lake (the lake is not hydrologically connected to the river) and traverses ranchlands before meeting the main stem below Warm Springs Dam.

 The 8-mile Malheur River Trail is one of the great riverfront walks in eastern Oregon, with exceptional larches and ponderosa pines in delightful glades. From the town of John Day drive south on Hwy 395 to Seneca, go east on FR 16 for 17 miles, turn south on gravel FR 1643 for 12 miles to Malheur Ford, and hike down the west side.

Lower, the ranchland Malheur can be seen 39 miles east of Burns at the Hwy 20 bridge. Downstream from hayfields there, the river flows 10 miles through a trail-less canyon of BLM and state land to Warm Springs Reservoir.

From Warm Springs Dam to Juntura, an 18-mile semi-wild canyon through BLM and state land is a little-known highlight of southeastern Oregon; take Hwy 20 to Juntura, go south on Juntura-Riverside Road 17 gravel miles to Riverside, and angle left on the access lane. Below Juntura, the Malheur and Hwy 20 wind among 35 miles of badlands and ranches to diversions near Harper, followed by the depleted river through pastures and farms to the mouth north of Ontario.

 The upper river has good fishing for wild redband and brook trout, with redband and hatchery rainbows from Warm Springs Dam to below Juntura. Here trout season is open year-round and excellent in autumn. More turbid, the South Fork is not fished much.

 Quite a surprise, the Malheur from Warm Springs Dam to Juntura has a typical summer dam release, May–October, of 500 cfs, offering a rare boating opportunity in this harsh desert. Fast Class 1–2 water tours a basalt canyon with scenic cliffs, rolling hills, and some hayfields with an abandoned railroad alongside. Two barbed wire fences posed serious hazards during my 2012 trip: one 11 miles after put-in and above Little Mosquito Creek, and one between two houses a mile above takeout. Lucky, I was able to slip over each. Put in at Riverside access (see above) and take out above Allen Diversion Dam; from Juntura drive south on Riverside Road 2.2 miles and go left on a rough lane for 2 miles to the rock-dam. Downstream, fences are troublesome to Juntura. For shuttles call Juntura's Oasis Cafe.

A nice 5-mile Class 1+ canoe/tubing reach below Juntura has summertime dam releases from the main stem and North Fork. To avoid Juntura area fences take Hwy 20 east from Juntura 2 miles and turn left for access at the old bridge. Take out at a pulloff 4 miles farther east on 20. Below there, flows continue through ranches and badlands to Harper, but fences and diversions are likely hazards.

NORTH FORK MALHEUR RIVER

Length: 62 miles
Average flow: 137 cfs
Watershed: 523 square miles

This fork rises on the Blue Mountains' southern flank, flows south to Beulah Dam, and joins the main Malheur at Juntura. From source to National Forest boundary, 23 miles are a National Wild and Scenic River through

North Fork Malheur River below North Fork Campground

fine ponderosa forest and an 800-foot-deep basalt canyon. Until the dam was built in 1935, Chinook and steelhead spawned here. Bull trout survive in remote reaches.

 To see the upper river, go south from Prairie City on Hwy 62 (South Side of River Road), in 9 miles turn left on FR 13, go 16 miles, bear right on FR 1600 for 2 miles, then left on the rough FR 1675 for 3 miles to a campground and another 2 miles to the trailhead. With girthy ponderosas, magnificent larches, and basalt talus slopes, the trail winds 11 miles downstream to a dead-end. A side trail in 3 miles turns right and ascends Crane Creek. The Little Malheur confluence is 14 miles below Crane Creek, followed in 8 miles by Beulah Reservoir.

To see the lower North Fork, drive to Juntura and take Beulah Road (gravel) up the lower North Fork 6 miles to a BLM campground, then along 2 miles of whitewater, then through 7 miles of ranches and juniper to Beulah Dam.

 Upper reaches support native redband and rainbow with excellent angling, especially in autumn, artificial lures only.

LITTLE MALHEUR RIVER

The steep wooded canyon of this North Fork Malheur tributary lies in Monument Rock Wilderness and was heavily burned in 2002.

Length: 31 miles
Average flow: 18 cfs
Watershed: 135 square miles

 An 8-mile trail here has all but disappeared after the Monument Fire; remaining sections are riddled with fallen logs and officially "unmaintained" (volunteers with saws are needed!).

Little Malheur River in Monument Rock Wilderness

Until further maintenance, I don't recommend this hike for fun, but the outing shows interesting results of a large fire: beyond an ocean of dead trees you can see tremendous amounts of wood in the stream, a mosaic of burned and spared areas, unburned waterfront refuges, large trees including 5-foot diameter larch that survived intense heat, abundant deer, and robust riparian recovery. From Prairie City drive south on Hwy 62 for 9 miles, go left on FR 13 for 12 miles, then left on FR 1370 for 5 gravel miles to the trailhead.

 The Little Malheur has native redband.

BURNT RIVER

Length: 85 miles
Average flow: 131 cfs
Watershed: 1,041 square miles

This stream's headwaters from the southeastern Blue Mountains gather in Unity Reservoir, then flow east 20 miles through foothill ranchland, gold mining refuse, and Burnt River Canyon. Farther down, the stream can be spotted along I-84 in channelized bends, with railroad encroachment and a massive quarry and cement plant alongside. The former salmon stream ends in Snake River backwaters of Oxbow Dam.

For Burnt River Canyon, take I-84 east from Baker City 26 miles to exit 327 (Durkee), go north 1 mile on Old Hwy 30, then left on Burnt River Canyon Lane—a 20-mile byway ascending the rugged drainage. Recreational miners dig and dredge here, and at the top of the canyon, east of Bridgeport, massive cobble piles illustrate a legacy of uncontrolled mining in the past.

Burnt River Canyon above Durkee

Lower Powder River Canyon along Hwy 86

POWDER RIVER

Length: 153 miles
Average flow: 534 cfs
Watershed: 1,603 square miles

The circuitous Powder drops east from Blue Mountain headwaters, ponds in Phillips Reservoir (Mason Dam), aims north through Baker City and beyond, then cuts abruptly southeast again to the impounded Snake near Richland.

The upper stream percolates through Oregon's largest wasteland of mining debris: 7 miles of tailings above Phillips Reservoir. At middle reaches, a nearly inaccessible 12 miles of private and BLM land is designated Wild and Scenic below Thief Valley Dam and, though well hidden, features volcanic outcrops, bald eagles, and rainbow trout. Diversion structures in the lower end of this reach extract virtually all water in summer; this may be the only National Wild and Scenic River with complete dewatering grandfathered-in.

In upper reaches Hwy 7 passes Mason Dam, and just below it a mile-long loop trail follows the clear stream in Powder River Recreation Area. Downstream, in central Baker City off Campbell and Grove Streets, Geiser Pollman Park offers access to the channelized waters. Below town, ranchlands blanket the Baker and Powder Valleys.

The Wild and Scenic section can be reached for a limited and weedy quarter-mile walk along the north bank below Thief Valley Dam. North of Baker City take I-84 exit 285, go north on Hwy 237 for 7.4 miles, right on Telocaset Lane 6 miles, right at the Thief Valley sign for 1.3 miles, then left on a dirt lane to the dam and path downstream. Below, private parcels are followed by obscure and beautifully wild BLM acreage; from Baker City go 6 miles north on I-84, turn east on Hwy 203 for about 10 miles, a quarter mile before the Powder bridge turn left on an unmarked dirt road crossing a cattle guard, continue 2 miles to Big Creek, and walk 0.5 miles down to the Powder.

At the lower river, some water is returned to a 13-mile roaded canyon; in north Baker City take I-84 exit 302 and go east on Hwy 86 for 20 miles. Remains of a massive 1984 slide can be seen at an interpretive sign 8 miles into the canyon, where a small lake remains from a debris dam that formed and quickly burst.

 Recreation areas below Mason Dam and in Baker City have stocked rainbows. Below Thief Valley the short public reach is fished for hatchery trout in late spring before algae thicken.

 The reach below Thief Valley is reportedly Class 4 with multiple fences at private land and with portages—not advised. For the lower river, *Soggy Sneakers* describes springtime Class 3 paddling (450–900 cfs at Richland). It looks like this would be a fine 6-mile rocky run even at low early-summer levels. The old Hwy 86 put-in, 20 miles east of I-84, is fenced at a new bridge; use BLM pulloffs 2 miles downstream. Take out along the road 1 mile above Slide Lake.

NORTH POWDER RIVER

Length: 25 miles
Average flow: 90 cfs
Watershed: 118 square miles

This Powder tributary begins in a glaciated canyon shaded with subalpine fir between Twin and Red Mountains—each 8,920 feet. Through old-growth conifers the river supports wild rainbows in a 6-mile reach of National Wild and Scenic River, from the source to National Forest boundary. Below, the North Powder mostly disappears in hayfield diversions.

North Powder River at lower National Forest boundary

I tried the difficult approach to this tiny Wild and Scenic River north of Baker City by taking Anthony Lakes Highway west of North Powder, going south on Foothill Road 3.6 miles, west on Bulger Flat Lane 2.6 miles, left on rough dirt for 0.5 miles to the bridge, then walking upstream on cow paths and a maze of tractor-logging tracks. Headwaters hiking is likely better via a long drive south of Elkhorn Crest off FR 73.

EAGLE CREEK

Highlight of the Powder basin, Eagle Creek is one of five stellar radial streams that encircle Oregon's Wallowa Range—

Length: 41 miles
Average flow: 316 cfs
Watershed: 196 square miles

granite-gleaming outlier of the Rocky Mountains right here in Oregon. Eagle Creek and the Imnaha, Wallowa, Lostine, and Minam Rivers flow from the state's largest protected wilderness and offer Oregon's most spectacular high-mountain streamfront hiking.

The creek begins in a glacial cirque beneath 9,595-foot Eagle Cap. Aiming south through alpine zones of flowered meadows and resinous forests, it picks up West Eagle and then East Fork Eagle Creek, which is larger as it plunges through a longer wonderland of highcountry than the main stem. Eagle's glacier-sculpted upper basin transforms to an incised canyon below the West Eagle confluence. Farther down at Little Eagle Creek, the river morphs to a foothills stream amid ponderosa pines, grass, and basalt, then is largely diverted before joining the Powder. Clear pools alternate with waterfalls and whitewater, native trout refuges, and old-growth forests in successive highcountry, canyon, and foothill habitats.

Eagle Creek downstream of East Fork confluence

East Fork Eagle Creek at trailhead

Columbia basalt flows occurring between 17 and 6 million years ago covered the area, but then seismic forces pushed the Wallowas up 5,000 feet, exposing them to erosion from rivers and glaciers, which peeled away the basalt to reveal a brilliant underlying core of granite that creates rapids in today's rivers.

From source to National Forest boundary, the main stem's 27 miles are a National Wild and Scenic River. Mining claims remain where suction dredgers operate. Plans for clearcuts (now on hold) prompted ranchers in the 1980s to organize to protect their water. The fine stream dodged another bullet when a hydroelectric dam was proposed on lower reaches—back-burnered for now.

Outstanding trails ascend the main stem and three forks. To reach low-elevation hiking from Baker City, take Hwy 86 to Richland, turn north on New Bridge Road, and drive 10 miles to the main stem at a campground and the lower terminus of Martin Bridge Trail (named for a limestone formation, not a bridge). This path ascends 6 roadless miles—enticing when high elevations are still snowed in—to an upper trailhead. It and higher tributary trails are best reached from the southwest; from I-84 north of Baker City take Hwy 86 east 12 miles, turn north on gravel 852 for 4 miles, left on 891 (FR 70) 5 miles, right on FR 7015, cross the creek, and turn right to upper Martin Bridge Trail.

To reach the East Fork, take FR 77 up the valley from the upper Martin Bridge trailhead for 3 miles, then go right on East Fork Road 6 miles to the trailhead. Before setting out, stroll from the end of the road to the river for a view of thousand-foot "Granite Cliff"—perhaps the finest stream-and-mountain view in Oregon. East Fork Trail climbs 11 miles to rapturous alpine country beneath Eagle Cap summit.

Back at the East Fork turnoff, take FR 77 upstream (closed at this writing) and west 6 miles to FR 7755, which climbs 5 miles to Boulder Park and a 7-mile trail to Eagle Lake (dammed at its outlet). Beyond the 7755 turnoff, FR 77 proceeds west 5 more miles to a switchback at the West Eagle Creek Trail, which climbs 7 miles to sublime Traverse Lake. Loop hikes of a week are good through Eagle Creek country, where fearsome mosquitoes wane after July.

PINE CREEK

On the southeast slope of the Wallowa Mountains, the West and East Forks of Pine Creek join and flow to ranchland

Length: 35 miles	
Average flow: 191 cfs	
Watershed: 277 square miles	

and a valley ribboned with cottonwoods, through the welcoming burg of Halfway, then northeast to the Snake River in Hells Canyon Reservoir. The valley and canyon east of Halfway is beautifully lush with riparian forest beneath summer's golden-dry mountains.

North Pine Creek tumbles south through a canyon exactly parallel to the Snake, just 3 miles away but dropping in the opposite direction. This is odd enough, but the route also perfectly matches the north-south alignment of the Imnaha River immediately northward, as if both adhere to fault lines, though such faults are not mapped there. Chinook and steelhead migrated to Pine Creek before Hells Canyon Dam went up; remote enclaves remain home to bull trout and native rainbows, now isolated by dams and diversions.

North of Halfway a local road parallels Pine Creek to headwaters and a mining district, with trails up East and West Forks. Downstream from Halfway, Hwy 86 follows the river and its riparian corridor, excellent for biking in spring or fall.

To reach North Pine Creek from Halfway, take 86 east 10 miles and turn north toward Joseph. This route follows the stream 12 miles with

Pine Creek downstream from Halfway

pulloffs, then climbs 11 miles to Hells Canyon Overlook (big view but the Snake River is hidden). The route connects with Imnaha Road for an extended scenic drive or bicycle expedition (if you're up for the 20-mile climb to the overlook) on quiet paved byways.

 Paddling Oregon lists a Class 3+ Pine Creek run in late spring (250–800 cfs) from the North Pine confluence down, dropping through 8 miles of continuous whitewater and brushy shores with log hazards.

IMNAHA RIVER

| Length: 73 miles, 83 with SF |
| Average flow: 510 cfs |
| Watershed: 851 square miles |

Like the Owyhee, the Imnaha occupies a remote hinterland at the state's eastern limits, but unlike that desert river, it flows through a lush world of clear water, conifers, cottonwood floodplains, and high mountains with glorious weather and cool nights all summer long. With no dams and with wildness all around, the Imnaha is a secluded whitewater gem in its mile-deep canyon. One might think of it as a delightfully intimate iteration of Hells Canyon, but narrower, greener, more accessible, and more immediately linked to snowy headwaters. The stream drops from 8,000 to 900 feet through an almost unparalleled range of habitats in such short length. Lower reaches are northeastern Oregon's banana belt—haven for wintering deer, elk, and bighorns. What else can I say? This rugged place is fantastic.

The Imnaha begins as the South Fork on the flanks of Eagle Cap Peak. Amid crags of granite, limestone, and basalt, it drops through meadows and old-growth. The middle reach flows directly north into semi-arid ranchland incised by steep tributary canyons. Rainshadowed by surrounding mountains, lowlands lie in arid contrast to adjacent peaks. The final 5 miles drop through rocky rapids and a fantasy landscape of cliffs and rock towers ending in the depths of Hells Canyon one bend upstream from the Snake/Salmon River confluence.

The Imnaha's route north uncannily mirrors the northbound route of the Snake itself, just a few miles east and separated by only a thin massif that forms the backbone of Hells Canyon National Recreation Area. The river's extraordinarily straight course is only the largest in a striking suite of paralleling stream alignments echoed in tributaries Big Sheep, Horse, Lightning, Cow, and Deep Creeks, plus the Grande Ronde tributary Joseph Creek and its branches. All flow north as if the landscape were streaked by a giant claw scraping the land, or as if a clustered alignment of seismicity were the common cause, yet Oregon's geologic map does not reveal faults to be the source of these curiously parallel canyons. Another possible explanation is water flowing down the dip of tilted basalt.

The Imnaha is the uppermost major Snake tributary still accessible to anadromous fish. Productive and pristine, this is a fine steelhead stream with native rainbow and bull trout, plus one of the Snake basin's surviving runs of Chinook. The *Interior Columbia Basin Ecosystem*

Imnaha River below Cow Creek Bridge

Management Project rates the Imnaha with a rare "high degree of aquatic integrity"—status shared with adjacent Joseph Creek along with the Minam, Wallowa, and Wenaha Rivers, together making this an outstanding region of natural rivers in the West. The Imnaha is also part of a distinguished group designated Wild and Scenic source to mouth, and perhaps the most splendid Wild and Scenic River with so much private land. To protect open space, the Nature Conservancy has acquired riverfront parcels once slated for sale as homesites above the village of Imnaha.

 For headwaters, drive east from Joseph 8 miles, turn south on FR 39, wind 28 miles, turn right on FR 3960, and drop 9 miles to Indian Crossing Campground at road's end. Superb trails head up the main stem 6 miles to the South/North Fork confluence, then up the South Fork's 11 miles of rapids and waterfalls, peaking at Hawkins Pass. Another trail climbs the North Fork 9 miles.

From Indian Crossing downward, Imnaha Road (FR 3960 then 3955) parallels the river 15 miles through Hells Canyon National Recreation Area with several campgrounds. Private land then accounts for most frontage along 26 miles to Imnaha village. To drive directly to this middle river, go to Joseph and then 30 miles east on paved Hwy 350 (Little Sheep Creek Highway) to Imnaha. Private land hugs the river for 7 miles downstream to Cottonwood Creek, then private and National Forest land mix for 14 gravel miles to Cow Creek Bridge. There the road climbs east, but an excellent west-side trail follows the lower Imnaha through a deepening canyon, 4 miles to the Snake River (thick with poison ivy).

 Anglers find stocked and native rainbows in upper reaches, summer–early fall. Steelhead run September 1–April 15, catch-and-release. The lower river has good fishing below Cottonwood Creek.

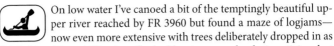 On low water I've canoed a bit of the temptingly beautiful upper river reached by FR 3960 but found a maze of logjams—now even more extensive with trees deliberately dropped in as fish habitat. The middle river, flanked by steep grasslands, is enticing, but landowners have aggressively barred access. *Paddling Oregon* lists a Class 4 run from Imnaha down with log hazards and steep rapids.

One of the more enjoyable whitewater canoe runs I've done was the lower Imnaha, 4 miles from Cow Creek Bridge to the Snake, but, to reach a takeout road entails continuing on the Snake for 23 big-volume miles to Heller Bar. I opportunistically scheduled my lower Imnaha exploration before rafting Hells Canyon, paddled my C-1 canoe down the stream, hid it at the mouth, walked back to the road at Cow Creek, and a week later rowed down the Snake and retrieved the canoe. But the lower Imnaha may have complexified after floods in 1996, or rockslides, or perhaps I got a Class 3-pass with low water; *Paddling Oregon* and others list challenging Class 4 rapids here. Definitely look first by hiking the trail.

GRANDE RONDE RIVER

The Grande Ronde winds through forests, grasslands, and canyons, and provides for native bull trout as well as depleted runs of Snake

Length: 209 miles, 173 in OR (including meanders cut-off by the State Ditch)
Average flow: 3,053 cfs
Watershed: 3,308 square miles

River Chinook and steelhead. Upper reaches gather water from the Wallowa-Whitman National Forest and pass through La Grande. After long farmland wanderings, the river drops again, meets the Wallowa, and cuts a striking canyon 3,000 feet deep with ponderosa savanna to Troy. The lower canyon continues another 47 increasingly arid miles, crossing

Grande Ronde River above Hwy 129 bridge

into Washington and joining the Snake at the base of Hells Canyon. Brilliant green in spring and early summer, the canyons are home to deer, bighorns, bears, and elk; bald eagles roost in winter.

The river once boasted world-class salmon and steelhead, now decimated by downstream dams on the lower Snake. A unique run of coho—much farther inland than typical—went extinct in 1987. But the lower river remains critical for Chinook spawning, and with relatively little hatchery influence, distinct breeding populations survive. Native rainbows, bull trout, and mountain whitefish hide in cool tributaries, and the *Interior Columbia Basin Ecosystems Management Project* ranked the lower Grande Ronde as the largest watershed east of the Cascades having highest ratings for aquatic integrity.

The upper river still suffers elevated temperatures owing to historic grazing, roads, railroads, and beaver eradication, but restoration with broad participation is making headway. As one of the more bizarre diversions anywhere, the river 7 miles below La Grande was shunted into the State Ditch in the 1860s as a means of dewatering 40 richly meandering miles of riparian wetlands through ranches. This shortcut has since captured the entire river and grown from 6- to 80-foot widths. Below, for 44 miles from the Wallowa confluence to the Washington line, the Grande Ronde is a National Wild and Scenic River and a State Scenic Waterway. The mid- and lower Grande Ronde benefits from cold-water inflow of the Wallowa, Wenaha, and Joseph Creek.

A mid-river tributary, Catherine Creek drains the southwestern Wallowas for 32 miles and in lower reaches follows the Grande Ronde's former course before the State Ditch was excavated. In the 1970s a dam on Catherine was considered but dropped. To see the creek, take Hwy 203 southeast from La Grande to Union and continue 8 miles to a state park campground and streamfront path. Back on 203, go another 4 miles, turn left on FR7785 for 6 miles to North Fork Catherine Trail and hike through old-growth conifers.

As the Grande Ronde's lowest tributary, Joseph Creek enters in Washington. The 49-mile-long stream harboring native rainbows and steelhead drops through pine savanna with cottonwoods. The nearly inaccessible canyon (though only a sliver of the creek) can be spotted from a distant Hwy 3 viewpoint 30 miles north of Enterprise. Joseph's lower section can be reached from Heller Bar on the Snake; drive up Grande Ronde Road 8 miles.

To see the upper Grande Ronde, take I-84 west from La Grande 4 miles to exit 252 where Hilgard Junction State Park has camping and access. Then take Hwy 244 west 8 miles to Red Bridge State Park in its beautiful ponderosa setting. Another 7 miles on 244 lead toward headwaters via Grande Ronde River Road.

For La Grande's Riverside City Park and festive summertime swimming beach, take I-84 exit 261, head west toward town on Island Avenue for 0.6 miles, turn right on Monroe, in 1 block go right on Spruce, and continue 1 mile. For access downriver, drive northeast of La Grande 20 miles on Hwy 82 to Elgin and turn right on Cedar Lane to the city park. Palmer Junction is farther downstream; from Elgin go west on 204 a few blocks, right on Palmer Junction Road for 16 miles, then 0.5 miles north of town for access.

Troy and the river below can be reached by taking Hwy 3 north from Enterprise (renumbered Hwy 129 in Washington). In 47 miles a lower-river access appears next to Boggan's Oasis Cafe. North of the bridge there, turn west on Grande Ronde Road, wind upriver 16 miles, turn left to cross the Redmond Grade Bridge to the east side, immediately turn upstream, and go 2 miles to the Troy access (Troy's bridge is closed, and access in town is private). Returning to the main river road, drive upstream 2 miles to Troy and continue upstream on gravel 7 miles to Mud Creek ramp or another mile to Powwatka bridge access.

For a shortcut to Troy, go north from Enterprise 33 miles, left at the sign for Flora, and follow signs to Troy via a steep gravel drop. Or, even shorter (from the west) but dustier, from the west end of the town of Wallowa go north at the sign for Troy (39 miles gravel). The lowest Grande Ronde mileage in Washington can be reached by driving north from Asotin; take Snake River Road to Heller Bar, then a gravel road for 3 miles up the Grande Ronde.

A few trails reach the river but none follow it; I prefer boat-in sites below the Wallowa confluence where ponderosa parklands invite freeform walking along shores and up ridgelines to glorious views. Watch for rattlesnakes.

 A premier fly-fishing stream, the Grande Ronde attracts anglers in spring/early summer for rainbows and in early spring and in fall for steelhead, Minam to Troy. Good fishing for stocked and wild steelhead September 1–April 15 extends to the mouth, with heavy use along Troy Road. Rainbow trout are popular in headwaters; smallmouth bass in the lower river. Drift boaters enjoy flows over 1,500 cfs. Bull trout and Chinook survive in small numbers, catch-and-release. Bull trout from the Wenaha winter in the Grande Ronde between the Wallowa confluence and Troy.

 This is a great intermediate raft trip, running high through spring, then excellent in summer for capable families and experienced canoeists. I used to regard the Grande Ronde as backup to the Rogue or Hells Canyon but have since come to really love this river.

In spring or early summer you can put in at Elgin, with a Class 3+ rapid 4 miles below, and float 16 miles to the mouth of the Wallowa and onward to Troy. However, the classic Grande Ronde journey extends from Hwy 82 (Minam) at the Minam/Wallowa confluence and runs 10 miles down the lower Wallowa River into the Grande Ronde, then 30 more miles to Mud Creek access (7 miles above Troy), Class 2–3. Over 10,000 cfs in May is intense; below 800 by August means some dragging. A deep canyon with basalt outcrops and rolling swales of ponderosa savanna grace the river as it riffles through wide gravel rapids, big waves, and tight bends. From La Grande take Hwy 82 north to Minam (14 miles beyond

Elgin) and launch on the Wallowa below the bridge (self registration and portable toilets/firepans required). The first 10 miles on the Wallowa have Class 2–3 hydraulics at high flows, followed by a wider Grande Ronde.

Most boaters cut the trip short at Mud Creek or Troy, but another 19 miles of perfectly beautiful Class 2 have a few powerful wave trains, a wide canyon of pines and grass, ranches, and occasional campsites down to Boggan's Oasis (intermediate access available). This is eastern Oregon's premier Class 2 day-trip in summer, but is scarcely used. The riverfront road is great for biking, or call Boggan's for shuttles.

Below Boggan's, 26 wilderness miles to Heller Bar are Class 2 with one Class 4 called the Narrows. Heavy turbulence here, especially at high flows, comes just 5 miles before Heller Bar. Rattlesnakes throughout! Altogether, a splendid 91-mile Grande Ronde journey from Minam beckons. For that matter, continue on the Snake another 25 miles to Asotin (why drive extra shuttle miles along a river if you can float?), for a 119-mile trip. For shuttles from the top, call Minam Raft Rentals.

The upper Grande Ronde—Red Bridge State Park down to Hilgard—can make an 8-mile Class 2+ run in late spring to early summer, however, *Soggy Sneakers* reports barbed wire fences, and midway a rifle range with its target-embankment at the river gave me pause. The reach from Hilgard to La Grande's city park is 9 miles of Class 2–4; you can avoid the difficult rapid at the takeout by exiting at the bridge just above.

WALLOWA RIVER

The Wallowa carries somewhat more flow than the Grande Ronde where the two meet, though the Grande Ronde

Length: 56 miles
Average flow: 1,508 cfs
Watershed: 927 square miles

runs much higher in spring, before snowmelt of the Wallowa Mountains kicks in. With its Lostine and Minam River tributaries, the Wallowa supplies crucial cool water to Grande Ronde fish.

Wallowa headwaters once buried in glaciers 20 miles long now offer some of the most scenic high-elevation terrain in Oregon. Ample precipitation raked from Pacific storms foams into streams across brilliant whitish-gray, erosion-resistant granite. The river drops into Wallowa Lake (which became a reservoir when the natural lake was dammed at the outlet), then past Joseph, Enterprise, a 30-mile ranching valley, and an 18-mile forested canyon to the Grande Ronde.

The Wallowa accounts for some of the Snake basin's best spring Chinook and steelhead habitat, plus mountain whitefish and rainbow trout. But "best" is relative. The river has been greatly simplified with levees and channelization; in 1908 the entire stream through one reach was shunted-over to accommodate a railroad.

In a tragic episode of Oregon environmental history, a rare but prolific run of sockeye salmon was extirpated here. First, a hatchery dam built for the Columbia's commercial fishing industry blocked the Wallowa in 1904, arresting this river's own extraordinary spawning run. Center of local

West Fork Wallowa River, lower gorge

controversy, the dam was dynamited in 1914, and a screen at Wallowa Reservoir's outlet was removed to allow an estimated 5 million fish access to the ocean. But most were flushed into irrigation canals. Another private dam was built at the outlet in 1918 and raised in 1929 for added irrigation. In 2000 the Oregon Water Resources Department declared this 35-foot blockage a "high hazard dam," and money was appropriated to fix it, but solutions are still pending. At the request of local irrigators, the reconstructed dam may include passage for reintroduction of sockeye. Now a rainbow trout fishery, the Wallowa also hosts hatchery and wild steelhead.

Visit the upper basin by hiking upstream from Wallowa Reservoir. Trails climb the forested West Fork valley 10 miles to glaciated Frazier Lake cirque basin. Nearby, Eagle Cap and Glacier Peak support the range's lasting remnant from the glaciers—Benson snowfield. A 10-mile loop to five lakes and down the shorter East Fork make an eyeful rivaling exquisite glacial lake basins of the Rockies or Sierra Nevada. The lower trail gets a dust cloud of traffic by horse packers and daily riders, but upper reaches are stunning. You can hike the entire loop but miss one of the more incredible gorges anywhere—hidden just off the main path: take the West Fork Wallowa Trail half a mile, turn right on the Chief Joseph Trail, then immediate right and cautiously follow user paths to the rim of the vertical-walled gorge.

To the west of the Wallowa headwaters, the trail up tributary Hurricane Creek offers views of the range's highest peaks: not the expected Eagle Cap but the white wall of Matterhorn, plus Sacajawea and Chief Joseph Mountains. From Hwy 82 in Joseph go west on Hurricane Creek Road 9 miles to the end.

Downstream, Hwy 82 follows the ranch valley and then a deepening forested canyon with pullouts for 8 miles to the Minam confluence. From that bridge the river drops 10 miles to the Grande Ronde; railroad tracks allow hiking on the right while a left-bank road ends in 2 miles at a state campground.

 Anglers walk the old railroad and catch rainbows, especially in the lower river from Rock Creek (6 miles above Minam) to the mouth. Steelhead peak March–mid-April, mostly from the Wallowa hatchery near Enterprise. Hwy 82 pullouts are used year-round. The river is fished from boats in spring and later by wading. Steelheaders congregate below the Big Canyon hatchery acclimation facility, 3 miles above Minam.

 The Wallowa above Minam makes a fine 10-mile Class 2 day-trip—one of only four Class 2 summertime adventures in Oregon east of the Deschutes basin. The canyon is beautiful and riffles delightful, even with the road. Adequate water may continue until August; the channelizing effect of both the road and railroad tend to concentrate flows. Take Hwy 82 west from the town of Wallowa 3 miles, turn south on Lower Diamond Lane, and go 0.3 miles to the bridge with informal access, river-right. Take out below the 82 bridge in Minam.

From there downstream, the lower 10 miles (Class 2–3) are prelude to the Grande Ronde float. At 1.5 miles, the Minam Roller at high flows introduces turbulence that runs 6 miles with Class 3 rapids. The Wallowa/Grande Ronde confluence lacks public access; boaters on the lower Wallowa commit to floating the Grande Ronde another 29 miles to Mud Creek or farther.

LOSTINE RIVER

Length: 32 miles
Average flow: 184 cfs
Watershed: 93 square miles

This Wallowa tributary tours mountain scenery through alpine meadows, U-shaped glacial valleys where ice extended 20 miles downstream, canyons of granite crags, and dense forests. Wild salmon and steelhead spawn, bull trout survive, and elk thrive in the upper basin. A 16-mile Wild and Scenic reach is followed by private forest and ranchland to the mouth. The once-vibrant Chinook run here dwindled to 13 fish in 1999, in part because of summer irrigation diversions. Improved flows have nourished recovery—back up to 3,000 fish in 2009.

 Hiking along the upper Lostine is a highcountry streamside delight. From Enterprise take Hwy 82 northwest 9 miles to Lostine, turn south on Lostine River Road, drive 7 miles on pavement through what might be Oregon's prettiest ranching valley, and 11 more on rough gravel past campgrounds and ending at Two Pan Trailhead. Then hike 6 miles through fir/lodgepole, along foaming cascades, at the edge of brilliant water tinted green with white granite in the bottom, and past high meadows encircled by mountains. An ideal 3-mile connecting trail crests in Alpine terrain while crossing to the East Lostine, then drops along that parallel course and loops back to Two Pan, 16 miles in all. Headwaters are also the best access to the range's landmark, Eagle Cap.

Upper Lostine River

Expect company here, though horse packers use these trails less than the heavily trammeled upper Wallowa.

  The Lostine has small native rainbows (lures only), best mid-summer through fall. Salmon must be released.

Waterfalls, logs, low flows, ranchland—no good boating here.

MINAM RIVER

Length: 51 miles
Average flow: 455 cfs
Watershed: 239 square miles

A westward sister to the Lostine, but larger and longer, the Minam's crystalline water drops from 7,000-foot peaks, passes limestone and granite outcrops, curls through green meadows in a glacial valley where ice once extended 21 miles, then courses into deep forests and old-growth ponderosa. Native rainbow and bull trout do well, while Chinook and steelhead spawn. Without ever passing through ranchland zones that the mid-elevation Wallowa and Lostine face, the Minam swirls into the forested Wallowa 10 miles above its confluence with the Grande Ronde, making the Minam-Wallowa-Grande Ronde system a vital habitat nexus for bull trout and surviving steelhead and salmon. Statewide, the Minam and even-more-exceptional Wenaha are the two largest rivers that remain nearly pristine, source to mouth.

But not entirely pristine. While the Minam's upper 39 miles are a rare National Wild and Scenic River entirely within wilderness, the lower 8 miles, owned by the timber industry, have been heavily logged, roaded, and splash-dammed with bedrock-blasting in the past. Public acquisition of this industry land would make the Minam the longest Oregon river to

Minam River 1 mile upstream of Wallowa River confluence

be entirely safeguarded. Potential for full restoration may be greater here than anywhere else.

 For the only roadside view, take Hwy 82 northeast from La Grande 33 miles and, 1 mile short of the Wallowa River bridge at Minam, take a hard right at an unmarked lane leading to an ODFW access (best to go to the Wallowa bridge and return 1 mile). Here, during low summer flows, a ford crosses to a north-side trail. Also, on Hwy 82, several miles back southwest toward La Grande and high on the mountainside, a gravel forest-industry road heads east above the Minam's south side—gated to vehicles, though hikers and mountain bikers are allowed. In 7 miles, at the National Forest boundary, this road connects with the Minam Trail that starts at the ODFW ford.

An epic river-valley hike is possible by walking up the neighboring Lostine 6 miles, crossing the divide to headwaters of the Minam, then down it 37 miles to the logging road. At that point, continue down the road to a Minam bridge. Here you can cross and walk the logging road several miles up to its gate at Hwy 82, but better—during low flows—continue down an east-side road to its end, pass through a fence, and follow a faint trail that becomes clearer and in 2.5 miles emerges at the ford and ODFW access 1 mile upstream from the Hwy 82 bridge over the Wallowa. This 50-mile hike is best done in late summer to safely ford and to find mosquito relief. Below highcountry, much of the route is heavily forested, but river views resume in the lower 15 miles. For shuttles call Minam Raft Rentals.

 Late summer fishing is good for wild rainbows; catch-and-release encouraged. Though state stocking has ended, plentiful brook trout in upper reaches can be confused with young bull trout; make positive identification (see Chapter 2). Bull trout must be released; keep the alien brookies.

WENAHA RIVER

Length: 22 miles, 38 with NF
Average flow: 390 cfs
Watershed: 295 square miles

One of the Northwest's wildest streams, the Wenaha flows east from the Blue Mountains to the Grande Ronde with no roads, dams, development, or diversions. All but 6 miles (also wild) lie in the Wenaha-Tucannon Wilderness. This riffling canyon-wonder of basalt walls and slopes soaring 2,000 feet transitions downward from Rocky Mountain–type coniferous forests to ponderosa pine savanna, all linked by riparian cottonwoods.

Prime habitat for bighorns, deer, black bears, mountain goats, bobcats, cougars, beavers, and bald eagles in winter, the basin also has plenty of elk. The river offers fine native rainbow habitat, probably Oregon's best bull trout refuge, and some of the region's finest Chinook and steelhead spawning beds in its main stem, Butte Creek, and North Fork. Cool water moderates high temperatures downstream in the Grande Ronde. Both the *Interior Columbia Basin Ecosystem Management Project* and Trout Unlimited list the Wenaha as a premier fishery. The entire main stem is a National Wild and Scenic River.

 For lower river access, drive south from Troy 0.7 miles and turn right to an ODFW campground near the Wenaha mouth. But to explore this gem, you have to walk or ride horseback. It's one of Oregon's premier river-hiking expeditions, at an easy grade, replete with river views and great campsites; there's no reason to journey to the great rivers of Idaho for the finest in wild-river backpacking. Flowers dazzle in May, though in springtime the ticks are out, and Butte Creek ford, 14 miles in, can turn you back. Summer is beautiful but hot. Poison ivy and rattlesnakes in the lower 4 miles warrant keeping your eyes on the

Wenaha River 13 miles upstream of Troy

trail, which owing to little use and nominal maintenance is often brushed over (more hikers please!). From Enterprise, take Hwy 3 north 33 miles, turn west at the sign for Flora, follow signs to Troy for 16 miles on pavement and then a gravel-road free-fall to the Grande Ronde, left to Troy, and right on Bartlett Road 0.3 miles to the trailhead.

The path runs 20 miles up to the North/South Fork confluence, then up the South Fork another 11 miles to Timothy Springs Campground (FR 6415 north of Palmer Junction). A side trail climbs Crooked Creek 12 miles.

 For anglers who like hiking, this might be the best bull trout fishing anywhere, catch-and-release in summer, with some rainbows and hatchery steelhead in the lower 7 miles, September 1–April 15.

 At the top of my to-do list, this would be one of the finest pack-raft or inflatable kayak, pack-in trips anywhere, with a few log blockages on low-but-doable flows well into summer (possible when the Grande Ronde runs 900 cfs at Troy).

This exquisite wild stream in the northeastern corner of the state makes a fine conclusion to any tour of the rivers of Oregon.

APPENDIX

For data methods, see the introduction to Part II.

LONG DAM-FREE REACHES OF RIVERS

*Listed by length in miles. *Indicates entire rivers that are free-flowing.*

John Day with NF: 284 miles
*Umpqua with South Umpqua and Castle Rock Fork: 226 miles
Owyhee: Duck Valley (ID) to Owyhee Reservoir; 190 miles
McKenzie with Willamette: Leaburg Dam to Willamette Falls Dam; 189 miles
Owyhee, SF: YP Ranch (NV) to Owyhee Reservoir; 180 miles
 Willamette with MF: Dexter Dam to Willamette Falls Dam; 177 miles
*Grande Ronde via State Ditch: 173 miles (low diversion dams possible)
Rogue: Lost Creek Dam to Pacific; 157 miles
*Nehalem: source to Pacific; 128 miles
Snake: Swan Falls Dam (ID) to Brownlee Reservoir; 116 miles
*John Day NF: source to main stem; 113 miles
*Siuslaw: source to Pacific; 109 miles
Snake: Hells Canyon Dam to Lower Granite Reservoir; 104 miles
*Coquille with SF: source to Pacific; 100 miles
Deschutes: Round Butte Dam to Columbia backwater; 98 miles
*Smith (Umpqua tributary): source to Umpqua Bay; 91 miles
*Sprague: source to mouth; 86 miles (low diversion dams possible)
*Imnaha with SF: source to mouth; 83 miles
*Donner und Blitzen: source to mouth; 78 miles

Additional entire rivers that are dam-free:
Yamhill with SF and Pierce Creek: 74 miles
Coos with SF and Williams: 73 miles
Siletz: 69 miles
Alsea with NF: 64 miles
West Little Owyhee: 63 miles
Chetco: 57 miles
Nestucca: 57 miles
Sandy: 57 miles

Illinois: 56 miles

Willamette, NFMF: 51 miles

Minam: 51 miles

Molalla: 51 miles

White: 49 miles

LONG RIVER TRIPS

Oregon's long river trips without major dams, or more than two portages, or Class 5 rapids (mostly Class 1–3 water).

John Day with NF: Hwy 395 to McDonald; 225 miles (one Class 3-4)

Willamette with lower 41 miles of McKenzie: Leaburg Dam to West Linn; 189 miles

Willamette with Middle Fork: Dexter Dam to West Linn; 177 miles

Umpqua with South Umpqua: Tiller to Reedsport; 176 miles (several Class 3 and one Class 4/portage, 27 miles tidal)

Rogue: Lost Creek Dam to Pacific; 157 miles (with several Class 4 rapids)

Snake: Swan Falls Dam (ID) to Farewell Bend; 116 miles

Nehalem: Timber Road to Pacific; 105 miles (two Class 4/portages, some Class 3, 9 miles tidal)

Snake: Hells Canyon, Hells Canyon Dam to Asotin; 104 miles (with big volume Class 4)

Deschutes: Hwy 26 to mouth; 98 miles (one portage by vehicle)

Siuslaw: near Siuslaw Falls to Florence; 97 miles (many logjams, 20 miles tidal)

Grande Ronde: Hwy 82 to Heller Bar on Snake River; 91 miles (one Class 4)

Owyhee: Rome to Leslie Gulch; 67 miles (Class 4, 11 miles reservoir)

Smith: Yellow Creek to Umpqua Bay; 67 miles (one portage, logjams possible, 21 miles tidal)

Yamhill with South Yamhill: La Grande to mouth; 61 miles

Coquille with SF: Baker Creek to Bandon; 60 miles (35 miles tidal)

Alsea: Mill Creek Park to Alsea Bay; 52 miles (12 miles tidal)

Santiam with South Santiam: Foster Dam to Buena Vista; 52 miles (two portages)

Santiam with North Santiam: Mill City to Buena Vista; 48 miles (one portage/ boat-slide)

Siletz: Moonshine Park to Siletz Bay; 45 miles (16 miles tidal)

BEST RIVER RUNNING

See the text of Part II of this book for details about this subjective list, and for a description of whitewater difficulty (Class) ratings. Each run may have one rapid greater than the Class listed here. Take all precautions discussed in the introduction to Part II and elsewhere. High water tends to raise the difficulty beyond what may be listed here. Within each whitewater class, rivers here are listed not in qualitative hierarchy but in the order that they appear in Part II.

Estuaries

Nestucca

Siletz

Tenmile Creek (southern, in Coos County)

New

Umpqua

Class 1–2

Nehalem: Spruce Run Campground to Morrison Eddy Campground

Alsea: Alsea village to tidewater

Siuslaw: Clay Creek to Richardson access

Smith, NF (Umpqua basin): mile 13 to mile 6 (up from mouth) (one portage)

Smith: below Yellow Creek to Smith River Falls (logjams)

Chetco: Low Water Crossing to Loeb State Park

Umpqua: North/South Umpqua confluence to Reedsport (with several Class 3 rapids)

Sixes: Sixes Campground to Hughes House

Elk: hatchery to Hwy 101

Rogue: Lost Creek Dam to Tou Velle State Park; Gold Hill to Grave Creek (2+); Foster Bar to Gold Beach

Willamette: Eugene to West Linn

McKenzie: Finn Rock to Dorris State Park; Leaburg Dam to mouth

Santiam, North: Mill City to mouth (a boat-slide at a dam)

Santiam, South: Foster Dam to mouth (two portages)

Molalla: Glen Avon to mouth

Clackamas: McIver to mouth

Sandy: Dodge Park to Lewis and Clark Park (one Class 3)

Deschutes: Warm Springs to Trout Creek

Crooked: Big Bend to Castle Rock Campground

Spring Creek (Williamson tributary): Collier Park up to source and back

John Day: Kimberly to McDonald (one Class 3-4)

Grande Ronde: Troy to Boggan's Oasis

Class 2–3

Kilchis: above Mapes Bridge

Wilson: milepost 15 to Vanderzanden access

Trask: Trask Park to Cedar Creek access

Drift Creek, 1000-Line Road to May Road, with log jams

Lake Creek: Deadwood access to Tide

Siuslaw: Richardson access to Tide

Coos, SF: Williams River to mile marker 6.2

Umpqua, North: Susan Creek to Cable Crossing; Lone Rock access to Winchester Dam

Willamette, NFMF: below lower FR 19 bridge to Westfir (weir portage)

McKenzie: Olallie to Leaburg Dam (Class 3+ in upper reach)

Santiam, North: Packsaddle Park to Mill City

Molalla: Table Rock to Glen Avon Bridge (Class 3+ with one Class 4)

Collawash: Fan Creek to mouth

Deschutes, lower: Trout Creek to mouth (big water)

John Day, NF: Hwy 395 to Monument

Snake: Pittsburgh Landing to Heller Bar (big water)

Grande Ronde: Minam (on Wallowa) to Mud Creek

Class 4

Wilson: Jones Creek to milepost 15

Siletz: Buck Creek to Moonshine

Elk: Butler Bar to hatchery (log hazards)

Chetco: Slide Creek to Low Water Crossing (with Class 5/portages)

Umpqua, North: Boulder Creek to Susan Creek

Rogue: Grave Creek to Foster Bar

Illinois: Miami Bar to Oak Flat (with Class 5)

Willamette, NFMF: FR 1925 to below second FR 19 bridge

Santiam, North: above Detroit Reservoir

Santiam, South: Upper Soda Creek to Foster Reservoir (portages)

Quartzville Creek: Yellowbottom to Green Peter Reservoir

Little North Santiam: Opal Creek Trail to Three Pools ("Opal Creek" run)

Clackamas: Three Lynx to Bob's Hole

Hood: Tucker Park to mouth

Sandy: Marmot Dam site to Dodge Park

Metolius: Lower Bridge to Monty Campground

Klamath: Spring Creek to Copco Reservoir (with Class 5)

Snake, Hells Canyon: Hells Canyon Dam to Pittsburgh Landing (big water)

Owyhee: Three Forks to Owyhee Reservoir (Class 5 above Rome)

BEST HIKING ALONG RIVERS

See Part II for details. Rivers are presented here in the order they appear in the book. Outstanding multiday, riverfront trails are found along the upper and lower Rogue, North Umpqua, Middle Fork Willamette, McKenzie, North Fork John Day, Wenaha, and Snake.

Salmonberry: on railroad grade

Trask: Upper Peninsula County Park

Drift Creek (Alsea tributary)

Sweet Creek (Siuslaw tributary)

Coquille, SF: at Coquille Falls

Panther Creek (Elk tributary)

Pistol mouth: beach walking

Chetco: Loeb State Park

Umpqua, North: 79-mile trail, especially good from Lemolo to Hot Springs

Rogue: Upper Rogue Trail; Lower Rogue Trail; Grave Creek to Foster Bar

Willamette: Ruth Bascom Trail; Willamette Park; Bryant Park; Molalla River State Park

Willamette, NFMF: Constitution Grove

Willamette, MF: Middle Fork Trail, especially lower end

McKenzie: Waterfalls Trail at Sahalie Falls; McKenzie River Trail

Little North Santiam: river trail

Clackamas: Riverside to Rainbow; Indian Henry to Fish Creek

Hood, EF: Sherwood area trail

Eagle Creek (Columbia tributary)

Sandy: upper river, with Ramona Falls

Salmon (Sandy basin)

Deschutes: Lava Island Falls area upstream of Bend

Metolius: upper river

Crooked, NF: off-trail

John Day, NF: headwaters

Silvies basin: Myrtle Creek Trail

Snake, Hells Canyon: east and west side trails

Owyhee: Three Forks, Military Grade Trail

Malheur: upper river

Malheur, NF

Eagle Creek (Powder basin): EF, upper main stem, West Eagle, and Martin Bridge Trail

Imnaha: lower, also SF and NF

Wallowa: WF and EF

Lostine: main stem and EF

Minam: source to mouth
Wenaha

BEST BICYCLING ALONG RIVERS

Rivers are listed in the order that they appear in the book; see Part II for details.

Nehalem: Spruce Run Park down to Foss Road
Nestucca: upper river road
Siuslaw: Siuslaw River Road, Hwy 126 upstream for 26 miles, Stagecoach Road
Smith (Umpqua basin): 80 miles from headwaters to mouth
Coquille, SF: Hwy 219 and 3348
Elk: 10 miles upstream from hatchery
North Umpqua: challenging mountain biking on hiking/biking trail
Willamette: Ruth Bascom Riverbank Trail in Eugene
McKenzie: upper river, challenging mountain biking on hiking/bike trail
Quartzville Creek
Clackamas: Upper Clackamas River Road
Deschutes: Benham Falls to Lava Island Falls; lower-river bike trail
Metolius: upper river
John Day, MF: upstream of Hwy 395
John Day, NF: downstream of Hwy 395
John Day, SF
Chewaucan: FR 33 above Paisley

BEST FISHING

See Part II and fishing guides for many additional sites. This list draws heavily, but not exclusively, from Gary Lewis' *Freshwater Fishing, Oregon and Washington*.

Brook trout: upper Deschutes
Cutthroat trout: Tillamook, Nehalem, Nestucca
Rainbow trout: Deschutes, Wood, Williamson, Crooked, Fall (Deschutes basin)
Steelhead: Wilson, North Umpqua, Sixes, Elk, Rogue, Sandy, Deschutes, Grande Ronde
Whitefish: Deschutes, Fall, Crooked
Shad: Umpqua, Coos

Chinook: Wilson, Trask, Nestucca, Chetco, Umpqua, North Umpqua, Rogue, Columbia, Sandy, Willamette, Clackamas

Coho: Nehalem, Umpqua, North Umpqua, Rogue, Clackamas

Smallmouth bass: Umpqua, South Umpqua, John Day

Yellow perch: Columbia

Carp: Columbia, Willamette

Catfish: Columbia, Willamette

OREGON'S FINEST NATURAL RIVERS

The Great Rivers of the West survey by the Western Rivers Conservancy identified the most outstanding natural streams of each western state. The survey (2008) focused on biology with consideration of recreation, and was based on a variety of documents plus interviews with biologists. See www.westernrivers.org or inquire with WRC.

"A" Rivers

Elk, with NF and SF

Illinois

Imnaha with SF

John Day with NF

Metolius

Rogue

Sandy and Salmon

Smith, NF (California's Smith River basin)

Snake in Hells Canyon

Umpqua, North, and Steamboat Creek

Wenaha

Willamette, NFMF

"B" Rivers

Chetco

Coquille, SF

Cummins, Rock, and Tenmile Creeks

Deschutes

Donner und Blitzen

John Day, MF

Joseph Creek

Kilchis

Lostine

Minam

Nehalem and Salmonberry

Owyhee, with MF, NF, and West Little Owyhee

Smith, NF (Umpqua basin)

White

"C" Rivers

Clackamas and Roaring

Drift Creek (Alsea basin)

Eagle Creek (Columbia tributary)

French Pete Creek

Separation Creek

Grande Ronde, lower

Hood

McKenzie, upper

Nestucca

Siletz

Sycan

Umpqua and South Umpqua

Wassen Creek

Whitehorse and Little Whitehorse Creeks

NATIONAL WILD AND SCENIC RIVERS

For more information, see *The Wild and Scenic Rivers of America* and www.rivers.gov.

Big Indian Creek (Donner und Blitzen tributary): 10 miles

Big Marsh Creek: source to mouth at Crescent Creek; 15 miles

Blitzen, SF: source to mouth at Blitzen River; 17 miles

Chetco: source to Siskiyou National Forest boundary; 45 miles

Clackamas: source to Big Cliff; 47 miles

Clackamas, SF: EF of SF to Clackamas River; 4.2 miles

Collawash: source of EF Collawash to Clackamas River; 18 miles

Crescent Creek: Crescent Creek Dam to Hwy 6 bridge; 10 miles

Crooked: Bowman Dam downstream for 8 miles; below Hwy 97 for 7 miles; 15 miles

Crooked, NF: source to 1 mile above Crooked River; 32 miles

Deschutes: Wickiup Dam to Bend; Oden Falls (near Hwy 20) to Billy Chinook Reservoir; Pelton Dam to Columbia River; 173 miles

Donner und Blitzen: SF Blitzen/Little Blitzen confluence to boundary of Malheur NWR; 17 miles

Eagle Creek (Powder basin): source to National Forest boundary; 27 miles

Eagle Creek (Clackamas tributary): source to National Forest boundary; 8 miles

Elk: NF/SF confluence to fish hatchery; 17 miles

Elk, NF: 6 miles above SF confluence

Elk, SF: 4 miles above NF confluence

Elkhorn Creek: 6 miles in Opal Creek Scenic Area

Fifteenmile Creek: source at Senecal Spring downstream; 11 miles

Fish Creek: source to mouth at Clackamas River; 14 miles

Grande Ronde: Wallowa River confluence to Washington state line; 44 miles

Hood, EF: Hwy 35 to Mount Hood National Forest boundary; 14 miles

Hood, MF: confluence of Clear and Coe Branches downstream; 4 miles

Illinois: Siskiyou National Forest boundary to mouth; 50 miles

Imnaha: NF/SF confluence to mouth; 68 miles

Imnaha, SF: source to mouth; 9 miles

John Day: Service Creek to Tumwater Falls; 148 miles

John Day, NF: source to Camas Creek near Hwy 395; 54 miles

John Day, SF: 47 miles, Malheur National Forest to Smokey Creek

Joseph Creek: Joseph Creek Ranch to Wallowa-Whitman National Forest boundary; 9 miles

Kiger Creek: source to Steens Mountain Wilderness boundary; 4 miles

Klamath: Boyle Powerhouse to California state line 11 miles

Little Blitzen: source to mouth at Donner und Blitzen River; 13 miles

Little Deschutes: source to 1 mile above Hwy 58; 12 miles

Little Wildhorse Creek: source to Wildhorse Creek; 3 miles

Lostine: source to Wallowa-Whitman National Forest boundary; 16 miles

Malheur: below Bosonberg Creek to lower National Forest boundary; 12 miles

Malheur, NF: source to Malheur National Forest boundary; 23 miles

McKenzie: source at Clear Lake to Scott Creek; 13 miles

Metolius: below Metolius Springs to Billy Chinook Reservoir; 29 miles

Minam: source at Minam Lake to Eagle Cap Wilderness boundary; 39 miles

Owyhee: Three Forks to 4 miles above Rome; 6 miles below Rome to Owyhee Reservoir; 86 miles

Owyhee, NF: Idaho boundary to mouth at Three Forks; 10 miles

Owyhee, SF: Idaho boundary to mouth at Three Forks; 24 miles

Powder: Thief Valley Dam to Hwy 203 bridge; 12 miles

Powder, North: source to Wallowa-Whitman National Forest boundary; 6 miles

Quartzville Creek: Willamette National Forest boundary to Green Peter Reservoir; 9 miles

Roaring: source to mouth at Clackamas River; 14 miles

Roaring, SF: source to mouth at Roaring River; 5 miles

Rogue: Crater Lake National Park to lower National Forest boundary; Applegate River to Lobster Creek; 125 miles

Salmon: source to mouth; 34 miles

Sandy: source to National Forest boundary; Dodge Park to Dabney State Park; 25 miles

Smith NF: source to California boundary; 13 miles

Snake: Hells Canyon Dam to 4 miles above Washington boundary; 67 miles

Sprague, NF: River Spring to Fremont National Forest boundary; 15 miles

Sycan: source to Coyote Bucket at Fremont National Forest boundary; 59 miles

Umpqua, North: Soda Spring Powerhouse to Rock Creek; 34 miles

Wallowa: confluence of Wallowa and Minam to mouth; 10 miles

Wenaha: source at NF/SF confluence to mouth; 22 miles

West Little Owyhee: source to mouth; 58 miles

White: source to mouth; 47 miles

Willamette, NFMF: Waldo Lake to National Forest boundary; 42 miles

Whychus Creek: source to 800 feet above McAllister Ditch; 15 miles

Whychus Creek tributaries including NF, SF, EF, WF, Soap Fork, Park Creek Fork: all in Three Sisters Wilderness; 27 miles

Wildhorse Creek: source to mouth of canyon; 7 miles

Zigzag: source to Mount Hood Wilderness boundary; 4 miles

STATE SCENIC WATERWAYS

See Oregon State Scenic Waterways map: www.oregon.gov/OPRD/RULES/Pages/waterways.aspx.

Clackamas: 66 miles in two segments

Clackamas, NF: 12 miles

Clackamas, SF: 4 miles

Deschutes: 199 miles in two segments

Elk: 11 miles

Elk, NF: 5 miles

Elk, SF: 5 miles

Grande Ronde: 42 miles

Illinois: 46 miles

John Day: 160 miles

John Day, NF: 56 miles

John Day, MF: 71 miles

John Day, SF: 29 miles

Klamath: 17 miles

McKenzie: 16 miles

McKenzie, SF: 21 miles

Metolius: 14 miles

Minam: 45 miles

Nestucca: 23 miles

Owyhee: 25 miles

Rogue: 161 miles in two segments

Sandy: 12 miles

Santiam, Little North: 7 miles

Umpqua, North: 40 miles in two segments

Waldo Lake: 0 river miles

Walker Creek (Nestucca tributary): 3 miles

Wallowa: 10 miles

Willamette, NF of MF: 43 miles

OREGON RIVERS CANOED OR RAFTED BY THE AUTHOR

Alsea: Alsea village to Salmonberry Road

Alsea: Mill Creek (below Alsea village) to Tidewater

Applegate: McKee Bridge to Cantrall Park

Chetco: Boulder Creek to mouth

Clackamas: Milo McIver Park to mouth

Columbia: Aldrich Point area

Coos, SF: Williams River to 6 miles above Dellwood

Coquille, SF: Siskiyou Forest boundary to Powers; Baker Creek to Coquille Myrtle Grove

Crooked: Bowman Dam to Castle Rock

Drift Creek: 1000 Line Road to May Road

Elk: Milepost 9 to Slate Creek; Bald Mountain Creek reach (4 miles); hatchery to mouth

Grande Ronde: Wallowa/Minam confluence to Boggan's Oasis

Goose Creek: Sparks Lake area

Hunter Creek: 5 miles to mouth

Illinois: Miami Bar to lower Oak Flat

Imnaha: Cow Creek Bridge to mouth

John Day: Kimberly to Cottonwood

John Day, MF: 8 miles above Hwy 395

John Day, NF: Camas Creek to mouth

Little Deschutes: La Pine State Park Road to Hwy 42

Luckiamute: 3 miles to mouth

Malheur: Warm Springs Dam to Allen Dam (Juntura); Horseshoe Bend reach (4 miles)

Marys: 1 mile to mouth

McKenzie: McKenzie Campground to Dorris State Park; Leaburg Dam to mouth

Metolius: Camp Sherman area

Millicoma, EF: below Glenn Creek to below Nesika County Park

Molalla: bridge above NF to mouth

New: Boice-Cope Park to Croft Lake access

Owyhee: above Rome

Pistol: 5 miles to mouth

Rogue: Lost Creek Dam to Tou Velle State Park; Gold Hill to mouth

Salmon: lower trailhead to Hwy 26

Sandy: Marmot Diversion Dam to Revenue Bridge; Dodge Park to Oxbow Park

Santiam, North: Packsaddle County Park to mouth

Santiam, South: Foster Dam to mouth

Sixes: Sixes Campground to Hughes House

Siuslaw: below Siuslaw Falls to Mapleton

Smith: Yellow Creek to Smith River Falls

Smith, NF, (Umpqua basin): above bridge #8 to below bridge #1

Snake: Swan Falls Dam to Weiser; Hells Canyon Dam to Lewiston

Sprague: Hwy 140 bridge to Chiloquin

Spring Creek (Williamson): source to mouth

Umpqua: North/South Umpqua confluence to Reedsport

Umpqua, North: Susan Creek to Cable Crossing; Lone Rock to Winchester; Hwy 99 to mouth

Umpqua, South: Tiller to mouth

Wallowa: Lower Diamond Lane to mouth

Willamette: source to West Linn; Clackamas confluence to Jefferson Street

Willamette, MF: Oakridge to Lookout Point Reservoir; Dexter to mouth

Willamette, NFMF: lower gorge to Westfir

Williams: lower 2 miles to Coos River

Williamson: above Collier State Park to Chiloquin

Winchuck: Bear Creek confluence to mouth

ORGANIZATIONS INVOLVED WITH RIVER CONSERVATION (PARTIAL LIST)

See addresses on the Internet. Search for additional organizations by river name. State-sanctioned Watershed Councils exist for most rivers.

American Rivers

American Whitewater

Audubon Society of Portland

Bend Paddle Trail Alliance

Calapooia Watershed Council

Central Oregon Flyfishers

Columbia Riverkeeper

Coquille River Watershed Association

Deschutes Land Trust

Deschutes River Conservancy

Freshwater Trust

Friends of the Columbia Gorge

Friends of Elk River

Klamath-Siskiyou Alliance

Lower Columbia Canoe Club

Native Fish Society

Nature Conservancy of Oregon

Oregon Environmental Council

Oregon Natural Desert Association

Oregon Wild

Pacific Rivers Council

River Network

Rogue Riverkeeper

Tillamook Estuaries Partnership

Trout Unlimited

Tualatin Riverkeeper

Umpqua Watersheds

WaterWatch of Oregon

Western Rivers Conservancy

Wild Salmon Center

Willamette Canoe and Kayak Club

Willamette Riverkeeper

ACKNOWLEDGMENTS

Editor Mary Elizabeth Braun of Oregon State University Press saw promise in this book from the beginning; many thanks to her, to all the excellent publishing staff at OSU, to Mollie Firestone for exceptional care in copy editing, to Erin Greb Cartography, and to Steve Connell for design.

With a rare combination of artistic skill and scientific knowledge, Ph.D. biologist and professor Bill Avery sketched the 50 plants and animals featured in Chapter 2. I'm privileged to have such fine original artwork accompanying my text and photos. Bill can be reached at averyw@ saclink.csus.edu.

Data about length, volume, and watershed area for the featured rivers were calculated by Matt Mayfield; many thanks to him and Amy Haak of Conservation Geography in Boise. As near as I can tell, ours is the first comprehensive tally of such basic data for Oregon rivers. Matt also produced the original drafts of the maps.

Many thanks also to Gregory Knight and Marieta Staneva of the Knight-Staneva Foundation for Sustainability and Future Environments, which covered some of my expenses. Adam Smith of the Whole Systems Foundation also championed my work; thanks to him, to Norton Smith, and to all the trustees of that foundation.

A long list of writers and explorers have traveled Oregon's rivers before me; deep appreciation to all who appear under *Sources* and especially the authors of two whitewater guidebooks: Willamette Kayak and Canoe Club contributors of *Soggy Sneakers*, and Robb Keller, author of *Paddling Oregon*. Jim Yuskavitch's *Fishing Oregon* was very helpful. Laurie Pavey of the Willamette Kayak and Canoe Club provided a thorough review and perceptive edit for accuracy, content, and language.

My friend Travis Hussey joined me for a number of adventures when Ann was not able to come; next to her, I can't think of a better and more capable paddling buddy—one who relished not only the comfort of being outside, but also the cold, the rain, the winter camping, and a few gripping moments.

Thanks also to Jeremy Monroe of *Freshwaters Illustrated* and his filmmaking brother, Mike, for their distinguished professional skills and for a short video they created about the book. Trips were also shared with Zach Collier of Northwest Rafting Company and ECHO River Trips—an outfitting professional who blends business with conservation in ways that should be emulated everywhere. Valued friend and river conservationist Don Elder joined with his paddle and boat as well, taking precious time from duties at River Network. Bob Allen of Umpqua Watersheds helped with my North Umpqua travels, and Ogden Kellogg led me to highlights of the middle Rogue.

A lot of people generously gave time for interviews; see Sources. Special thanks to Stan Gregory, stream ecologist at OSU. Several experts read the entire manuscript and many specialists reviewed portions; thanks to Lesley Adams, Bill Bakke, Kelly Burnett, Paul Burns, Molly Chaudet, Julie Chick, Zach Collier, Romain Cooper, Greg Currie, John DeVoe, Jeff Dose, Jim Eisner, Don Elder, Paul Engelmeyer, Pete Giordano, Eric Hartstein, Kevin Hoskins, Bob Hunter, Travis Hussey, Andy Kerr, John Kober, Patrick Kolodge, Doug Markle, Jim McCarthy, Scott McEwen, David Moryc, Jim Myron, Laurie Pavey, Stan Petrowski, Grant Richie, Jim Rogers, Chuck Sams, Bill Sedivy, John Shipp, Barbara Ullian, Dan Valens, Ann Vileisis, Grant Weldenback, Travis Williams, and Allen Wilson.

Going way back, my revered friend Bob Peirce led the way on some of my first Oregon river trips with seasoned capability that still holds me in awe. His friend and mine, Bob Potter is remembered with great honor and appreciation for his passion and committed vocation in stewarding the rivers that we love.

I save the greatest gratitude for my wife, Ann Vileisis, who helped me throughout with brilliant ideas, smart and thorough editing skills, encouragement even though it meant time apart that neither one of us liked, support in our daily living, and best of all—stellar company as she expertly kayaked, canoed, or rafted on trips that this book enticed us to do. She managed to accomplish all this while working on a challenging book of her own, plus engaging with our shared zest in endless opportunities for conservation in the community and region where we live.

SOURCES

Abell et al. 2000. *Freshwater Ecoregions of North America*. Island Press.

Allen, David and Colbert Cushing. 2001. *Streams: their ecology and life*. Academic Press.

Augerot, Xanthippe. 2005. *Atlas of Pacific Salmon*. University of California Press.

Alt, David D. and Donald W. Hyndman. 2000. *Roadside Geology of Oregon*. Mountain Press.

Barnosky, Anthony D. 2009. *Heatstroke: Nature in an Age of Global Warming*. Island Press.

Bastasch, Rick. 1998. *The Oregon Water Handbook*. Oregon State University Press.

Bend Paddle Trail Alliance. About 2010. *Deschutes Paddle Trail Guide*.

Csuti, Blair, et al. 2001. *Atlas of Oregon Wildlife*. Oregon State University Press.

Defenders of Wildlife, et al. 1998. *Oregon's Living Landscape*.

Dettinger, Michael D., Lynn Ingram. January 2013. "Megastorms Could Drown Massive Portions of California." *Scientific American*.

Gregory, S.V., Swanson, F.J., McKee, W.A., and Cummins, K.W. 1991. "An Ecosystem Perspective of Riparian Zones." *Bioscience*, 41, 540–551.

Hawley, Steven. 2011. *Recovering A Lost River: Removing Dams, Rewilding Salmon, Revitalizing Communities*. Beacon Press.

Hay, Keith G. 2004. *The Lewis and Clark Columbia River Water Trail: A Guide for Paddlers, Hikers, and other Explorers*. Timber Press.

Hobbs, Stephen D. et al, eds. 2002. *Forest and Stream Management in the Oregon Coast Range*. Oregon State University Press.

Huntington, Charles, Willa Nehlsen, Jon Bowers. March 1996. "A Survey of Healthy Native Stocks of Anadromous Salmonids in the Pacific Northwest and California." *Fisheries*.

Jones, Philip N. 2007. *Canoe and Kayak Routes of Northwest Oregon*. The Mountaineers.

Keller, Robb. 1998. *Paddling Oregon*. Falcon.

Kerr, Andy. 2012. *National Wild and Scenic Rivers and State Scenic Waterways in Oregon*. The Larch Company, unpublished report.

_____. 2000. *Oregon Desert Guide*. The Mountaineers.

_____. 2004. *Oregon Wild*. Oregon Wild.

Lichatowich, Jim. 1999. *Salmon Without Rivers*. Island Press.

Loy, William G. ed. 2001. *Atlas of Oregon*. University of Oregon Press.

Miller, Marli Bryant. 2012. *Geology of Oregon & the Pacific NW*. Mountain Press (forthcoming).

Moyle, Peter B. 2002. *Inland Fishes of California*. University of California Press.

Northwest Environmental Advocates. 1992. *Columbia River—Troubled Waters*. Advocates, brochure.

Noss, Reed F. and Allen Y. Cooperrider. 1994. *Saving Nature's Legacy*. Island Press.

Olson, Larry N. and John Daniel. 1997. *Oregon Rivers*. Westcliffe.

Oregon Department of Fish and Wildlife. 2012. *Oregon Conservation Strategy*.

_____. 2010. *Oregon Native Fish Status Report*.

_____. 1993. *Oregon Wildlife Diversity Plan*.

_____. 2009. *Fishing, Hunting, Wildlife Viewing, and Shellfishing in Oregon*.

Oregon Department of Parks and Recreation. 1995, with updates. *Willamette River Recreation Guide.*

_____. *Willamette River Water Trail Guide.* About 2011.

Oregon Department of Water Resources. 2010. *Integrated Water Resources Strategy.*

Orr, Elizabeth L. and William Orr. 2012. *Oregon Geology.* Oregon State University Press.

Orr, Elizabeth and William Orr. 2005. *Oregon Water: An Environmental History.* Inkwater Press.

Palmer, Tim. 1996. *America by Rivers.* Island Press.

_____. 1997. *The Columbia.* The Mountaineers.

_____. 1991. *The Snake River: Window to the West.* Island Press.

_____. 1993. *The Wild and Scenic Rivers of America.* Island Press.

Peter, Susan, et al. 2002. *Exploring the Tualatin River Basin.* Oregon State University Press.

Reeves, Gordon H., Kelly M. Burnett, Stanley V. Gregory. 2002. "Fish and Aquatic Ecosystems of the Oregon Coast Range," in *Forest and Stream Management in the Oregon Coast Range.* Oregon State University Press.

Schoonmaker, Peter K. et al. 1997. *The Rain Forests of Home: Profile of a North American Bioregion.* Ecotrust.

Sullivan, William L. 1999. *Exploring Oregon's Wild Areas.* The Mountaineers.

University of Oregon Institute for Sustainable Environment, U.S. Forest Service, et al. 2008. *Rogue Basin Climate Change Impact Report.*

U.S. Bureau of Land Management. 2001. *Deschutes River Boater's Guide.*

_____. About 2001. *John Day River Recreation Guide.* Bureau of Land Management.

_____. 2011. *Owyhee, Bruneau, and Jarbidge Rivers Boating Guide.*

_____. 1993. *Rogue River Float Guide.*

_____. 2012. *Wallowa and Grande Ronde Rivers Boater's Guide.*

U.S. Forest Service. 2005. *Final Environmental Impact Statement: Special Use Permits for Commercial Operations on the Lower Rogue and Lower Illinois Rivers.*

_____. 1992. *Draft Environmental Impact Statement: Elk Wild and Scenic River Management Plan.*

_____. 2002. *North Umpqua Trail.*

_____. 2004. *North Umpqua Wild and Scenic River Users Guide.*

U.S. Forest Service, Pacific Northwest Research Station. 1997. *Highlighted Scientific Findings of the Interior Columbia Basin Ecosystem Management Project.*

Western Rivers Conservancy. 2008. *The Great Rivers of the West.* By Tim Palmer and Ann Vileisis.

Wildlife Society. 1994. *Interim Protection for Late-Successional Forests, Fisheries, and Watersheds.*

Willamette Kayak and Canoe Club. 2004. *Soggy Sneakers.* Pete Giordano, ed., The Mountaineers, Fourth Edition (also earlier editions).

Williams, Chuck. 1980. *Bridge of the Gods, Mountains of Fire.* Friends of the Earth. (Columbia River Gorge).

Wolf, Edward C. and Seth Zuckerman, eds. 2003. *Salmon Nation.* Ecotrust.

Wood, Wendell. 1991. *A Walking Guide to Oregon's Ancient Forests.* Oregon Natural Resources Council.

Yuskavitch, Jim. 2001. *Fishing Oregon.* Falcon.

INTERVIEWS

Adams, Lesley, Rogue Riverkeeper

Anderson, Stephen, The Nature Conservancy

Bach, Leslie, The Nature Conservancy

Bakke, Bill, Native Fish Society

Burns, Paul, Forest Service, Siuslaw River

Chaudet, Molly, Forest Service, Deschutes River

Collier, Zach, Northwest Rafting Company

DeVoe, John, Oregon WaterWatch

Dose, Jeff, fisheries biologist, Umpqua National Forest (retired)

Elder, Don, River Network

Frissell, Chris, fisheries biologist

Giordano, Pete, river outfitter, paddler, editor of 4th edition *Soggy Sneakers*

Gregory, Stan, stream ecologist, Oregon State University

Heller, David, U.S. Forest Service (retired)

Kober, John, Pacific Rivers Council

Kolodge, Patrick, BLM, John Day River

Lee, Patricia, Steamboat Inn

Markle, Doug, fisheries biologist, Oregon State University

Martin, Marli, geologist, University of Oregon

Moryc, David, American Rivers

O'Keefe, Thomas, American Whitewater

Pavey, Laurie, Willamette Kayak and Canoe Club

Peirce, Bob, river runner and conservationist

Richardson, Jason, Weyerhaeuser

Rogers, Jim, Friends of Elk River

Vandiver, Alan, Forest Service, Rogue River

Wallin, Phil, Western Rivers Conservancy

Weekley, Faye, U.S. Fish and Wildlife Service

Weldenbach, Grant, BLM, Klamath River

Williams, Jack, Chief Scientist, Trout Unlimited

Williams, Travis, Willamette Riverkeeper

Wilson, Allen, outfitter, Chetco River

ABOUT THE AUTHOR

Tim Palmer has written 23 books about rivers, the American landscape, conservation, and adventure travel. He has spent a lifetime paddling, hiking, exploring, and photographing along streams, and his passion has been to write and speak on behalf of river conservation. He has paddled on more than 350 rivers nationwide, including 50 in Oregon.

Recognizing his contributions in writing, photography, and activism, American Rivers gave Tim its first Lifetime Achievement Award in 1988, and Perception Inc. honored him as America's River Conservationist of the Year in 2000. California's Friends of the River recognized him with both its highest honors, the Peter Behr Award and the Mark Dubois Award. *Paddler* magazine named Tim one of the 10 greatest river conservationists of our time, and in 2000 included him as one of the "100 greatest paddlers of the century." In 2005 Tim received the Distinguished Alumni Award from the College of Arts and Architecture at Pennsylvania State University. Topping off these honors, he received the National

Photo by Ann Vileisis

Conservation Achievement Award ("Connie") for communications given by the National Wildlife Federation in 2011.

Tim's *Rivers of America* was published by Harry N. Abrams and features 200 color photos of streams nationwide. *The Columbia* won the National Outdoor Book Award in 1998, and *California Wild* received the Benjamin Franklin Award as the best book on nature and the environment in 2004. The *Heart of America: Our Landscape, Our Future* won the Independent Publisher's Book Award as the best essay and travel book in 2000.

Tim lives in Port Orford, Oregon, and has explored rivers on foot and by canoe and raft throughout the state.

Before becoming a full-time writer, Tim worked for 8 years as a land-use planner. He has a bachelor of science degree in Landscape Architecture, and is an Associate of the Riparia Center, Department of Geography, Pennsylvania State University, and a Visiting Scholar with the Department of Geography at Portland State University. He speaks and gives slide shows for universities, conservation groups, and conferences nationwide. See his work at www.timpalmer.org.

ABOUT THE PHOTOS

Most photos were taken with film, and none were digitally manipulated to change the color or content of the scenes. Tim used Canon A1 cameras with fixed-focal-length lenses, 17–200 mm, and a Canon 5-D digital camera. Most film was Fuji Velvia, which captures colors largely as they are in nature.

INDEX

page numbers followed by p *refer to photographs or drawings*